RUDOLF STEINER'S ESOTERIC TEACHING ACTIVITY

Rudolf Steiner, Munich, 1906

RUDOLF STEINER'S
ESOTERIC TEACHING ACTIVITY

Truthfulness
Continuity
New Form

HELLA WIESBERGER

SteinerBooks
An imprint of Anthroposophic Press
402 Union Street #58, Hudson, NY 12534
www.steinerbooks.org

Copyright © 2019 by SteinerBooks / Anthroposophic Press, Inc.

All rights reserved. No part of this publication may be reproduced, stored in a retrieval system, or transmitted, in any form or by any means, electronic, mechanical, photocopying, recording, or otherwise, without the prior written permission of the publisher. Originally published in German as *Rudolf Steiners esoterische Lehrtätigkeit. Wahrhaftigkeit – Kontinuität – Neugestaltung* by Rudolf Steiner Verlag, Basel, Switzerland, 1997.

Translated by Rita Stebbing, John Wood, Matthew Barton, and Marsha Post (see page 277 for more on textual sources).

Cover image: *Group X, No. 2, Altarpiece* ("Paintings for the Temple"), oil and metal leaf on canvas, 1915, by Hilma af Klint (Guggenheim, New York)
Design: Jens Jensen

Heartfelt thanks to Dr. Julius Zoll for his dedicated preparation of the original text for this volume and to Marsha Post for her attention to detail in her translation of the previously untranslated chapters.

LIBRARY OF CONGRESS CONTROL NUMBER: 2019937972

ISBN: 978-1-62148-241-3 (paperback)
ISBN: 978-1-62148-242-0 (eBook)

Contents

	Introduction	vii
1.	Rudolf Steiner in the History of the Esoteric Movement	1
2.	Rudolf Steiner as a Teacher of Esotericism	12
3.	Research into Occult History	52
4.	Rudolf Steiner on the First Section of the Esoteric School, 1904–1914	76
5.	The Structure of the Esoteric School	79
6.	The Movement, the Esoteric School, and the Society	92
7.	Separation of the Esoteric School from the Theosophical Society	101
8.	The Second Section of the Esoteric School, 1904–1914	114
9.	Establishing the Cognitive–Ritual Section	119
10.	Ritual in Rudolf Steiner's Esoteric Work	149
11.	The Meaning and Spiritual Origin of the Cognitive Ritual	184
12.	Esoteric Research into the Hiram–John Individuality	195
13.	Was Rudolf Steiner a Freemason?	211
14.	Clarifying Rudolf Steiner's Connection with Theodor Reuss	217
15.	The Esoteric School and a New Beginning after the War	237
16.	Adolf Arenson: A Circular to the Members and a Letter to Albert Steffen	247
17.	Concluding Remarks	255
	Index of Names	267
	Bibliography and Recommended Reading	271
	Bibliographic Sources for this Volume	278
	About the Author	279

Introduction

Rudolf Steiner (1861–1925) represented his pioneering insights for the new spiritual development in books, essays, and numerous lectures that were, mostly, recorded by stenographers. Historically, his starting point was Goethe and the German idealists. In 1882, the youthful age of twenty-one-year-old Rudolf Steiner was assigned the task of editing Goethe's natural–scientific writings for Kürschner's "German National Literature." He was called to Weimar to edit the large Sophia Edition of Goethe's works from 1890 to 1897. From 1897 to 1900, he published the *Magazine for Literature* in Berlin and was active as a teacher and lecturer in the Workers' Instructional School and in several other circles. During this early time he also published a number of philosophical books on Nietzsche, Goethe's worldview, the development of philosophy in the nineteenth century; and above all his foundational *Philosophy of Freedom* (1894).

In autumn 1900 (his fortieth year of life), the Berlin theosophists invited Rudolf Steiner to lecture on the recently deceased Friedrich Nietzsche. During that lecture, Steiner perceived that he had entered a circle in which "people had a great interest in the spiritual world." Immediately after the lecture he was asked to give another, so he spoke on Goethe's fairytale, "The Green Snake and the Beautiful Lily." In his *Autobiography* he remarks, "In *that* lecture I spoke of the fairytale from a purely esoteric perspective. This was an important experience for me. I was able to speak with words created directly from the spiritual world. Circumstances in

Berlin had thus far limited me to hinting about spirit, allowing it to shine only through my presentations" (p. 202). After the lecture, he was asked to present weekly lectures throughout the six months of the winter of 1900/01, which Steiner continued during the following winter. This led to him being asked at the end of 1901 if he would be prepared to assume leadership of the Theosophical Society Berlin Branch. The Count and Countess Brockdorff (its leaders until then) wished to step down owing to their age. When his condition was granted (that Marie von Sivers would be allowed to work with him in this task), he agreed, and thus became a member of the Theosophical Society.

The Theosophical Society had been founded in 1875 in New York City and lived according to the spiritual content communicated through Helena Petrovna Blavatsky, aka "HPB" (1831–1891). After 1879, the headquarters of the central leadership was located near Madras in Adyar, India. The German Branches were connected to the European Section with its headquarters in London. After Scandinavia, France, Holland, and Italy had established their own sections of the Society, there were growing efforts in the German Branches to establish their own Section. Richard Bresch, a member of the Leipzig Branch, approached Count Brockdorff with a recommendation: "Now that Dr. Steiner is president of the Berlin Lodge, he can also be the General Secretary of the German Section." Rudolf Steiner accepted this, and the German Section was established in October 1902 with Steiner as General Secretary, overseeing around a hundred members. Steiner's activity was a result of the fact that the German Section and its 2,500 members were expelled from the Theosophical Society in 1912/13. The Section was then reestablished as the Anthroposophical Society.

None of these external happenings influenced Rudolf Steiner's teaching, but (to a certain degree) only *how* he taught. The *what* continued to flow from *The Philosophy of Freedom*. The *how* resulted from the fact that, around turn of the century, the theosophists were

Introduction

the only group of people who could follow his spiritual–scientific presentations unhindered by strong biases. Those who had come together through the Theosophy could develop imaginations of the spiritual world that would make it possible for them to understand, because H. P. Blavatsky had already struck a hole in the materialism of the time through her work in the 1880s.

Initially Rudolf Steiner had to speak in a way *they* could understand; consequently he used the Indian-influenced terminology of Theosophy. Nonetheless, this was soon replaced (mostly in his public lectures) by terminology appropriate to contemporary times. Steiner in no way communicated only established theosophical doctrine in his lectures, but rather what he could say from his own research (see chapters 1 to 3). This is what the members wanted to hear and why they invited him into the Theosophical Society. The central leadership of the Theosophical Society in India had passed to Annie Besant, who was unable to tolerate the fact that the entire German Section had been expelled.

Soon after the German Section had been established, Steiner was asked, in part by some of those who already belonged to the English Esoteric School, to present esoteric instruction. Thus, he engaged in this and formed, within its framework, his own School in 1904 (see chapters 4 to 7). Although the connection with the English Esoteric School was tenuous (because Steiner led his School completely at his own discretion), it had become so weak that he felt the need to eliminate that connection again in 1907. Also, as leader of the Eastern School of Theosophy, Annie Besant had acted in an inappropriate way esoterically.

With the development of the Esoteric School, Rudolf Steiner found it necessary to take up a symbolic–cultic way of working. Because this should be connected with Freemasonry tradition, he allowed himself to be certified at a high degree in the order of Freemasonry. This was the Memphis–Misraim Rite led by John Yarker, who had already negotiated with H. P. Blavatsky about such a matter.

Thus, in 1906 the second division in the Esoteric School arose, the members of which also belonged to the first division, though not necessarily the other way around. In contrast to the first division, this second division was not a part of the order. Steiner had "absolutely nothing" to do with anything that otherwise took place in the order. Because the only existing connection with the order was organizational in nature, there was no reason to end that connection again (see chapters 8 to 14).

With the outbreak of World War I in 1914, all activity of the Esoteric School came to an end, since closed events were considered suspicious during the war. Moreover, the passionate agitation of the time was not conducive to esoteric work. Following the war, the situation changed to such a degree that the old forms of esotericism were no longer viable, whereas the development of newer forms required time. With the reestablishment of the Anthroposophical Society at Christmastime in 1923, Rudolf Steiner began to realize the new forms (see chapters 15 and 16).

We must never forget that Rudolf Steiner's presentations of esoteric content clearly avoid an easy, accessible establishment for the ordinary day-to-day consciousness; this is part of its nature. In addition, in an attempt to understand the motives of his actions in those intimate connections, we are far more dependent on lovingly entering what little he had to say about it. This book attempts this, as much as possible, by assembling and editing the collected commentaries on Rudolf Steiner's esoteric teaching activity.

I

RUDOLF STEINER IN THE HISTORY OF THE ESOTERIC MOVEMENT

FREE ESOTERICISM: A QUESTION OF METHODOLOGY

> *[Rudolf Steiner] has become the pioneer in this very area in which, through his indications, human beings have for the first time been allowed freedom.*[1]

As the first modern scientist of the suprasensory, Rudolf Steiner was completely thrown back upon his own resources. He taught only what he could vouch for through personal experience. Looking far ahead of his time he had discerned that the turning point of the end of the nineteenth century was not only the beginning of a new century, but also the beginning of a totally new epoch, when humanity would be faced with social upheavals of unimagined magnitude. He saw that with the increasing awareness of the individual, a tremendous struggle for freedom would ensue; through the ever more prevalent influence of the agnostic and pragmatic ways of thinking of the mechanical–materialistic sciences, great advances would certainly be made but, at the same time, the last vestiges of ancient inherited wisdom, which sees the creative–spiritual world as the origin and goal of all existence, would be lost. The inevitable

---

1 From Marie Steiner's preface to Rudolf Steiner, *The Stages of Higher Knowledge*, CW 12, p. viii.

result of this would be a universal devastation of the spiritual and a feeling of meaninglessness in life.

Through this insight Rudolf Steiner was convinced that this historic process, necessary for general progress, can be met by only one thing: a view of the world and of life founded on individual awareness, oriented toward what is spiritually creative. Thus he developed modern Spiritual Science (or Anthroposophy) through his own firsthand knowledge of the suprasensory guidance of the world and human destiny, and lived and taught in accordance with the spirit of modern times, according to the precept *freedom* and through the spirit of modern science in the realm of the suprasensory, the esoteric.

With this basic aim, he effected at the same time a historic turn in the esoteric movement, for this movement had acquired its store of wisdom from a consciousness springing from other sources. It was derived from the so-called archetypal wisdom that had been revealed to humanity during primeval times and had endowed it with an extensive control over the material powers of existence. As long as human beings still acted without individual responsibility, in full accord with the intentions of the spiritual worlds, this wisdom was a part of the heritage of knowledge belonging to the whole of humankind. But when, on the road to the development of personality, egoism arose, and the unquestioned connection with the suprasensory worlds faded, the suprasensory knowledge, which was a source of power, had to be protected from misuse. It was withdrawn into the mysteries. But from there it directed the public life of culture for a long time, even into the beginning of the Christian era. Through Christianity and growing intellectualism, when the progressive cultural consciousness directed its attention increasingly strongly toward the cognition of the laws of the material universe, the mysteries gradually lost their dominant position and were finally extirpated as public institutions. Since then, the ancient wisdom of the mysteries could only be cultivated within restricted, secret circles. There it was strictly guarded until, in the nineteenth century, the signs of the times demanded that a spiritual counterpart be set against the purely materialistic–agnostic way of thinking of civilized society.

This task had given rise to a question that had become a weighty problem for the esoteric movement of the nineteenth century. Should this body of knowledge remain secret or would it be better to make it generally known? This question touched the pulse of existing practice so deeply that a decision could not be made immediately to popularize them; to prevent their misuse, truths had been handed on since early times higher only to those who had been specially prepared to receive it. A compromise solution was tried, first testing, as it were, public reaction to the announcement proclaiming the existence of spiritual worlds and beings. Thus came about the spiritualistic-mediumistic movement of the 1840s to the 1870s. The result was certainly different from what had been expected but, nevertheless, the dam of strict secrecy had been broken and it now became inevitable that at least the main truths should be openly revealed. This came about through the Theosophical Society founded in 1875 by a Russian, Helena Petrovna Blavatsky, and an American, Henry Steel Olcott.

These two experiments certainly gave rise to sensational movements (Spiritualism and Theosophy), but in a deeper sense, they must be considered to have failed in their intention, mostly because the cultural norm of natural–scientific thinking rejected the mediumistic way as unscientific. This was justified inasmuch as this way signified not only a going back to former stages of consciousness, but also a curtailing of the free choice of the individual. On the other hand, mediumism had up till then been the only surviving method of spiritual investigation.[2]

---

2   For more see *The Occult Movement in the Nineteenth Century*, CW 254. Compare also the two lectures translated from CW 52, "The History of Spiritism" and "The History of Hypnotism and Somnambulism," Berlin, May 30, 1904, and June 6, 1904. Other lectures in this series have not yet been translated.

While this dilemma was still being faced by the occult movement at the end of the nineteenth century, the problem had been solved by Rudolf Steiner along his own individual path to the spirit. He had gained the crucial understanding that suprasensory knowledge and reality can unite in a healthy way with modern civilized life only when the method employed ensures that exactness and independence are equally achieved, as with modern natural science. He had not acquired this knowledge from the traditional teaching guarded by the occult societies, but from what he had acquired quite naturally through his childhood experiences and by mastery over the mechanical–materialistic manner of thought he had encountered in his natural–scientific upbringing.

Based on this knowledge he made his first task the development of a method of suprasensory investigation founded entirely on natural–scientific principles. By strict self-discipline, leading from sense-imbued thinking to thinking free of the senses, he found the necessary certitude regarding the spirit as such. At the same time he recognized freedom as an actual experience and as the bearer of true morality. Thinking that is free of the senses thus became for him the starting point for a scientifically clear connection to the suprasensory world and for a science of freedom as the basis of "ethical individualism."

The logical extension of the inner experience of the "I" led, furthermore, to the perception of the macrocosmic representative of "I"-being, the Christ Spirit, whose nature is expressed in true freedom and love. Thereby, Rudolf Steiner had also paved the way to the understanding of the two Christian ideals appropriate to our time: freedom and love, which he constantly referred to as the basic impulses behind the central event of humanity's development, the Mystery of Golgotha. And connected with it is humanity's greatest task: "to transform the Earth into a cosmos of freedom and love" (Düsseldorf, Apr. 18, 1919, CW 110).

This relationship of the human "I" to the World-"I" is later touched on by Rudolf Steiner in a lecture given in Dornach on May 24, 1920 (CW 74): "The 'ethical individualism' of my *Philosophy of Freedom* is, in reality, founded upon the Christ impulse in humanity, although this is not expressed in the book." He also said later that, at the present time, the only way to directly convey the original wisdom springing from initiation is to preserve one's association with Christ (Stuttgart, March 7, 1920, CW 197). This association, acquired through sense-free thinking in what Rudolf Steiner calls "the emancipation of the human being's higher consciousness from the fetters of every authority,"[3] provides the necessary condition whereby esotericism could be set free in a wholesome way from attachment to certain brotherhoods. If, in the past, one had been able to penetrate to the world of spiritual realities only through a dimming of one's consciousness, and under the guidance of a spiritual leader whose authority had to be unconditionally acknowledged, now, through Rudolf Steiner's pioneering deed, every serious aspirant can achieve this in a clear state of consciousness and with free responsibility for his or her own actions.

The only condition attached to this, to which everyone is obliged individually, is activity of soul and spirit. This is essential not only for the individual, but for the general progress of humanity. Indeed, this is so to such an extent that civilization must cease altogether unless every single person is prepared to bring to it a new impulse through a renewed knowledge of the spirit. This was expressed by Rudolf Steiner decades ago (Dornach, July 2, 1920, CW 198).

It is just in this matter of activating the will of the individual to social responsibility that anthroposophic Spiritual Science differs so fundamentally from the ancient wisdom guarded in the esoteric brotherhoods. For concepts springing from the latter source, proceeding as they do from revelations from a period in human history

---

3   Letter to Rosa Mayreder, Dec. 14, 1893, in *Briefe Band II: 1890–1925* (letters, vol. 2), Dornach 1953 (CW 39).

still rooted in a group soul consciousness, can provide no new, valid social impulses. On the other hand, no new impulses can be developed where no knowledge arises through initiation. For this reason Anthroposophy can be explained through social necessity as an instrument to produce new spiritual revelations, which take into account the consciousness of the individual. It had become a task of culturally historic importance to make the new revelations of the spirit understandable to human beings, especially those that had appeared after the end of the Kali Yuga period in 1899. Through this, the greatest event of humanity's history—the Mystery of Golgotha—was rendered accessible again, and to this end Rudolf Steiner dedicated his efforts. He remarked on one occasion, "Anyone who cannot understand Anthroposophy in this sense is unable to understand it at all" (Dornach, Dec. 20, 1918, CW 186). Therefore, when he began lecturing about the social question, he appealed to his hearers' power of discernment:

> Who can speak about the burning questions of the moment in a really modern and pertinent way, so that it goes to the heart of the matter? You cannot discover this in the rituals and statutes of this or that Masonic or Confessional Body. One would like to see a capacity for discernment taking hold of people. (Dornach, Dec. 15, 1918, CW 186)

In this same connection he asserted that the spiritual current he represented had never been dependent on any other, and that he was therefore not obliged to anyone to be silent about anything that he thought should be spoken about at the present time:

> A pledge of silence cannot be imposed on those who are not indebted to anyone else for their store of spiritual insight. This forms the basis for discriminating between this and other movements. Those who would assert at any time that what is proclaimed by anthroposophically oriented Spiritual Science differs from the sense of what is expressed in my book *Theosophy* (the words of which I can personally certify) are saying

something untrue, whether it is through ill will or not. Insofar as I am concerned, such judgment might be made in ignorance of the circumstances, or frequently a person might not have been present and were judging from outer appearances only. Nonetheless, those who have been with us for a while and state something different, using another spiritual movement to substantiate what they say about (for example, a past event or connection of this movement) but actually know the circumstances here—they are lying. Those are the facts of the case. Either a person is stating an untruth through ignorance of the circumstances or telling a lie while knowing those circumstances. This is how all opposition toward our movement should be understood. Thus, I must emphasize repeatedly: I need to remain silent only about things that I know may not be divulged because people today are unripe to receive them. However, there is nothing that I must remain silent about because of a pledge or anything of that sort made to anyone. Nothing has ever entered this movement that has come from anywhere else. This movement has never been spiritually dependent on any other; such connections were only external. (Dornach, Dec. 15, 1918, CW 186)

This statement leads to the question: why did Rudolf Steiner then link to other movements at all, when he felt obliged to reject both the old method of keeping everything secret, as well as the old practices used in their investigation? This contradiction is only solved when one takes into account the two main rules of esoteric life that Rudolf Steiner always worked to comply with when at all possible. They are the rules of absolute truthfulness and of preserving continuity. These two rules were placed ever and again before the souls of his esoteric pupils.[4] He adhered to the rule of absolute truthfulness in that he taught only those things he knew to be true through his own investigation. He followed the rule of preserving continuity by not simply putting something quite new and better in the

---

4 Disclosed by a member of the Working Committee of the Esoteric School, in a letter from Adolf Arenson to Albert Steffen, Dec. 24, 1926.

place of the less perfect, but by linking in every case to an already existing situation and seeking to transform it into something more perfect. This signified an awakening to life within him of the deepest Christian concept, the concept of resurrection. If we are able to experience within ourselves how the present can be carried over into the future in a living way, thus fulfilling the Gospel words that we should remain related to one another not only in the body through the blood, but should relate to one another in the soul life through the spirit, then the way to an understanding of the Mystery of Golgotha has been discovered.

Much could be gained, according to Rudolf Steiner's conviction, if people of a later generation would take their guidance from the dead, whereby a continuity of development would be consciously preserved. When he wrote about Goethe, he completely ignored his own opinion and attempted to express only the thoughts originating from Goethe; he wrote a theory of knowledge of Goethe and did not give his own philosophy of life. Just as in the case of Goethe's world conception, he also immersed himself in the thought worlds of Friedrich Nietzsche and Ernst Haeckel, for we are able to attain to true knowledge only if we do not absolutely insist on our own point of view, but submerge ourselves in the spiritual views of others. And only after he had struggled to work in this way for twenty years to gain the right, so to speak, to work on the living, did he begin to disseminate Spiritual Science in public. For then no one could any longer rightly maintain: This occultist speaks about the spiritual world because he is ignorant of the philosophical and natural-scientific achievements of the age.[5]

This path, so unusual to ordinary understanding and perception, was incomprehensible to Rudolf Steiner's opponents, and was understood only with difficulty by friends sympathetic to a spiritual-scientific view. Because he was aware of this difficulty, he took

---

5 See *The Connection between the Living and the Dead*, Berne, Nov. 9, 1916, CW 168; see also the autobiographical sketch of 1907 in *Correspondence and Documents 1901–1925*, CW 262.

pains again and again to make clear, at least to his anthroposophic friends, that the spiritual current to which he adhered had never depended upon other currents, and that certain connections had been only outer ones. He admitted, however, that the distinction had been made more difficult through historical happenings. However, although it might appear to superficially that it would have been more advisable to found the Anthroposophical Society independently of other societies, the connections were nevertheless justified in terms of karma.

This remark makes it evident that the linking up with other societies that took place at the time, was necessitated by the interplay of forces arising between the polarities of *freedom* and *love*, as they are justifiably expressed in esoteric life as *truthfulness* and *continuity*. Working toward truth and knowledge requires freedom, but at the same time, what has been recognized as true must link in fellowship to what already exists in the world. It is significant that even Rudolf Steiner's great strength was not always sufficient to reconcile the polarities of a life devoted in freedom and truth to the search for knowledge while trying to preserve continuity in the cause of fellowship. This was objectively unattainable because, where continuity is concerned, the world is involved, and though Rudolf Steiner respected continuity in a far greater measure than is normally the case, nevertheless, he could not sacrifice truthfulness to the cause of fellowship. When this became an acute problem in the Theosophical Society it led to separation.

Only by failing to consider Rudolf Steiner's discernment toward these polarities of esoteric life can misunderstandings and wrong judgments occur with regard to his spiritual independence. But, beyond all such fleeting opinions, the historical importance of Rudolf Steiner's cultural act—that of creating, through his method of spiritual investigation, a science that allows freedom to be found in the realm of the esoteric—will become increasingly acknowledged.

Here it might be objected that, through the creation of his Esoteric School, Rudolf Steiner did impose a rule of *secrecy* after all. This argument is not justified, however, for, in Steiner's view, it was never a case of keeping anything secret in the usual sense of the term, not even in the Esoteric School. For him it was a matter of upholding a truly scientific attitude that, in the cultural life of our time, demands as a matter of course that serious knowledge can only be acquired step by step. For example, no one who has not received the requisite grounding can be instructed in the higher stages of geometry. Whereas this is clear to everyone in the case of geometry, the most widespread belief is that in the realm of suprasensory knowledge everything can be comprehended and judged without any kind of preliminary requirements.

Solely in accordance with this impartial and methodical approach, Rudolf Steiner's way of teaching ranged from what was completely free and public to what was conditional. The common basis of all these stages of instruction subsisted in what he proclaimed as his "act of inauguration," which occurred at the commencement of his public activity on behalf of a science of the suprasensory.

"I will build on the strength that enables me to lead the pupils of the spirit along the pathway of development. This will be the sole meaning of my act of inauguration."[6]

The Esoteric School served this purpose in its particular way insofar as its pupils received their instruction entirely in accordance with their individual needs and capabilities. It existed, from 1904 until the outbreak of World War I in the summer of 1914, in three sections. True to the law of esotericism (to maintain continuity as far as possible and in as far as this lay in the direction of personal intentions), it was connected with what already existed. The first section was connected to the Esoteric School of Theosophy of the Theosophical Society; the second section, the cognitive–ritual

---

[6] Letter of Aug. 16, 1902, to the representative of the German theosophists, Wilhelm Hübbe-Schleiden, from *Briefe II* (not translated).

section, was connected to a Society with Freemason ritual forms; this kind of connection for the third section is not known. It was reported that only twelve proven pupils of Rudolf Steiner belonged to it—pupils with whom questions about the spiritual existence of the anthroposophic movement were discussed.[7]

---

[7] As reported orally to Hella Wiesberger by Emil Leinhas and Günther Schubert. See Rudolf Steiner's statement to Marie Steiner on the three classes of the "Independent School for Spiritual Science" (chapter 15 in this volume).

2

Rudolf Steiner as a Teacher of Esotericism

One cannot separate Rudolf Steiner's works from his biography. Everything he taught was personally accomplished and developed by him, in the same way that, by his own testimony, his major philosophical work, *The Philosophy of Freedom*, contained "personal experience in every line."[1] He developed the book's philosophical outlook in relation to the nature of pure thinking, as his own personal point of departure. Twenty years later, he proposed it as the necessary starting point for those "who wish to undergo their own esoteric development," formulating this in the following simple yet vivid terms:

> A great figure of the Enlightenment was held to have expressed something of great importance when he said in the eighteenth century: "People, dare to use your faculty of reason!" Today, a still greater phrase needs to resound in our souls: "People, dare to see your concepts and ideas as the beginnings of your clairvoyant faculties!"

True sight could not develop if one had not already had a "grain" of clairvoyance in one's soul (initially in one's concepts and ideas) that can be developed to greater and unlimited extent. This is the reason it is important to understand that clairvoyance really begins with mundane things. "We need only to grasp the

---

1 Letter dated Nov. 4, 1894, to Rosa Mayreder, in *Briefe II* (Letters), 1891–1924, CW 39.

suprasensory nature of our concepts and ideas," becoming clear that these enter our soul not from the sensory world, but from worlds of spirit (Helsinki, May 29, 1913, CW 146). Steiner himself developed his scientific outlook and ethics of freedom from this grasp of the suprasensory nature of concepts and ideas; he was also able to realize ethical individualism in the realm of esoteric research through the resulting "emancipation of higher human consciousness from the chains of all authority."[2] He regarded it as his special task to make individual research the sole basis of his work. From the beginning of his spiritual–scientific endeavors, he stressed that what he developed in this field would be oriented to "the starting point initiated in *The Philosophy of Freedom*" (Dornach, Oct. 27, 1918, CW 185). This remark accords with the statement during that same period about pure thinking as the core idea in that book: "I regard this pure thinking as the first still shadowy revelation of spiritual stages of knowledge."[3]

Until Rudolf Steiner embarked on his work, secrecy and strict personal tutelage governed all serious paths into suprasensory worlds. He was the first to initiate a modern path to spiritual knowledge without dependence on authority. In order to make this path available to humanity as a whole, the results of his spiritual research were always reported alongside an account of the method by which he had gained them. He once referred to this as follows: "We can distinguish two aspects of what is now called Anthroposophy. One is the type of thinking used or the mode of enquiry and research involved. The other is the content, the results of the spiritual research insofar as it has been possible to elaborate them."[4] Development of these two aspects occurred, naturally, as a gradual process.

---

2   Letter of Dec. 14, 1983, to Rosa Mayreder, op. cit.
3   Essay, "Spiritual Science as Anthroposophy and the Contemporary Theory of Knowledge," 1917, in: *Philosophy and Anthroposophy*, CW 35.
4   Dornach, June 5, 1920; not yet included in the Collected Works (CW).

1. The Epistemological Foundation

The capacity to meet the reality of the conceptual realm is something I have presented as primary philosophical experience, saying also that such an experience allows us to stand in the world as a confluence of the human "I" and the content of the spiritual world. I have tried to show that this experience is just as real as sensory experience. The spiritual content of Anthroposophy has grown from this primary experience of spiritual insight.[5]

In his *Autobiography*, Rudolf Steiner related how, even as a child, he experienced the world as dual reality: "I had two notions that, although somewhat vague, played a great part in my inner life before I was eight. I distinguished between things and entities 'one sees' and those 'one does not see.'" And although the world of spirit was as self-evident for him as the world of the senses, he felt the need for a "kind of justification" of this other realm of experience: "I wanted to be able to tell myself that my experience of the spiritual world was not illusory but as real as that of the sensory world." The eight-year-old then had an experience that helped orient him. He discovered a book on geometry in his village schoolmaster's classroom; and entirely on his own, he began to explore mathematical ideas enthusiastically. He felt an inner joy at "being able to grasp something purely in the mind." And it struck him that, as in geometry, when the soul "experiences things through its own powers alone" then inevitably one gains inner knowledge of the spiritual world. Looking back to his relationship with geometry he saw "the first surfacing of an outlook" that gradually developed and assumed a "fully conscious form" when he was about twenty.[6]

---

5   Review of "Alois Mager's book *Theosophy and Christianity,* Nov. 1924, in *Der Goetheanumgedanke inmitten der Kulturkrise der Gegenwart* (The Goetheanum idea amid the present cultural crisis), CW 36.

6   *Autobiography,* CW 28, ch. 1.

Following this experience of geometry he sought increasingly to develop his powers of thinking. He tried to delineate every thought clearly, to avoid its being pulled in some uncontrolled direction by any vague, passing feeling. He also wished to form a clear view about how "human thinking relates to the creative life of nature."[7] Thus his striving for knowledge focused tirelessly on the scientific outlook of the time, and on philosophical views of the nature of knowledge, that informed the intellectual life of the second half of the nineteenth century.

In science, Charles Darwin and Ernst Haeckel's theories of natural evolution of living creatures and humankind were having a revolutionary impact and had radically undermined traditional views of divine creation. Rudolf Steiner witnessed how a great many people began to question past ideals and religious convictions, being compelled to believe that if scientific views were correct, then human beings must be the product of natural necessity. In this case, all ideals and religious persuasions would be illusory, and freedom would be impossible.[8] In philosophy, the prevailing view was that we come up against certain limits to knowledge, which human consciousness cannot move beyond. Thus it must accept these limits and forego any knowledge of what lies as true reality beyond the world it creates within itself.

Rudolf Steiner was unable to embrace contemporary evolutionary theory wholeheartedly because it failed to take any account of the autonomous existence and activity of the spirit. Nor could he accept the postulate of limits to knowledge. His own experience of cognition told him that when sensory reality is "properly known," it shows itself to be a manifestation of spirit; "if we deepen our thinking sufficiently, we can live in a spiritual reality that we experience inwardly and recognize in life."[9]

---

[7] *Autobiography*, CW 28, ch. 2.

[8] Public lecture in Stuttgart, May 25, 1921, in *Beiträge zur Rudolf Steiner Gesamtausgabe* (contributions to the Rudolf Steiner collected works), no. 116, 1996.

[9] *Goethe's Theory of Knowledge*, p. 2 (CW 2).

He became ever more convinced, therefore, that a new worldview was needed to do full justice to both halves of reality—nature and spirit. He was clear from the outset that the scientific value of this new outlook would depend on the soundness of its epistemological basis. Only when a theory of knowledge, as a foundational science of the diverse sciences, was able to show that they are all predicated on the very nature of cognition itself, would it be possible to clarify the relationship of each scientific domain to the world, and thus arrive at a true worldview. In contrast to previous theories of knowledge (none of which, he found, had dispensed with underlying assumptions) this required proof through "analysis of the act of cognition delving back into its ultimate elements" that "our thinking can attain everything necessary for explaining and fathoming the world."[10] This fundamental idea was already present in his very first written attempt to reformulate Fichte's *Science of Knowledge* in 1879, written during the period between his completion of secondary education and the start of his studies at Vienna's technical college.[11]

At the beginning of the 1880s, Steiner was commissioned to edit and write commentaries on Goethe's scientific writings for Kürschner's German National Literature series; and in doing so, he explored Goethe's epistemological approach to diverse fields of research. It became ever clearer to him that his own outlook was in harmony with Goethe's worldview. He therefore wrote his first epistemological work as a supplement to Goethe's scientific writings—*Goethe's Theory of Knowledge: An Outline of the Epistemology of His Worldview* (1886, CW 2). Nearly forty years later, when he reissued this text in 1923, Steiner wrote in the preface to the new edition that this text still seemed to him to be the "basis and justification of all he had subsequently stated and published," since it speaks of the nature of cognition as releasing us from the sensory world and pursuing a path into a world of spirit.

---

10 *Truth and Science*, preface, CW 3.
11 In *Beiträge...* (contributions...), no. 30, summer 1970.

Looking back to his initial basic research at various later points, he always stressed that his principal question at the time concerned the extent to which one can prove the reality of spirit at work in human thinking. To solve this question, he set himself the task of comprehending the nature of human thinking itself. To do so, he first set aside all visions of a spiritual world available to him. In his words, "Regardless of how convincing subjective visions might be, however intensely they arise before the soul, we are not justified in concluding objective validity from their subjective emergence, unless we can also make a bridge from sure scientific foundations to the world of spirit.

By every means possible he tried to discover the real nature of human thinking, until he realized that we can properly understand this thinking only if we see in its highest expressions something that is accomplished "independently of corporeal organization." This meant that already in the "most mundane daily life" there is a "suprasensory" element, if we can only raise ourselves to pure thinking, where we are not governed or determined by anything other than the contents of thinking itself; rather than what proceeds from bodily processes as the natural necessity of instincts, will impulses, and so forth.[12] He had therefore gained the certainty needed to bridge scientific and spiritual knowledge: "I tried to build this bridge already in my introductions to Goethe's scientific writings [1883–1897]. Then I pursued this particularly in my little book *Truth and Science* [1892] and my longer book *The Philosophy of Freedom* [1894].... I believe that this *Philosophy of Freedom* confirmed for me nothing less than the suprasensory nature of human thinking."[13]

In Steiner's view, therefore, he had found proof that our capacity to penetrate the reality of the spiritual realm can be epistemologically substantiated just as fully as the way we penetrate sensory reality. For him this justified the claim of exact scientific procedure in developing according to the "model of pure thinking," the stages

---

12 Public lecture, Stuttgart May 25, 1921, in *Beiträge...*, no. 116, 1996.
13 Op. cit.

of higher knowledge that pass through Imagination, Inspiration, and Intuition.

> In my spiritual–scientific writings I present processes of cognition that lead, through spiritual experience and observation, to concepts of the spiritual world in just the same way as our senses and the rationality associated with them lead to concepts of the sensory world, and the human life unfolding in it. In my view this can be justified as truly scientific only if there exists proof that the process of pure thinking itself is already the first stage in processes by means of which suprasensory knowledge can be attained. I believe that I have given such proof in my earlier writings.[14]

After developing Anthroposophy (at that time still called *Theosophy*) over a ten-year period, Steiner was asked to give a lecture on theosophy at the fourth international philosophy conference in Bologna (April 1911). The lecture was titled "Theosophy's Psychological Foundations and Epistemological Stance."[15] He concluded his observations with the following words:

> The soul disposition of the spiritual researcher can only be understood as a state in which the illusion of ordinary consciousness is overcome, giving rise in the soul to an incipient experience of the core and essence of the human being in free release from the corporeal organism. Everything else that can then be achieved through practice is only a deeper delving into the transcendent, in which the "I" of ordinary consciousness really resides, although it may be unaware that it does. Spiritual research is therefore proven to be epistemologically conceivable. This conceivability, of course, will be acknowledged only by those who can accept that our so-called critical theory of knowledge maintains the impossibility of a leap in consciousness solely by failing to penetrate the illusion that the core human entity is imprisoned in the body and can receive

---

14 Essay, "Spiritual Science as Anthroposophy and the Contemporary Theory of Knowledge," 1917, in *Philosophy and Anthroposophy*, CW 35.

15 Quoted in *Philosophy and Anthroposophy*, CW 35.

only sensory impressions. I am aware that my epistemological comments here offer only rough indications. However, it may be possible to see from these suggestions that they are not isolated instances; but, in fact, arise from a fully developed underlying epistemological outlook.

2. Public (Exoteric) Accounts of Spiritual Training

> *I wish to build on the power that enables me to help spiritual pupils embark on self-development. That must be the whole import of my inaugurating deed.*[16]

Toward the end of the nineteenth century, Rudolf Steiner became ever more certain that if suprasensory knowledge (which he saw as essential for the flourishing of further human development) were to become common currency in a form fully appropriate to modern consciousness, then it would have to be conveyed other than in purely scientific and philosophical ways. He therefore wondered how to "express the inner truths of my vision in a way that could be understood by the modern age."[17] Having wrestled with this question, he resolved to go public with detailed accounts of the world of spirit.

To really get a sense of the gravity of this decision, we should recall that at that period suprasensory knowledge was known as something to be cultivated only within strictly closed circles, in the form of ancient traditions and symbols. An initial breach had been made in this tradition of secrecy by H. P. Blavatsky's publications; but among the general public there was greater interest in sensational phenomena such as somnambulism, mediumism, and spiritualism. Rudolf Steiner inevitably rejected such things, because of his view of higher human powers of cognition. His spiritual insight

---

16 Letter of Aug. 16, 1902, to Wilhelm Hübbe-Schleiden. Published so far only in the first edition of *Briefe II* (letters), Dornach 1955.

17 *Autobiography*, CW 28, chapter 23.

showed him that "supposed perception," which fails to acknowledge pure thinking as a kind of model, and moves in the realm of spirit without the same degree of careful reflection and inner clarity as sharply delineated thinking, "cannot lead us into a real world of spirit."[18] At the time therefore, since prevailing scientific circles repudiated anything suprasensory as wholly suspect, great courage was needed for a well-known writer in the fields of science and philosophy to publicize his detailed perceptions of suprasensory realities and to claim scientific respectability for them.

When, in the final year of the nineteenth century, he began to act on this decision, he took his point of departure from a cultural legacy that he had long regarded as one of the "most profound texts in world literature. This was Goethe's mysterious fairytale, "The Green Snake and Beautiful Lily" (Munich, May 22, 1907, CW 99). He saw this tale as an expression of the fact that Goethe had always regarded the human faculty of knowledge as capable of development, and that this indicated nothing other than the principle of initiation: "Initiation therefore means nothing other than enhancing human capacities to ever-higher levels of knowledge and perception; and thus achieving deeper insights into the true nature of the world" (Berlin, Oct. 24, 1908, CW 57).

In his essay "Goethe's Secret Revelation: In Celebration of the 150th Anniversary of Goethe's Birth, August 1899," Steiner began by transposing the content of the fairytale's images into modern concepts. He showed that the fairytale is concerned with the great question of how to develop the powers of our psyche in a new era in which we seek to rise from an earthly realm to a spiritual realm. The solution to this riddle, he said, is hinted at in the story. Previously there were only two states of soul that enabled people to reach suprasensory realms, both involuntary. One was through creative imagination, which is a reflection of suprasensory experience; and

---

18 Essay, "Spiritual Science as Anthroposophy and the Contemporary Theory of Knowledge," 1917, in *Philosophy and Anthroposophy*, CW 35.

the other arises when conscious perception is darkened and weakened, in the form of superstition, visions, and mediumistic states. The time had arrived, said Steiner, for a new state of awareness that could be consciously and intentionally created. This, however, required "the snake," representing sensory forms of knowledge, to gain the insight that the highest can be achieved only through selfless devotion and sacrifice. As soon as the snake is willing to give up her own, self-referential existence, her body forms itself into a bridge over the great river, uniting the two realms of sensory and spiritual reality, and allowing all to pass over it.[19]

No one is likely to have noticed at the time that this transposition of Goethean images into modern conceptual language was also a significant step in cultural history, although this became ever more apparent as time passed. Just one year later, in the fall of 1900, Rudolf Steiner was invited to give lectures to a group of people who, although not scientists, were profoundly interested in real spiritual knowledge. This was the Berlin group of the Theosophical Society, which H. P. Blavatsky and others had founded in America in 1875, and that relocated its headquarters to India shortly afterward. In this group of Berlin theosophists, who were open to detailed accounts of spiritual insight, Steiner was now able to speak "very esoterically" of things he had only hinted at in his essay on Goethe's fairytale. "For me it was an important experience to be able to speak in words informed by the world of spirit, having previously been compelled by circumstances...to allow the spiritual realm to shine through what I had to say in only a veiled way."[20]

This lecture on the fairytale became the "seed" of the anthroposophic movement. The first, decisive phrase in the tale, "The time has come!" is uttered in a mighty voice by the "old man with the

---

19 The essay of 1899 is in CW 30, *Methodische Grundlagen der Anthroposophie* (Methodical Foundations of Anthroposophy).

20 *Autobiography*, CW 28, chapter 30.

lamp," a figure who guides and directs all that occurs. That phrase gained added force from the growing realization of the tale's second phrase: "One person alone does not help, but rather he who unites with many at the right time." Teacher and pupils have a mutually enhancing effect. With this in mind, after being invited in the spring of 1902 to take on the role of General Secretary of the new German Section of the Society, and just before accepting it, Rudolf Steiner described how he saw his task in a letter to a representative of the German theosophists. "I wish to build on the power that enables me to help spiritual pupils embark on self-development. That must be the whole import of my inaugurating deed."[21] From then on, with increasing intensity, he elaborated his Spiritual Science, at the same time developing an association geared to cultivating this work and representing it publicly.

Whereas his essay on Goethe's fairytale (1899) could only hint at the new initiation principle, this was now clearly documented in the first two series of lectures he gave to the theosophists in Berlin, published as *Mystics after Modernism* (CW 7, 1901) and *Christianity as Mystical Fact* (CW 8, 1902). In the foreword to *Mystics after Modernism*, he expressed his conviction that the modern achievements of science need enhancing into true mysticism, stating that it is perfectly possible to be both a "faithful adherent of the scientific worldview" and yet at the same time also seek "the paths of the soul" that lead to an appropriate mysticism. Indeed, one can gain a full understanding of natural phenomena only if one acknowledges the spirit as true mysticism does. Likewise, in his foreword to *Christianity as Mystical Fact*, which examines Christianity in the context of the mysteries, and thus in terms of initiation, he wrote: "I hope I have written no single line that I could not justify in terms of a truly self-comprehending examination of nature, nor one that agrees with the crassly materialistic view of many modern scientific thinkers."

---

21 *Goethe's Theory of Knowledge*, CW 2, Preface to the new edition 1924.

As his work continued, his insight into the nature of Christianity, its "mystical fact," became ever more profound and was accentuated in relation to the path of schooling. The death of Christ at Golgotha enabled the power of Christ, previously found only in spiritual heights, to unite with earthly evolution. Since then, there lives within the soul of each of us the strength to find the path into the world of spirit by our own resources. By contrast, before that event, this was possible only by adhering to the authority and instructions dispensed by teachers in the mystery schools.

It is therefore due to the Golgotha event that we can attain higher knowledge through spiritual self-education. This can happen, though, only if we make ourselves into appropriate instruments. Just as no one can see that water contains hydrogen and oxygen (which have quite different properties from water) by mere external observation, and without chemical analysis, so we cannot recognize the true reality of the soul and spirit without using methods of spiritual–scientific research to release soul and spirit from external corporeality. This, however, is a different kind of process, one that takes place within the soul and must be prepared in its most profound depths (Norrköping, Sweden, July 13, 1914, CW 155).

The guidance and instruction necessary for this could not, however, be taught publicly until the required forces of the consciousness soul developed, as they did increasingly from the fifteenth and sixteenth centuries. Only in consequence of this did it become possible for a scientist with spiritual vision to elaborate the methodology of the path of knowledge and teach this methodology in public. For a modern spiritual researcher who works in this way, the time of the old prophets is now past. As a "sober investigator," the researcher desires only to draw attention to what is needed in order to pursue studies of the human soul's profundities. The spiritual researcher says: "I have found this; and if you search for it, you too will find it!" In Steiner's view the time would soon come when people would regard a spiritual researcher, like a chemist or biologist, as a "sober investigator." The only difference is that the spiritual researcher inquires into a realm that closely concerns every human soul (ibid.).

As we move on into the future, the importance of Rudolf Steiner's work will inevitably be seen primarily in the methodology he developed for all of us, as a pioneer in his field. Prior to this, no such method existed for independent and reproducible verification of the reality of the world of spirit. *Theosophy* (1904) was Steiner's first written introduction to the suprasensory foundations of the world and humanity. It has a final chapter entitled "The Path of Knowledge" in which he first publicly described the conditions necessary for pursuing a spiritual–scientific methodology. In this first account, he stressed, above all, that higher faculties of cognition can proceed only from thinking, since this is the highest capacity that we possess within the sensory world. Immediately after this, in ongoing essays, he began to describe specific stages on this path, later published in *How to Know Higher Worlds*. Its first sentence states: "In each of us slumber capacities by means of which we can acquire knowledge of higher worlds." In further publications, in particular the major work *An Outline of Esoteric Science* (1910), and in many lectures, besides publicizing ongoing new research findings, he also kept adding new aspects of the path of spiritual schooling.

We can see the importance Rudolf Steiner himself ascribed to these public accounts of the path of schooling from statements such as the following:

> In our time, the principle of initiation has undergone a great change, insofar as it can be achieved to a certain degree and level without direct personal instruction by virtue of the fact that today one can present the principles of initiation in the public domain; I did this in *How to Know Higher Worlds*. Anyone who makes earnest efforts to follow and experience what is described there can make a great deal of progress in relation to the principle of initiation (Berlin, Feb. 3, 1913, CW 144).

It would be a misunderstanding, however, to conclude from these words that anyone interested in Spiritual Science must embark on spiritual schooling. Steiner expressed his view about this in a personal letter as follows: "Theosophy is necessary today.... However, it would be undesirable for every theosophist to decide to become an esoteric pupil. This would be rather as if everyone thought they had to become tailors because everybody needs clothes."[22] He also stated this in public: "I would expressly point out that there is no need for every person to become a spiritual researcher to gain the proper soul benefit from Spiritual Science, or Anthroposophy."[23]

Although he was very concerned to help spiritual pupils embark on self-development, the primary need, as he saw it, was for knowledge of the reality of the spiritual world to increasingly inform humanity in general through the publicizing of spiritual–scientific research results. However, he considered it essential that this should occur in a way appropriate to the nature of such knowledge, and not in some diluted or popularized form. For this reason, he said, he had intentionally given his writings a character that required real efforts of thinking to engage with their content. He was clear that such activation of thinking already contained the seeds of spiritual schooling.[24]

In another context one even finds the following remark: "I do not lecture on Theosophy for any external reason but because this is the first stage of Rosicrucian initiation" (Munich, June 6, 1907, CW 99). By "Rosicrucian," however, he did not mean the return to some historical body of knowledge, but rather a further evolving and living Rosicrucianism. For this reason, too, what is presented in *How to Know Higher Worlds* as "the most suitable path" into the spiritual

---

22 Letter dated Sept. 20, 1907, in CW 264, *From the History and Contents of the First Section of the Esoteric School 1904–1914*, CW 264.

23 "Human Life from the Perspective of Spiritual Science (Anthroposophy)" in *Philosophy and Anthroposophy*, CW 35.

24 *An Outline of Esoteric Science*, CW 13, preface to the 16th–20th German editions.

spheres should not be confused with what can be called the Rosicrucian path. "Our stream," which encompasses a far broader field than that of the Rosicrucians, should be designated simply as "modern Spiritual Science," or as "anthroposophically oriented Spiritual Science of the twentieth century" (Karlsruhe, Oct. 6, 1911, CW 131).

After years of tireless lecturing throughout Europe, and thus developing more widespread understanding for Spiritual Science, Steiner was then able to start presenting his research method in the more precise thought forms of a science of cognition. *An Outline of Esoteric Science,* published in 1910, has two main sections: "World Evolution and the Human Being" and "Knowledge of Higher Worlds," in which he proposed study of spiritual–scientific communications as a sure path leading to sense-free thinking. He stated that there is also another way "that is still more sure and above all more focused, yet at the same time harder for many people"; that is, the path he outlined in his epistemological writings, especially in *The Philosophy of Freedom.* Although these texts made no reference to Spiritual Science, they showed, he said, that pure thinking, working on its own terms, can give us insight into the world, life, and human nature.

> These texts stand at a very important intermediate stage between knowledge of the sense world and that of the spiritual world. They offer what thinking can achieve if it raises itself above sensory observation without as yet engaging in spiritual research. Those who allow these writings to work upon their whole soul already stand within the world of spirit, except that this world reveals itself to them as a thought world. Those who feel able to let this intermediate stage work upon them are pursuing a sure path; and through it they can achieve a sense of higher worlds that will subsequently bear the finest fruits for them.[25]

One can say that this reference to the epistemological writings as intermediate stage between perception of the sensory world and of the spiritual world is a bridge leading to the account that Steiner

---

25 Op. cit., in the chapter "Knowledge of Higher Worlds."

next elaborated, of the three-level, cognitive method of imagination, inspiration, and intuition. In April 1911, at the philosophers' conference at Bologna mentioned earlier, he gave a lecture on "Theosophy's Psychological Foundations and Epistemological Stance."[26] In his subsequent books, *The Riddles of Philosophy* (with its final chapter entitled "From Philosophy to Anthroposophy," 1914), *The Riddle of Humanity* (1916), and *Riddles of the Soul* (1917), he further elaborated the epistemological and philosophical foundations of his anthroposophic spiritual research. These writings include several key essays published between 1916 and 1918 (all in CW 35), as well as his reflections published in 1922 in the weekly *Das Goetheanum* on a cycle of ten lectures, containing a particularly incisive, concentrated formulation of the spiritual research method and the knowledge of the world and the human being gained through it.[27] In 1923, four more essays followed, *On the Life of the Soul*.[28] There he stressed repeatedly that there was an entirely organic train of development starting from basic epistemological views expressed in *Truth and Science* and *The Philosophy of Freedom* through to the content of Spiritual Science or "Anthroposophy."

Not only in publications but also in public events (conferences, School for Spiritual Science courses, and so forth), he described the method used for gaining spiritual–scientific insights, showing how these can make the diverse sciences more fruitful. At the first School course at the Goetheanum, he once again pointed out, as he had done in 1910 in *An Outline of Esoteric Science*, that there are two different means to describe the path of knowledge. "In *How to Know Higher Worlds*, the path described for entering suprasensory realms is safe and sure; it is described in a way that makes it suitable for those without any real scientific training or experience" (Dornach

---

26 Quoted in *Philosophy and Anthroposophy*, CW 35.
27 *Cosmology, Religion, and Philosophy*, CW 25.
28 In *Der Goetheanum-Idea inmitten der Kulturkrisis der Gegenwart* (The Goetheanum-idea in the midst of the cultural crisis of the present), CW 36.

Oct. 3, 1920, CW 322). But someone who wishes to pursue the path of knowledge as a scientist should engage with what is presented as pure thinking in his *Philosophy of Freedom*, proceeding from this via the other pole of knowledge, perception, toward imagination. Steiner regarded this path as more appropriate for Western culture. The exercises for cultivating this path are, however, the same in nature as those in *How to Know Higher Worlds* and in *Soul Exercises*. They are all based on meditative engagement with symbolic images, metaphors, and ideas, as also described in the lecture at the philosophy conference in Bologna in 1911.

It was clear to Rudolf Steiner from the very outset that true spirit knowledge must be incorporated into mainstream science for the sake of all cultural progress. In the difficult years after World War I, this moved him and his colleagues to establish courses that could awaken interest and understanding of the science of the spirit and its methodology in people with a scientific background. In words that can move us today because they still largely apply, he spoke of his efforts in this direction, looking back at the ways he had been trying, for more than twenty years, to explain to the world how spiritual researchers arrive at their findings.

> If I have not had greater success in eliciting a general response to this anthroposophically oriented Spiritual Science; if it has repeatedly been necessary instead to speak to those without scientific training, who are therefore not so used to attending to details; and if it has not really been possible to speak to those with a science background, then in my experience this is due largely to these scientists themselves. Up until now they have shown very little inclination to listen to what spiritual researchers have to say about their paths to knowledge. Let us hope that this may change in future. You see, it really is essential to find an upward path by accessing deeper powers than those that are clearly incapable of helping us progress because, basically, they have led us into cultural decline (Stuttgart, Mar. 18, 1921, CW 324).

3. Internal (Esoteric) Accounts

> *My sole endeavor is this: to communicate what I am able to investigate in suprasensory worlds to contemporary humanity, in a form of knowledge aware of its due responsibility toward modern science. I present what, as I see it, is either entirely appropriate to modern humanity at its current stage of intellectual maturity, or other things for which certain groups of people are in the process of acquiring maturity through (esoteric) preparation.*[29]

It was not at all because Rudolf Steiner, an esotericist par excellence, wished to withhold certain spiritual truths from the public that he also worked as an esoteric teacher. The esoteric, as he presented it, was for him, rather, a specific form of expression of what, as true esoteric life, ultimately cannot be uttered in words at all, but can only be experienced. If it is necessary to reach for words in order to chart the paths that lead to such experiential capacity, this depends a great deal on the teacher's ability to formulate such things. "One says it first exoterically, then esoterically, and in speaking in both an exoteric and esoteric way, one is, as it were, resorting to two different dialects of an inexpressible language" (Dornach, Oct. 18, 1915, CW 254). This means that "there is no absolute boundary between exoteric and esoteric, but one flows into the other" (Stuttgart, June 12, 1921, CW 342). And this is because "at the moment we find a form of expression for the inner nature of something, we have rendered the esoteric as exoteric. The esoteric, therefore, can never be communicated in any other way than exoterically."[30]

Often over the years Steiner spoke of the objective difficulty involved in transposing what he saw in spiritual vision into the

---

[29] Oct. 1924: "Simple aphoristic notes on the book *Reformation or Anthroposophy*" by Edmund Ernst, in CW 36.

[30] See *Beiträge...* (Contributions...) nos.51/52, Michaelmas 1975, p. 35.

conceptual language of modern times. An example is the following: "If we approach language with the great treasures of wisdom that are unveiled in our souls and try to pour into words what is inwardly revealed to us, a battle arises with this really very weak instrument of language, which in certain respects is hugely inadequate" (Bern, Sept. 2, 1910, CW 123).

The reason such a "fierce inner battle" is involved in this process becomes clear in his short essay "Language and the Spirit of Language."[31] It is because—in working our way through from merely conceptual thinking to revelatory vision—the soul discovers the living power of the spirit of language.

> Those who gain this type of vision remove themselves from what can be expressed in language. Their vision initially does not find its way to their lips. If they reach for words, they immediately sense that the content of their vision changes. If they wish to communicate their visions, their battle with language begins. They try everything possible within the realm of language to form a picture of what their vision shows them. From sound qualities to turns of phrase and syntax they search the field of language. They fight a tough inner battle. They have to acknowledge that language has its own idiosyncratic willfulness. It can express all sorts of things as it wishes, and we have to submit to its willfulness so that it incorporates what we perceive.
>
> In trying to pour spiritual vision into words, we do not, in fact, encounter an indeterminate, malleable element that we can form as we like, but instead a living spirit, the spirit of language. If we battle honestly in this way, the best, the loveliest outcome can emerge. A moment arrives when we feel that the spirit of language takes up what we have seen in vision. The words and phrases we reach assume something of a spiritual quality. They cease "meaning" what they usually mean and slip into the content of vision. Then something like a living dialog with the spirit of language unfolds. Language

---

31 Contained in CW 36.

assumes a personal character and we engage with it as with another human being.³²

If we consider the wealth of research findings that Steiner communicated during more than two decades, we can get a sense, in regard to what he said above, of the spiritual achievement necessary to transpose the suprasensory realities he perceived into the language of modern thought. This was essential for speaking of them in public; for only in that form could modern awareness accept them, or cast doubt on, or reject them, in full freedom. By contrast, there were other conditions governing the representation of spiritual realities that cannot yet "be revealed in the form of ideas," either at all, or only at certain times.³³ Such communications required a group of people who wish to pass from the exoteric to the esoteric. In other words, people who were prepared to undertake to engage with such truths with the degree of responsibility appropriate to their nature. This is indicated in the note stating that certain communications depend on "particular groups of people" who "are in the process of acquiring maturity through (esoteric) preparation."

We can see from the history of such groups taught by Rudolf Steiner, that he met with some disappointment in this respect; and that here, too, as a result, the trend toward the exoteric became ever stronger over time. The first group for such esoteric preparation was called the Esoteric School.³⁴ It was established at the same time as accounts of the path of schooling were published in the book *Theosophy*, in the essays comprising *How to Know Higher Worlds*,

---

32 In *Das Goetheanum,* July 23, 1922.

33 Essay, "Die Freie Hochschule für Geisteswissenschaft. I" (The Free School for Spiritual Science, I.) (Dornach, Jan. 20, 1924) in CW 260a.

34 This school existed from 1904 until the outbreak of World War I in the summer of 1914. Initially it was administered as a department of the Theosophical Society's Esoteric School of Theosophy directed by Annie Besant. When Annie Besant sought appointment as the president of the T.S. in 1907, and used esoteric matters for her campaign, Rudolf Steiner, in agreement with her, dissolved this administrative connection at the Munich Congress. For more on this, see chapter 7 of this volume.

and in *The Stages of Higher Knowledge* in 1904/05. The aim of the Esoteric School was to help "spiritual pupils embark on the path of self-development" through specific instruction. Such a school was also necessary because the whole cultural situation at the beginning of the century showed clearly that spiritual–scientific teachings would fall on "half-deaf ears" without a foundation of people who wished to make spiritual development a key aspect of their lives.[35]

Initially there was a very small number of esoteric pupils; this made it possible for them to receive personal instruction. This was in line with Rudolf Steiner's principle that only individual developmental processes exist, rather than development in general: "There is only development of one or the other person, or of a third, a fourth or a thousandth" (Berlin, Oct. 31, 1910, CW 125).

Schooling instructions in published texts, by contrast, have to be general in character. Between 1910 and 1913, in his *Four Mystery Dramas*, he resolved in exemplary artistic form the problem of how individual developmental processes could be represented. After the initial performance of the first of these plays, *The Portal of Initiation: A Rosicrucian Mystery*, based on images contained in Goethe's fairytale, he referred as follows to the two ways of representing the path of schooling: "Whereas the book *How to Know Higher Worlds* contains, as it were, the starting point and the secret of every person's self-development, *The Portal of Initiation* relates the secret of a single individual's development, that of Johannes Thomasius."

Accounts in *How to Know Higher Worlds* and *An Outline of Esoteric Science* inevitably "have an abstract, semi-theoretical character, despite their specificity," because they are applicable to every human individual. By contrast, the play was able to offer "a far more intense, lifelike, and real" representation, because it was "far more individual." He was convinced, in fact, that he would no longer need to speak of many things "in the realm of the esoteric, the occult," if all that was contained in the Rosicrucian play "took

---

35 Letter dated Apr. 16, 1903, to Marie von Sivers in *Correspondence and Documents 1901–1925*, CW 262.

effect in the souls of our dear friends and diverse other people" (Berlin, Oct. 31, 1910, CW 125).

After the outbreak of the World War I in the summer of 1914 it seemed better to close the Esoteric School, because closed meetings might have seemed suspicious under war conditions. Nevertheless, people continued to ask him for personal esoteric instruction. He complied with such requests in many personal conversations, although he already considered that personal instruction was no longer needed, since there was now enough published schooling material available. In the preface to the fifth edition of *How to Know Higher Worlds,* dated September 7, 1914, he stressed the following:

> At the time (1904/05, when the essays comprising that book were written) it seemed clear to me that much of what the book did not contain could be received through "personal communication." Today, a great deal has now been published, to which I referred in this way. Such references may not have entirely excluded possible misconceptions in readers, however. For instance, some may have attributed much greater importance than necessary to the personal relationship that a person seeking spiritual schooling has with a particular teacher. I hope that I have succeeded in this new edition in emphasizing more clearly that, under the spiritual conditions prevailing today, it is much more important to gain a full, direct relationship with the objective world of spirit than with the personality of a teacher. In spiritual schooling such a teacher will increasingly exercise the function of a guide or helper, as is the case, in line with modern views, in any other field of study.

Steiner was compelled to stress this again within the Anthroposophical Society in the spring of 1917, when former members of the society accused him in a public journal of giving people harmful exercises.[36] At the time he categorically refused to continue to give esoteric advice in private conversations. In future, everything must be done in full transparency in the public domain. He stated

---

36 In "Psychische Studien" (Psychological studies), 44, Leipzig, 1917.

that there was sufficient schooling material available (one should just read *How to Know Higher Worlds*) and that he would soon show that private conversations of this kind were no longer in the least necessary for esoteric practice: "They will soon be entirely replaced."[37] In fact this happened seven years later, when the Esoteric School was reestablished in an entirely new form as the "School for Spiritual Science at the Goetheanum."

Steiner's intention, as voiced within the Anthroposophical Society at this time, to bring the mode of esoteric tuition fully into line with contemporary ideas, clearly led to his repeated emphasis in a public lecture of that year (Berlin, Oct. 19, 1917, CW 72) that Anthroposophy aimed to live entirely in accordance with the transparency demanded by the *zeitgeist*. He continued by saying that although much still (in 1917) seemed like "the old institutions,"[38] this was only insofar as certain preparations were necessary in order to understand subsequent developments. The eighth edition of *How to Know Higher Worlds*, published soon after this (May 1918) was consistent with this stated aim. As previously in the preface to the 1914 edition, it made clear that "statements regarding the need for an esoteric pupil to receive personal instruction should be understood to mean that the book itself offers personal instruction." And the article entitled "Former Secrecy and Modern Disclosure,"[39] published two months later, in July 1918, concludes with these words:

> We live in an age in which suprasensory knowledge can no longer remain a secret possession of the few. It must instead become the common possession of all who sense in their souls a need to fathom the meaning of life. This need is already far more active and widespread in unconscious depths of soul than

---

37 Lectures in Stuttgart on May 11 and 13, 1917, in CW 174b; Munich, May 19, 1917, in CW 174a; Leipzig, June 10, 1917 (not yet published in the CW).

38 This comment may refer to specific relics on Society management of the theosophical time.

39 In *Philosophy and Anthroposophy*, CW 35.

many are aware. This will increasingly manifest as a need for greater worth to be accorded to suprasensory cognition, giving it equal status with scientific inquiry.

In 1923/24, when Rudolf Steiner set about reconfiguring the whole anthroposophic movement in line with necessary public transparency, and released for publication typescripts of lectures previously available only to members, he sought also to reestablish the Esoteric School in accordance with this principle. The "Free School for Spiritual Science at the Goetheanum" was to be the first public esoteric school, for "secret societies are no longer possible today; our modern era requires something different," and "steps would be taken" to insure "'that what they do will be known as widely as possible" (Dornach, Jan. 30, 1924, CW 260a). The only reservation, self-evident, was (as applies equally in the public school system) that no one would be admitted to a higher level of study without first becoming conversant with the lower ones. Accordingly, Spiritual Science was to be cultivated within the Anthroposophical Society in the form of ideas, because it is appropriate for people today to encounter the spiritual world through ideas initially. In the three classes of the School for Spiritual Science, students were also to be led upward by degrees into realms of the spiritual world that "cannot be revealed in the form of ideas.... Here we encounter the need to find the means of expressing imaginations, inspirations, and intuitions."[40]

In fact, because of the death of Rudolf Steiner one and a half years later, only the first of the planned three esoteric classes could be established; and only "the first section of this first class," as he noted in the last of the Dornach Class lessons, the nineteenth. In these Class lessons, esoteric instruction was no longer divided (as it had been in the former Esoteric School) into personal exercises and lectures for all; but was given in the form of meditative verses, and their exegesis, in wording that was the same for all who attended

---

40 Essay, "Die Freie Hochschule...I." (The free school ...I.), (Dornach Jan. 20, 1924) in CW 260a.

(CW 270/1–4). These meditations differ from the exercises for morning and evening only in that they are not bound to a specific time ("Questions and Answers," Dornach, Apr. 22, 1924, CW 316).

4. The Esoteric Exercises

> *The aim of contemplation (meditation) of symbolic pictures and feelings is, specifically, to develop higher organs of perception within the human being's astral body. These organs are initially created from the substance of this astral body.* (An Outline of Esoteric Science)

If we wish to perceive the higher worlds we need healthy organs of perception, just as we do in the physical world. The prime concern of every mode of esoteric training has thus always been to develop such organs *carefully*. All of the exercises Rudolf Steiner gave also focus on achieving this. There are numerous accounts of how to do this in his works—most fundamentally in *How to Know Higher Worlds*, which also explains the effects of the exercises, for "the principles of true esoteric science include being fully aware of what we are doing when we devote ourselves to it. We should not undertake or practice anything without knowing its effect. An esoteric teacher giving someone advice or instruction will always also describe its effect on the body, soul, and spirit of those seeking higher knowledge."

The extent to which we can fulfill the first requirement of the spiritual–scientific schooling method (development of the astral body's organs of perception) is repeatedly described as follows. During daily life we are entirely given up to external impressions acting on our senses and reason. The astral body participates in this, since it is fully immersed in the physical body while we are awake. Even when it leaves the physical body as we fall asleep, it is still subject to the aftereffect of these forces. It adheres to the elasticity of the physical body rather than to its own laws, and is therefore prevented from developing its own organs. If this is to change, something "very specific" must be accomplished with the physical body while we are awake, so that this can be imprinted in the astral body and subsequently resonate during the night. For this change to happen, we must take our inner life in hand through a methodical schooling: "This is called meditation, concentration, or contemplation. These are exercises governed by instructions that are as strict in the schools where they are taught as, say, the regulations governing how to examine objects under a microscope in laboratories, etc."

The nature of the exercises is based on teachers applying "all knowledge" about the effects of the exercises that has been gathered over millennia of human experience. Such teachers know that these exercises work intensively to cause the astral body, on emergence from the physical body during sleep, to liberate itself from the aftereffects of the latter and acquire its own intrinsic form; or in other words, gradually unfold the organs necessary for higher perception. If the wrong exercises are done, however, then "forms contrary to nature" are built into the astral body; perverted forms in disharmony with the greater context of the world. This is why those who decide to undertake such exercises also take on a great responsibility.[41]

This is no doubt one of the key reasons that Steiner repeatedly stressed that the spiritual–scientific method is the most appropriate one for Westerners. Although the human significance of such exercises is the same in all schools of initiation, they were focused more on schooling the powers of thinking in pre-Christian times, and more on schooling forces of heart and soul in the time since Christ. Since the fourteenth century, however, because of the changed nature of the times, a "special kind of 'will-culture,' or will exercises" were introduced in the so-called Rosicrucian schools (Nuremberg, June 19, 1908, CW 104). The special nature of the will-culture is characterized as follows:

---

41 Hamburg, May 30 and 31, 1908, CW 103; Nuremberg, June 18 and 19, 1908, CW 104; Munich, Aug. 24, 1909, CW 113.

Thought exercises, on the one hand, and will exercises, on the other—these are the practices that open the portal to the suprasensory world.... Thought exercises entail becoming aware of the will's influence on thinking; will exercises involve observing the influence of thinking on our will.... The contents of our thoughts, which we usually consider their most important aspect, must be allowed to take a backseat while we learn consciously to apply our will to our thinking (London, Apr. 14, 1922, CW 211).

The three main types of initiation method that have developed through the post-Atlantean period are characterized as having these differences, along with the changing nature of the teacher–pupil relationship. Thus we have the ancient Eastern yoga method, the Christian–Gnostic method, and the Christian–Rosicrucian method, or its continuation as the spiritual–scientific method. Before Steiner gave these accounts, however, he first clarified that there are other methods besides that of ancient Indian schooling, which at that time was the only path discussed in the Theosophical Society. This clarification was also immediately published. In the journal *Lucifer–Gnosis* (May 1905), in a very positive review of the recently published German translation of Annie Besant's lectures, *Path of Discipleship*, Steiner stressed that the path outlined there is appropriate for people of Indian ancestry, and that this fact should not go unmentioned. While there is but "one truth," he said, and the highest summit of knowledge and life for all times and all people is also a "single" one, it would be wrong to think that the path of discipleship can be the same for people in modern Europe as for the people of India:

> Whereas intrinsic nature remains the same, forms change in this realm. Consequently, it must be seen as natural that various matters are presented in the journal articles titled "How to Know Higher Worlds" differently from the way they appear in lectures Annie Besant presented for the people of India. The path described in this journal has developed in the esoteric

schools of Europe since the fourteenth century as rightful adaptation to Western life and the stage of development of Europeans. And Europeans can be successful in such endeavors only if they pursue this path as directed by their own esoteric teacher.

This does not mean there is no point in Europeans becoming acquainted with what is appropriate for the Indian people:

> The current stage of development for Europeans requires them to acquaint themselves with everything through their rational faculties. To progress, reason must compare and contrast, measuring what it possesses against what is more distant from it. It must hearken to the beneficial guidance given to our brothers in the Far East. This is why books such as this one should be gladly welcomed, and not because the same can be done in Europe. (CW 34)

Shortly after this, in essays in the same journal entitled *The Stages of Higher Knowledge* (CW 12), Steiner began to describe the three possible modes and methods of initiation embodied in ancient Eastern yoga, Christian–Gnostic, and Rosicrucian initiations. He stated that he would soon give a "precise account" of the differences between these three methods, and under what circumstances it might be possible for an esoteric pupil "even in modern Europe, not to pursue the Rosicrucian, but the Eastern path, or the older Christian path; although the Rosicrucian path is the most natural one for our times." This latter, he said, was not only just as Christian as the older Christian path, but could also be undertaken by people "who believe they stand at the summit of a modern, scientific worldview." This precise account was never forthcoming, however, because Rudolf Steiner's workload meant that the journal ceased publication. From then on, though, in lectures to theosophists, he repeatedly described the stages involved in each of these three methods.[42]

---

42 See, for example, the Stuttgart lecture cycle of Aug. 1906, published as *Founding a Science of the Spirit*, CW 95.

5. Meditative Verses:
The Heart of the Esoteric Exercises

> *One would have to write a great many books to fully exhaust the meaning of these verses, for besides there being meaning in every word, there is meaning in the symmetry of their words, the way they are arranged, the intensifications at work in them, and much more; and therefore, only long, patient devotion to them can fully fathom what they contain.*[43]

Since the spiritual–scientific method for developing astral organs of perception starts with imagination, this requires us to open ourselves to as many symbolic and pictorial ideas as possible. These do not have to be only inwardly visualized images, however; they can also be words that embody profound cosmic truths in compressed form (Vienna, March 28, 1910, CW 119).

The real heart of Rudolf Steiner's esoteric teachings consisted in such cosmic truths repeatedly formed anew into meditative verses. As yet we still cannot fully assess the significance of this accomplishment for modern spiritual life; it would require comprehensive evaluation of his whole creative oeuvre in the realm of language. He himself once said that Anthroposophy presented him not only with "formal tasks of knowledge," but also with "historically creative tasks"; and by this he meant forming language into an appropriate instrument for presenting spiritual perceptions (Dornach, Sept. 29, 1921, CW 343).

Many years before this statement, he had spoken of the increasing trend of applying abstract language to merely material things, saying that this trend was one of the reasons that led to an inauguration of the spiritual world stream at the turn of the nineteenth to twentieth centuries. "If one had waited another hundred years, our

---

43 "Pictures of the Apocalyptic Seals and Columns" in *Rosicrucianism Renewed: The Unity of Art, Science, and Religion: The Theosophical Congress of Whitsun 1907*, CW 284.

words could no longer have expressed what Spiritual Science has to say." This had required "hearkening to the most favorable moment" for seizing the opportunity to "impress new words" on everything through Spiritual Science, giving all words a "new imprint"; and in fact "really renewing language itself" so that people could regain a sense that certain words refer not merely to tangible or visible things, but also to what leads us upward into higher worlds (Berlin, Oct. 19, 1907, CW 284). And in the public lecture "Spiritual Science and Language" (Berlin, Jan. 20, 1910, CW 59), the following lofty aim was presented: "Spiritual Science will be able to appropriate suprasensory worlds through thought; will develop the capacity to pour the thought into the sound and pattern of speech, so that our language can also once again become a means to communicate what the soul perceives in the suprasensory realm."

Repeatedly, in various contexts, Steiner suggested that our understanding of how everything arose from the "Word" (an instinctive insight in ancient times) could be regained only by penetrating the sound-forming, creative powers of speech. Until the time came, when idea and sound content in language fell asunder, all ancient wisdom and all scholarship had really been only a rewriting of the phrase that underpinned the secret of the whole cosmos: "In the beginning was the Word" (Dornach, Apr. 9, 1921, CW 204). The need for Spiritual Science to rediscover this insight is expressed succinctly in this sentence: "Essentially, all of Spiritual Science is a search for the lost Word" (Berlin, Apr. 25, 1916, CW 167). This is a matter, ultimately, of becoming aware of the lofty developmental goal that is called the "mystery of the creative Word"; or in other words, the knowledge that just as everything first arose from the divine Word, so in humanity's far-distant future the human word itself will become creative.

> Once the Earth has transformed into Jupiter, the Word will become creative in the mineral realm; in the Venus planetary embodiment, the larynx will bring forth plants; and so it

will continue until we are capable of bringing forth our own kind.... In the Earth's future evolutionary stages, we will be able to produce in an enduring way what today we are able only to speak.

Using a metaphor, he sought to show how this could be possible:

> I am speaking to you here. You hear my words, my thoughts, which are first within my soul, and that I could also conceal from you if I did not transpose them into words. I transpose them into tones. If the air were not spread out between us, you would be unable to hear my words. The moment I speak a word here, the air in the room moves. Every time I speak, my words make the whole air resonate in a certain way; the air vibrates in conformity with my words. Let us take this a little further. Imagine that you could make the air fluid and then solid. In fact, it is already possible today to make air solid; water can exist as steam or gas, can then cool and become fluid, and in turn become solid in the form of ice. Imagine now that I speak the word "God" out into the air. If, at the moment when the sound waves of this word were present, you could solidify the air, then a shape, such as a shell form, would fall down. With the word "world" a different waveform would fall down. You would be able to pick up my words, and every word would correspond to a crystallized air form. (Kassel, June 28, 1907, CW 100)

Accordingly, everything originally arose from the Word, the "choral harmony and interplay" of divine spiritual beings, with the aim of creating the human being, the human form. "The human being [the origin of the human form] is a divine ideal and divine aim."[44] There are various pointers in Steiner's collected works to the connection of this human form with the most profound secrets of evolution. At one place he even said that realizing this human form is no less than "the meaning of all earthly evolution." According to

---

44 See "What is revealed when one looks back at our past life between death and a new birth?" (Reflections of Jan. 18, 1925) in *Anthroposophical Leading Thoughts*, CW 26.

him, it is the spiritual foundation of the Earth, though not "in this or that form as image of the human race, but as a universal ideal of humanity" (Leipzig, Sept. 4, 1908, CW 106). One should remember, however, he continued, that a "huge difference" exists between this ideal form, as that of the "I"-evolving human being, and the physical body. "The physical body is what occurs within the human entity as physical and chemical processes. In the human being today this takes place within the human form, which is, however, something thoroughly and absolutely spiritual."[45]

Our task today is to collaborate in the realization of this divine ideal. If this human form is eventually to become capable of being reproduced by the human word itself, we must start preparing this now by working on language to make the human word creative. "The word, language, is what we already bring forth from ourselves as preparation of the future nature of the human being." For what we speak remains in the akashic record. "It is the first foundation of the future human being" (Berlin, Oct. 2, 1905, CW 93a).

From this perspective, meditative phrases not only have the potential to offer help for our spiritual development; they can also enable us to participate consciously in preparing this goal of human evolution. This is because they are "spiritually articulated" words and can engender "word resonances" that accord with the resonances of thought in the akashic material (Berlin, Dec. 28, 1905, CW 264; Munich, Oct. 28, 1906, CW 94).

This is because the words in such phrases conjure, and are imbued with, sound qualities, as something of intrinsic importance in esoteric life. "At the moment when a thought is reconfigured into a word, even if the word itself is only invoked in thought as in a word meditation, the word imprints itself in the world ether"; whereas the thought itself does not; "otherwise, we could never become free beings in pure thinking" (Dornach, Mar. 13, 1921, CW 203). In meditation, therefore, when the sound qualities of words come alive

---

45 Op. cit.

inwardly, every letter, every turn of phrase can have an effect upon the soul; and, in consequence, the gateway to the world of spirit can open (Vienna, Feb. 22, 1907, CW 97). Similarly, many years later, he reiterated this; if one can become aware that there is "more than speaking" in the word, then the word can become something enabling us to perceive "the first connection, the first dialog with the divine." Thereby, he added, since "this is, as it were, a path from the subjectivity of thinking to objectivity," something "spiritually objective can flow into the word (Dornach, Sept. 27, 1921, morning lecture, CW 343)." This points to the second stage of schooling, that of inspiration; "through inspiration it becomes possible to acquire awareness of an outer soul–spiritual world around us, a soul–spiritual objectivity" (Stuttgart, Sept. 3, 1921, CW 78).

Although Rudolf Steiner often referred to the meditative phrases and verses he gave using the Indian term mantras[46] or "mantric verses," there are key differences between them and what are regarded as mantras in India. In Hinduism, the world's oldest religion, this term refers to sacred texts in Sanskrit; in particular, the part of the Vedas containing hymns relating to acts of worship and sacrifice; or to the tantra (mantra yoga) formulae consisting of letters and syllables from the Sanskrit alphabet, whose meaning is found by combining them in particular ways with corresponding intonations. The content of Rudolf Steiner's meditative verses, by contrast, consists of meaningful thought configurations. He did, however, agree with the Indian view according to which illumination lies concealed within a mantra as a tree lies hidden in a seed, and that, as soon as illumination takes effect, the mantra is endowed with a wonderful power through which it develops the cosmic energy latent in it.

---

46 The word *mantra* is formed from the first syllable of *manana* ("to think" and "human being") and *tra* in *trana* ("liberation from the chains of the world of maya"). The word *mantra* thus means, literally, "something that brings liberation when one thinks on it." See Arthur Avalon (Sir John Woodroffe), *The Garland of Letters*.

"Tantra believes that some of the chief mantras were not created by human brains but exist eternally, and that the seeker can attain perfection by reciting them."[47] This accords with Steiner's statement that meditative phrases are based on "centuries of experience of the masters of wisdom and of the harmony of feelings"; this is why not every thought content is suitable as meditation material, but only "if given by the masters of wisdom and of the harmony of feelings" (Berlin, Jan. 28, 1908, CW 96). Tantric "recitation" here becomes an inner speaking and hearkening appropriate to modern human consciousness.

While the mantric tradition is certainly rooted in ancient Indian practice, other ancient cultures continuing through to the Christian era knew of the occult power of speech sounds.[48] However, the real origins of this, according to spiritual–scientific research, lead back even long before ancient Indian culture to Atlantean times. At that period, in a great school of adepts, which flowered during the fourth of the so-called Turanian epochs, skills in "occult speech" had developed alongside reading of the "occult script," in a tradition that has continued through to the present day.[49] At that primal stage of mantric practice, said Steiner, it was possible to exert mighty influences through the great power contained in words in those times. Since Atlanteans had not yet developed rationality, the mystery leaders had been able to use tone combinations, symbols, and phrases to put their pupils in a state in which the godhead could directly illumine them. This was no longer possible

---

47 Swami Nikhilananda, *Hinduism: Its Meaning for the Liberation of the Spirit.*

48 Primarily in Judaic esoteric doctrine (the *Q'abbalah*). For instance, see Gershom G. Scholem, *On the Kabbalah and Its Symbolism*; also *Jewish Gnosticism, Merkabah Mysticism, and Talmudic Tradition.* See also: Roelof van den Broek (ed): *Gnosis and Hermeticism from Antiquity to Modern Times.*

49 Something similar is described in Blavatsky's *Secret Doctrine* (vol. I.). She stated that priests of those times had succeeded in invoking their gods in the latter's own language, consisting not only of words, but of tones, numbers and figures. This, she said, is the language of invocation, otherwise known, in India, as mantras.

after the great Atlantean flood. Because of the great change in awareness that had arisen as a result of the flood, it was necessary to start transposing the primal, unified, Atlantean wisdom into rational thought mode, and to teach it in ways that were appropriate to diverse, evolving national cultures (Leipzig, Feb. 17, 1907, and Dusseldorf Mar. 7, 1907, CW 97).

This change also made it necessary to develop a new level of mantra practice. To attain higher knowledge, the breathing process had to be trained through yoga, since at that time thought lived in deeper regions of human nature than did the word. Thought raised itself into language only gradually, said Steiner; today it has lifted itself beyond the word (Vienna, June 3, 1922, CW 83). This gradual rise of thought into the region of the word meant that experience of thought increasingly focused on words borne on the breath, rather than on the breathing process as such. Therefore, what was expressed in words, lifted in this way by the breathing process, began to be formed into "simple, word-laden verses." At that point, efforts were made to live fully within the "word chime" or "word tone" (Dornach, Oct. 2, 1920, evening lecture, CW 322).

In this sense Arthur Avalon, a classic connoisseur of Indian mantra lore, refers to a mantra as "power in tonal form."[50] What is generally called a mantra, he says, "are the particular tones used in worship and sacred practice, consisting of certain letters, or letters arranged in a particular sequence of tones, whose representative symbols they are."[51]

The strong dominance of tonal and musical elements in Eastern mantric practice is something that Blavatsky accentuated. She said that the "mystic language" lives in the mantra, or rather in its tones (the tones of the speech sounds); for, in her words, the tone is the "first of the keys that open the gateway of intercourse between

---

50 Arthur Avalon (Sir John Woodroffe): *The Serpent Power* (retranslated from German).

51 Arthur Avalon: *The Garland of Letters.*

mortals and immortals."[52] In the West, she said, we have little idea, however, "of the powers that lie concealed in the tone, in the akashic resonances that can be invoked by those who know how to utter certain words." In relation to the best-known mantric formula, AUM, she stated, "*Om* is of course *Aum,* which can be spoken in two, three, and seven syllables, invoking a range of various vibrations.... The seven meanings and the seven effects depend on the intonation given to the whole formula and to each of its syllables."[53]

Rudolf Steiner devoted a whole lecture to this ancient Eastern prayer, or knowledge utterance (Dornach, Apr. 1, 1922, CW 211). There he showed how, in ancient Eastern yoga, people sensed the inner dome of the head by sounding on the inhalation the vowel tone between "ah" and "o," or between "ah" and "oo." By doing this they could grasp the revelation of the cosmic Word—what surges and weaves as dynamic creativity through the world, since the head is an image, or reflection, of the whole universe. Then, sounding the consonantal tone "m" on the exhalation, they breathed out an affirmation of the cosmic word in absolute devotion to the universe. In this way they were able to perceive that "*inhalation is revelation, exhalation is affirmation;* 'aum' is the merger of revelation and avowal or affirmation, or enlivening within oneself the cosmic mystery, the affirmation of this cosmic mystery in oneself." Steiner described how the path to this experience has changed in our current era:

> The tone has risen higher and is expressed in real, tangible, and specific (in contrast to intellectual) thought. Thus we can say that inhalation becomes thought, while exhalation becomes will-enacted realization of a thought. In other words, we separate what was once inhalation-as-revelation and exhalation-as-avowal into thought exercise and will exercise. By this means, likewise, in thoughts (but in the kind we practice

---

52 Blavatsky, *The Secret Doctrine,* vol. 1.
53 Ibid., vol. 3.

in meditation) we gain revelation; and in the will exercises that we also carry out we avow or affirm what has been revealed to us. For people today, what was once experienced only in the breathing process and was formed as vowel tone in the inhalation process, and as consonantal tone in the exhalation process, now unfolds in a more inward way in the soul, in an inwardly contemplated thought; it then is permeated by the will in devotional dedication to the universe. The process is the same, but has been shifted into the soul realm, internalized. Nevertheless, the process still involves perceiving our inner experience of the universe and its mysteries, and affirming, avowing this universe and its spiritual foundations.

Whereas ancient Eastern wisdom consisted in gaining the highest inspiration through breathing and mantra exercises, based on the intrinsic interplay between *melos* and inner experience of the breathing process (Dornach, Sept. 29 and Dec. 2, 1922, CW 282, and Dornach Oct. 2, 1920, evening lecture, CW 322), when we seek inspiration today, "merely logical connections" must become a "musical connection within the thought itself" through exercises that are purely soul–spiritual in nature (Dornach, May 27, 1922, CW 212). Regarding the difference between an Eastern and Western approach to mantras, Steiner stated clearly on one occasion that in Eastern mantras "a music living in these verses is heard or uttered in the soul"; whereas in Western culture this must happen in a soul–spiritual way, so that we "do not fall into this kind of chanting or reciting of mantric verses or repeated phrases." (Berlin, Feb. 28, 1918, CW 67)

It is clear from this that mantric practice has changed according to human evolution. During an esoteric class, Steiner once spoke of the fundamental effect of the Christ event on mantric practice, and a participant in the class recorded it in his notes as follows:

> Because the Word became flesh, the mode of instruction in the esoteric schools changed also. In the pre-Christian era, the Word was not yet active. Teachings were imparted in silence;

and silently, in images, pupils received communications from the spiritual worlds in visions.... In responsible modern esoteric schools, centered on the Christ power, teaching can be given only through the Word. In former times, dialog with divine–spiritual worlds could come about only through mantras, through sound. Now, however, we can prepare to unite with the Christ power through the meaning-imbued word within us. Words should be winged messengers that bear us upward into worlds of spirit.[54]

In a lecture given shortly after, this principle was exemplified in relation to the archetypal Christian prayer, the Lord's Prayer:

[Sevenfold human nature] was explained to the Turanian initiation pupil by requiring him to listen to a tonal scale as metaphor for the seven human bodies, in combination with an aroma scale and the picturing of certain colors. What lay in the sevenfold harmony scale rose up in him as inner experience invoked and mediated by what was outwardly present. The great religious founders poured this into certain phrases, and the greatest of them poured it into the Lord's Prayer. Each person who says the Lord's Prayer receives its effects. It is a prayer, which is not a mantra as such [in the sense of an exercise using speech sounds]. It will still retain its significance after thousands upon thousands of years have passed, for it is a thought mantra. The effect of the Lord's Prayer was poured into thoughts. The effect of the Lord's Prayer remains, for this effect lies in the mighty nature of the thoughts themselves. (Berlin, Feb. 18, 1907, CW 96)

Everyone who prays the Lord's Prayer can receive its effects. It is not a mantra as such, although it can have mantric powers. It is a thought mantra. Naturally it had its greatest power in the original language (Aramaic). But since it is a thought mantra, its power will never fade, even if translated into a thousand languages (Leipzig, Feb. 17, 1907, CW 96).

---

54 Esoteric lesson, Munich, Dec. 5, 1909, CW 266/I.

This formulation points to the fact that there must be a huge difference between Eastern speech–sound mantras that cannot be translated and spiritual–scientific thought mantras.[55]

The extent to which the concept of a "thought mantra" corresponds to the current stage of language evolution, and must therefore also apply to the nature of Rudolf Steiner's mantric verses, becomes clear in his highly significant comments in the lecture in Dornach on Apr. 13, 1923 (CW 224). There he described the evolutionary process of human speech from its origination in Atlantean times through to our own day: its advance from a "will language" in Atlantean times to a "feeling language" in the post-Atlantean epoch up to the ancient Greek era and on to a "thought language" in our own times.

This great evolutionary trajectory ended with the loss, necessary for the development of human freedom, of an experience of the creative powers of speech sounds and the capacity to form language in a living way. A new impulse is needed. Since the Mystery of Golgotha, this can be only the Christ impulse, which is so decisive for earthly evolution. This impulse involves spiritualization; or in other words, an evolutionary return, or involution. Whereas the path progressed previously from the word to thinking, as spiritualization begins we must start with thinking and find our way back to the real formative powers at work in words.

We must seek the path from concept to Word. A different experience is involved when, without speaking outwardly, we have within us, not the content of a merely abstract concept, but a living experience of the speech sound, whichever language it happens to be (Dornach, Sept. 30, 1921, a.m. lecture, CW 343).

A quite different and quite particular kind of formative speech power will then come to the fore, Steiner said, so that the Christ

---

55 As Indian mantras are understood, a mantra ceases to be one when it is translated; "the words heard or spoken in the translation are not the tone of the *devata* (divinity) and do not invoke the latter. We do not use the same tone (as in the Sanskrit mantra), but rather the translation into another language, with other tones and speech sounds." Arthur Avalon: *The Garland of Letters* (here retranslated from the German).

impulse can itself become the creative power in language (Dornach, Apr. 13, 1923, CW 244 and Pforzheim, March 7, 1914, CW 152). Accordingly, a new mantric culture could be inaugurated only with thought mantras, in which the thought content conceived as meditation is poured into fitting speech sounds. If we look at all of Rudolf Steiner's work in this context, we can recognize his great efforts at reconfiguring and reenlivening language in his writings and talks, his poems and mantras, and above all, in the movements of speech sounds rendered visible in the new movement art of eurythmy. We can recognize him not only as a great spiritual teacher and researcher, but also as a great artist who sought to shape the Word in a way that could once again mediate and convey the spirit.

3

RESEARCH INTO OCCULT HISTORY
THE GREAT SPIRITUAL LEADERS OF HUMANITY

THE MASTERS OF WISDOM AND OF THE HARMONY OF SENSATIONS AND FEELINGS IN RUDOLF STEINER'S WORK

The exercises given in the Esoteric School for inner development should also lead to knowledge of the "Masters of Wisdom and of the Harmony of Sensations and Feelings," as the actual founders and leaders of the Esoteric School. These supreme beings, active already on higher planes (as said in a letter[1] dated Jan. 2, 1905), "have already completed the path that the rest of humanity still has to tread.... They work on the physical plane through the 'Messengers' they have appointed." Imparting an understanding of these lofty spiritual leaders of humanity is an essential motive that extends from the beginning, throughout not only the esoteric but also through the whole of Rudolf Steiner's teaching activity.

At the first General Meeting of the German Section in October 1903, Rudolf Steiner outlined his future program as "esoteric historical research," a part of which was to comprise the teaching of great spiritual leaders of humankind. Esoteric historical research from the three aspects of body, soul, and spirit shows how bodily existence is determined by the great cosmic natural forces, how the personal element plays a part in history, and how the universal spirit of the cosmos interweaves in human destiny by directing its life into

---

1 To Anna Wagner, in CW 264.

the higher self of a great leader of humanity, thus influencing the whole of humankind:

> That is the path followed by the life of the spirit; it flows into the leading personalities' higher selves, who then impart it to their brothers and sisters. From one incarnation to the next the higher selves of men and women are progressing and thereby continue to learn in ever greater degree how to make the inner self into a missionary for the divine world plan. Through esoteric historical research one will become aware of how the leaders of humanity develop to such a height that they can take over a divine mission; one will comprehend how Buddha, Zarathustra, and Christ came to their missions.[2]

At the next General Meeting, in October 1904, the theme of world leaders was taken up again with many references to the fact that, to understand the subject properly, one must differentiate between Masters of the past, present and future.

Masters of the Past, Present, and Future

After references such as those in the lectures of October 7 and 24, 1904, this fact was again dealt with in detail on October 28, 1904,[3] with the justification that, although most people already knew it, one should nevertheless continually remind oneself that:

> During the course of our fifth Great (post-Atlantean) epoch,[4] an important step will be taken for all of evolution—specifically, that the leaders of humanity, or *manus*, will arise from

---

2 "Okkulte Geshichtsforschung" (Esoteric historical research) by Rudolf Steiner in *Lucifer–Gnosis* (in CW 34).

3 *Esotericism and World History in the Greek and Germanic Mythology*, Dornach 1955.

4 The terms *Würzelrasse* and *Unterrasse* (translated in English as *root race* and *subrace*) were usual for various phases of the evolution of humanity. Rudolf Steiner used these terms in the early years of his activity in the Theosophical Society. Gradually, he replaced *Unterrasse* with *cultural epoch* or *cultural period*. He translated *Würzelrasse* as *great epoch*.

the ranks of humankind itself. All the great leaders, or *manus*,[5] who have helped humankind in its progress during the preceding great epochs, who gave the great impulses, did not undergo their development only on Earth, but also partly on other heavenly bodies, and thereby they have brought to Earth from other worlds the impulses they wished to impart to humankind. The manus of the Lemurian race and those of Atlantis, as well as the principal manu assigned to our fifth great epoch, are superhuman individuals who have undergone special training on other planets to become the leaders of humanity.

On the other hand, such highly evolved individuals are developing among humanity itself during our fifth great epoch that they can become leaders of humanity from the time of the sixth great epoch onward. In particular, the chief leader of the sixth great epoch will be a human being, just as we ourselves are human beings, only he will be one of the most advanced—indeed the most advanced of all. It will be a being that began development during the middle of the Lemurian epoch, when humanity was only just coming into existence. This being was always a human being among other human beings, but could develop more quickly and went through all the stages of human development. That will be the basic characteristic of the manu of the sixth great epoch. Such beings have to undergo the most manifold initiations. They have to be initiated again and again.

Because of this, during the fifth great epoch there were always initiates—those who had been initiated so they could, as it were, go their own independent way. This had not been the case throughout the whole of the Lemurian epoch, nor during the whole of the Atlantean epoch. During those epochs, those who assisted human progress, the rulers and leaders of the state and great religious communities, were under the influence of higher beings. During the course of the Lemurian and Atlantean epochs they depended entirely on those exalted beings who had undergone their training on other planets. Humanity will only be given its freedom during the fifth great epoch. During this epoch we will have initiates

---

5   *Manu* comes from the Sanskrit root *man*, to think.

who are certainly in contact with higher beings, but who have not received their comprehensive instructions worked out in such detail. The initiates of the fifth great epoch will increasingly be given freedom regarding the details. Directions will be given in general, not only to the initiates, but also to those who receive inspiration from them. They will receive the impulses in such a way that they will have to work from their own initiative. (Berlin, Oct. 28, 1904)

A few months after this exposition, we again find an emphasis on the fact that the leaders of humanity and Masters of the fifth great epoch—the post-Atlantean epoch—will arise from the ranks of human beings: "Now he will become one of the Masters who is able to pass through all the phases of humanity but in more rapid succession, and is able to raise himself to become a leader of humankind."[6] Such individuals will then become the "true" Masters of Wisdom and of the Harmony of Sensations and Feelings. The direction of this endeavor is revealed as follows:

> The task we have today is to grasp the esoteric in the purest element of thought, in Manas. To comprehend what is spiritual in the finest distillation of the brain is the true mission of our age. To make this thought so powerful that it acquires something of an esoteric strength itself—that is the task that has been set us in order that we may assume our rightful position in the future. (Düsseldorf, March 7, 1907)

This is also expressed in the answer to a question once asked about where the initiates of humankind can be found today, when a life's work such as theirs is at stake: "Spiritual truths have now to be grasped by human thought. If you were to meet these initiates today you might not find in them anything of what you are seeking. They had their tasks more in earlier incarnations. Today human thinking must be spiritualized."[7]

---

6   Berlin, May 5, 1905, in *Nachrichtenblatt* (The news), 1936, nos. 44–50.
7   Friedrich Rittelmeyer, *Rudolf Steiner Enters My Life*.

The Twelvefold, Sevenfold, and Fourfold Activity of the Masters

Until the separation of the first Esoteric Study Group from the Esoteric School of Theosophy in the year 1907, Rudolf Steiner gave the names of four Masters who were especially connected with the theosophical movement: the two Masters from the East, Kut Hoomi, and Morya, and the two Masters from the West, Christian Rosenkreutz and the Master Jesus. After the separation he only spoke of the two Masters from the West.

If one asks why only four Masters—respectively two—are named, whereas according to other statements, twelve constitute The Great White Lodge, (Cologne, Dec. 3, 1905, typescript), and if it is further stated that never more than seven of these are incarnated at any one time (Berlin, Oct. 10, 1905, CW 93a), then it will be evident that certain rules are connected with the numbers 12, 7, and 4. To begin with there is a fixed relationship between 12 and 7, expressed thus in notes of a privately held class lesson of Marie von Sivers in Berlin on July 3, 1904[8]:

I	II	III	IV	V	VI	VII
1						
2	2					
3	3	3				
4	4	4	4			
5	5	5	5	5		
6	6	6	6	6	6	
7	7	7	7	7	7	7
	8	8	8	8	8	8
		9	9	9	9	9
			10	10	10	10
				11	11	11
					12	12
						13

---

8 Berlin, July 3, 1904. In *Beiträge*... (Contributions...), nos. 67/68.

When we contemplate the development of a planetary system, the following has to be taken into account: Such development proceeds so that two things always interchange with one another: evolution and involution. And now we have to contemplate the seven from the point of view of evolution and involution.

When it comes to the turn of the next planet each of the ruling planets has to move on one stage further. Eight is the further development of seven. When a planet develops further, it turns into the next one. When it arrives at the seventh stage no further step is possible. If seven were to become eight, it would present a stage already attained, and it would be merely a repetition of the first; it is the seven on another level. In moving forward we find that the leaders themselves have undergone a change. We have twelve rulers and a thirteenth who is superfluous. This thirteenth causes the whole planet to change into its first condition, but on a higher level.

With twelve it finishes. So it is that in every sequence of a planetary chain we have twelve exalted leading spirits, not seven. In the first of these the eighth is not active, and so on. (Our concepts are a part of lower Devachan. These beings are beyond our conception and therefore it is not a question of something proceeding from something else, but of their relationship to one another—it is beyond time.)[9]

These beings have been designated the twelve Rulers through certain symbols—for example, the signs of the zodiac, through which the Sun passes. Corresponding to the macrocosmic stages is the enhancement of consciousness occurring in the microcosmic development. Thus the number twelve has always been a decisive factor and there have always been twelve universal leading spirits: the twelve Tribes of Israel, the twelve Apostles, the twelve Knights of the Grail. Twelve is thus the sacred number underlying all things, in both the macrocosm and the microcosm. Seven of these are actively engaged and five of them have other tasks to perform. For the physical planet only the number seven comes into question and that is

---

9 Concerning space and time in connection with the numbers seven and twelve, see the lecture: Munich, Aug. 31, 1909, CW 113.

the reason why, of the twelve principles, only seven principles of humankind are taught.[10]

These stated facts (that only seven of the twelve leading spirits are of importance for the physical realm) and replies to questions on May 29, 1915 (CW 264), make it clear why one speaks, within the Theosophical Society, of seven masters: Kut Hoomi, Morya, Jesus, Christian Rosenkreutz (called the Count of Saint Germain since his incarnation in the eighteenth century), Hilarion, Serapis, and the so-called Venetian Master. These seven were regarded as the seven rays of the Logos, and to each was ascribed a special way of working according to the kind of ray that was attributed to him. It was said of Christian Rosenkreutz, for instance, that as a representative of the seventh ray he worked by means of ceremonial magic. Rudolf Steiner apparently rejected this idea in a lecture in Berlin on June 20, 1912 (CW 133), when he stated that the individuality of Christian Rosenkreutz, "whom we acknowledge as the leader of the occult movement leading into the future," is often misunderstood, even by esotericists, and that he would certainly never transmit his authority by means of an exoteric cult.

However, as shown by the lecture of July 3, 1904, in Berlin and responses to questions on May 29, 1915, in Dornach (previously quoted), Rudolf Steiner also spoke of the Masters' sevenfold activity. In response to a question from another member about this sevenfold quality, he answered, "Two are active in the East, two in the West, two in the Center, but one moves about."[11] "In the Center" does not refer to Central Europe but to the Mediterranean region as the center of the world. Viewed globally, Central Europe belongs to the Western portion of the world. Consequently, Steiner

---

10 See *Cosmic Memory*, CW 11. There it is indicated that there are twelve stages of consciousness, of which, however, only seven can be described. The eye of the seer can perceive five further stages, but it is impossible to describe them.

11 Reported by Friedrich Rittelmeyer.

always spoke of the two Masters of the West in reference to those who represented Central Europe.

The various references to the reincarnations of the Masters may also appear controversial at first glance since we are told that such highly developed individualities are already released from earthly incarnations, but are also told of actual incarnations of certain Masters having a special mission, even to the extent that their physical bodies are preserved, and that death does not occur (CW 264). This apparent contradiction, however, shows only that the work of the Masters is varied and complicated and that their office comprises many different ranks—for example, bodhisattva and buddhahood—as described often by Rudolf Steiner.[12] This dual possibility of being incarnated or not is exemplified, for instance, in *The Temple Legend:*

> The masters, as a rule, are not persons known to history; they sometimes incarnate when necessary into historical personalities, but in a certain sense this is a personal sacrifice. The level of their consciousness is no longer compatible with any work for themselves—and preservation of a name does after all involve work for oneself. (Berlin, Dec. 23, 1904, CW 93)

> When the present-day "leaders of humanity" go about in the world in their human guise, they are not recognized by what they are in the outer world. When from the theosophical standpoint we speak of the "Masters of Wisdom and of the Harmony of Sensations and Feelings," people would often be surprised to see in what simple, unpretentious human form these "Masters of Wisdom and of the Harmony of Sensations and Feelings" pass through all countries. They are present on the physical plane, but do not give their most important teachings there, but they impart them on the spiritual plane. Those who wish to hear them, to receive their teachings, must have access to them not only in their physical body of flesh, but in their spiritual form (Munich, Aug. 24, 1911, CW 129).

---

12 See, for example, the lecture in Berlin on Oct. 25, 1909, in *The Christ Impulse: And the Development of Ego-Consciousness*, CW 116.

The foregoing passage clearly illustrates the need to be wary when judging and reflecting on statements by Rudolf Steiner concerning the incarnations of the Masters, especially when transmitted defectively or inauthentically. We must also consider the fact that the Masters do not appear only in physical incarnations, but also by means of incorporation, inspiration, or the astral. Eugenie von Bredow's report of an Esoteric Class lesson, in which the Master Kut Hoomi was being discussed, indicates this: "This incarnation did not occur in a particular individual, but his power was active first in one place and then in another. (Berlin, Dec. 13, 1905)

It is clear that the occult phenomena at work here are difficult or impossible to grasp with the ordinary intelligence. No doubt, the manifold guises in which the Mahatmas appeared to H. P. Blavatsky and other TS members were necessarily the cause of such great misunderstandings. Rudolf Steiner, however, never doubted the possibility of materialization. Friedrich Rittlemeyer records a conversation with him:

> A conversation particularly fresh in my memory took place after a Group Meeting. Dr. Steiner spoke about the previous incorporations of the Master. "A man in the room approaches you," he said. "You give him your hand and speak with him. He leaves the room again, but you do not notice that he leaves the house." Regardless of how readily Rudolf Steiner replied to such questions, he nevertheless gradually steered the conversation away in two different directions—first toward the side of the most important present-day task, the spiritualization of thinking, and then in the direction of historical connections.

The Seven Great Life Secrets and the Masters

If we now proceed in our inquiry regarding the activity of the Masters in human affairs from a consideration of the relationship of twelve to seven to the question of the relationship of seven to four, we are faced with a still more complicated problem. To elucidate this we must start with the letter to Günther Wagner on December 24, 1903, contained in supplement 3 of this book. This letter was in reply to a request for a fuller explanation of the indication given at the first General Meeting of the German Section in Berlin, October 1903, where it was stated that each of the seven "races" had a mystery to solve. The reply to Günther Wagner commenced with the following sentence quoted from *The Secret Doctrine* by H. P. Blavatsky: "Of the Seven Truths and Revelations, or rather 'revealed secrets,' only four have been handed to us, since we are still in the Fourth Round."

This sentence is from Blavatsky's commentary to the ten stanzas of the "Dzyan" book, which, as the basic source of theosophical knowledge of the universe, forms the main part of *An Outline of Esoteric Science*. The remaining content consists solely of the commentary thereto. In general Rudolf Steiner was very critical of the commentaries by H. P. Blavatsky, but of the Dzyan stanzas themselves he has always spoken with great esteem.[13]

The following is the first stanza, translated by Rudolf Steiner into German:[14]

> The Eternal Mother, wrapped in her ever-invisible robes, had slumbered once again for seven eternities.
> Time was not, for it lay asleep in the infinite bosom of duration.
> Universal mind was not, for there were no *ah-hi* to contain it.
> The seven ways to bliss were not. The great causes of misery were not, for there was no one to produce and get ensnared by them.
> Darkness alone filled the boundless All, for Father (law, necessity), Mother (world substance) and Son (ordered world, substance, cosmos) had not awakened yet for the new wheel and the pilgrimage thereon.
> The seven sublime Lords and seven Truths had ceased to be, and the universe, the son of necessity, was immersed in

---

13 For example, in the lecture given in Düsseldorf, Apr. 12, 1909, CW 110.
14 From a notebook of 1903. Archive no. 427, pp. 580–581.

> *paranishpanna* to be exhaled by what is, and yet is not. Naught (supra-existence) was.
>
> The causes of existence had been done away with; the visible that was, and the invisible that is, rested in eternal nonbeing, the one being (supra-existence).
>
> Alone, the one form of existence (supra-existence) stretched boundless, infinite, and causeless in dreamless sleep; and life pulsated unconsciously (blissfully) in universal space, throughout that All-presence sensed by the "open eye" of the *dangma*.
>
> But where was the *dangma* when the *a-laya* of the universe was in *paramartha* and the great wheel was *anupudaka?*
>
>> *ah-hi* = soul of the *dhyan-chohans*[15]
>> *paranishpanna* = perfection
>> *dangma* = seer
>> *a-laya* = world soul
>> *paramartha* = perfection
>>   (*parama* = above all things, *artha* = comprehend)
>> *anupadaka* = without parents

The full text of H. P. Blavatsky's commentary on the sixth verse of the preceding first Dzyan stanza mentioned by Rudolf Steiner in his letter to Günther Wagner (Dec. 24, 1903) is as follows:[16]

> The seven sublime Lords are the seven Creative Spirits, the Dhyan–Chohans, who correspond to the Hebrew Elohim. It is the same hierarchy of Archangels to which Saint Michael, Saint Gabriel, and others in Christian theology belong. Only, while Saint Michael, for instance, is allowed in dogmatic Latin theology to watch over all the promontories and gulfs, in the esoteric system, the Dhyanis watch successively over one of the rounds and the great root races of our planetary chain. They are, moreover, said to send their bodhisattvas, the human correspondents of the Dhyani Buddhas, during every round and race. Out of seven truths and revelations—or rather revealed

---

15 *Dhyan-Choans* = Archangel.
16 Blavatsky, *Secret Doctrine*, vol. 1.

secrets—only four have been handed down to us, as we are still in the fourth round, and the world also has had only four buddhas so far. This is a very complicated question, and will receive ampler treatment later on. So far, "there are only four truths, and four Vedas," say Hindus and Buddhists. For a similar reason, Irenaeus insisted on the necessity of four Gospels. But as every new root race as the head of a round must have its revelation and revealers, the next round will bring the fifth, the following the sixth, and so on.

According to Blavatsky (confirmed by Rudolf Steiner's letter of December 24, 1903, to Günther Wagner), only four of the seven truths, or revelations, have as yet been bestowed on the world. Whereas each revelation needs someone to reveal it, there must have been only four buddhas. It must remain an open question as to whether, and in what way, these four buddhas are identical with the four masters spoken of by Steiner in the Esoteric School; he once equated, however, the ranks "master" and "buddha" (Lugano, Sept. 17, 1911, CW 130).

We are here directly confronted with the question of the relationship of the masters to the buddhas or, respectively, to the bodhisattvas; Steiner refers to both as "great spiritual leaders of humanity," and he says of both that they form a unity of twelve whose task it is to regulate the further evolution of the world, and to teach humankind the importance of the Christ impulse for human progress. A condition for the closer study of this question is, undoubtedly, an acceptance of the fact that the designations "master," "buddha," and "bodhisattva" are not personal names but denote stages or titles in the hierarchy of the initiates, attainable by a human being who goes through the necessary development. In a lecture in Berlin on October 1, 1905 (CW 93a), the concept *bodhisattva* means "one who has absorbed all earthly experiences into oneself so that one knows how to use everything and has thus become a creator." The sages of this world, therefore, are not yet bodhisattvas, because a sage is still unfamiliar with some matters. After working for a long time as a teacher of humankind within the rank of bodhisattva, one ascends to the degree of buddha; one no longer needs to incarnate but works in a purely spiritual way to further evolution.

As Rudolf Steiner sometimes uses the term *bodhisattva* and sometimes *master* when speaking of the same person (Lugano, Sept. 17, 1911, CW 130)—Zarathustra, for example—and once equates the rank of buddha with *master,* one assumes the designation "Masters of Wisdom and of the Harmony of Sensations and Feelings" refers to the rank called *bodhisattva* or *buddha* in the Eastern traditions. However, Steiner has often stated that, to understand the actual relationships, we are presented with a very complicated structure, the outcome of the intervention of beings of the higher hierarchies.[17]

Understanding what even H. P. Blavatsky calls "a very complicated question" about the relationship of seven to four is elucidated only through Rudolf Steiner's description of what he calls "the seven great life secrets." H. P. Blavatsky calls these "the seven truths and revelations, or rather revealed secrets." In the letter by Rudolf Steiner already mentioned, he calls them "the seven esoteric root truths." In the notes of a lecture it is stated, "We speak of seven great secrets. There are seven great mysteries that reveal the seven great phases of life. Their name is "The Unutterable" (Berlin, Oct. 28, 1903).[18]

During the General Meeting, ten days earlier, Rudolf Steiner referred to this "in the sense of a certain occult tradition." This tradition had then already appeared in a literary form through the work of the English esotericist C. G. Harrison. In the six lectures in *The Transcendental Universe* (1894), Harrison took a stand

---

17 For the "bodhisattva question," see Steiner, *Spiritual Hierarchies and the Physical World,* CW 110; *The Christ Impulse and the Development of Ego-Consciousness,* CW 116; *Esoteric Christianity and the Mission of Christian Rosenkreutz,* CW 130, as well as T. H. Meyer, *The Bodhisattva Question.*

18 Unpublished notes.

against Blavatsky's Theosophy from the perspective of traditional European–Christian occultism. He had to admit, however, that *The Secret Doctrine* "affords valuable information about prehistoric civilizations and religions, hinting at certain secrets, the very existence of which was unsuspected and some of which have been tested by a process known to occultists and found correct" (lect. 1). In the sixth lecture, Harrison dealt with the "seven great mysteries." These mysteries, it is said, are valid for all stages of consciousness and cannot be explained in words "but require the use of a symbolic system, the nature of which the writer is not at liberty to explain." In a relevant footnote they are enumerated as follows: 1) abyss; 2) number; 3) affinity; 4) birth and death; 5) evil; 6) the word; and 7) godliness.

In the very fragmentary notes from the first years of Rudolf Steiner's lecturing in Spiritual Science, those seven mysteries are usually discussed only in part, and Harrison is never mentioned by name. In later, even more concrete statements, they are dealt with only partially, so that it is impossible to recognize that a sevenfold unity is being discussed.[19] Only three references allude to all seven mysteries as Harrison enumerates them. This is in the Paris lectures of May and June of 1906. The reference in the June 13 lecture follows: "There are seven life secrets, of which no one outside of the occult brotherhoods has ever spoken. Only in the present epoch has it become possible to speak of them exoterically. They are also known as the "unutterable" secrets."

The seven mysteries are...

1. the mystery of the abyss;
2. the mystery of number (may be studied in the Pythagorean philosophy);
3. the mystery of alchemy (understood through the works of Paracelsus and Jakob Böhme);

---

19 See: *Secrets of the Threshold*, CW 147; *Inner Reading and Inner Hearing*, CW 156; *Goethe's* Faust *in the Light of Anthroposophy*, CW 273.

4. the mystery of birth and death[20];
5. the mystery of evil (dealt with in the Apocalypse);
6. the mystery of the Word, the Logos;
7. and the mystery of godliness (the most hidden of all).

Based on notes by Marie von Sivers from her private lessons (Berlin, July 2, 1904),[21] it follows that in the case of these seven great mysteries or esoteric "root truths," we are not dealing just with concepts in general that "run like a red thread through the whole esoteric movement" (Paris, May 5, 1913, CW 150), but that high spiritual beings stand behind those concepts. Accordingly, the seven possible relationships that the Trinity of Father, Son, and Spirit enters can be understood as actual beings, and the names by which these seven possible "relationship beings" are designated relate again to the names of the seven life mysteries.

In the first lectures on spiritual–scientific cosmology,[22] we find, described in a basic way, how all of evolution is controlled according to three principles: *consciousness, life,* and *form,* and how each of these three principles passes through seven stages, or phases. The stages of life named therein correspond, furthermore, with the seven great mysteries of life. Knowing about these and the soul experiences that accompany them form the two integral halves of initiation and, consequently, the content of Anthroposophy as the modern science of initiation (Dornach, Dec. 30, 1914, CW 275). Whereas we constantly hear in Rudolf Steiner's Spiritual Science about the seven stages of consciousness and form (called the seven principles of the human frame and Earth's structure), this is not true to the same extent in the case of the seven stages of cosmic life. Evidently, this is connected with the fact that the

---

20 This fourth mystery was recorded in the report from Édouard Schuré only as "The Mystery of Death," which may have been an error in the notes.

21 *Beiträge...* (Contributions...), nos. 67/68, 1979.

22 Berlin, Oct. 17–Nov. 10, 1904, *Beiträge...* (Contributions...), nos. 67/68, 69/70, 71/72.

planetary spirit does not reveal its inner reaction (Berlin, Nov. 3, 1904). This is probably the reason the seven life secrets are called "unutterable" (which must be extremely difficult to describe), as indicated in the Munich lectures of December 4, 1907 (CW 98), and in Dornach, December 30, 1914 (CW 275).

The notes of a November 1, 1904, lecture in Berlin[23] provide the most decisive indication that the relationship of seven to four concerns both the seven mysteries themselves, as well as the revealers of the mysteries, the masters. According to this, the main characteristic of the seven life secrets is their application to all cycles of evolution because of their constant recurrence; indeed, they recur "in every round and epoch of Earth's evolution, and likewise in all cyclic developments within human beings themselves." This indication explains for the first time the statement in the letter to Günther Wagner on December 24, 1903: "...number four of the previously mentioned seven truths is derived from the seven esoteric root truths; of these seven partial truths (the fourth being considered as complete), one is divulged (as a rule) to each race [i.e., epoch]."

We can draw the following threefold conclusion from this: First, the seven root truths, or secrets, are relevant to the great evolutionary cycles of the planetary chain (Saturn–Sun–Moon–Earth–Jupiter–Venus–Vulcan). Second, for all of Earth's evolution, the fourth mystery (that of birth and death) applies. And third, because the seven mysteries always recur, they also apply to every sevenfold division within the whole of Earth's evolution, but only as partial truths within the much larger fourth mystery (Dornach, Nov. 3–4, 1917, CW 273).

This question arises from this: *How does the present time and the work of Rudolf Steiner stand in relationship to the seven great mysteries of life?*

---

23 *Beiträge...* (Contributions...), nos. 69/70. 1980.

Rudolf Steiner's Work in Relation to the Fifth of the Seven Great Life Secrets

Since the seven great mysteries of life apply to all cycles of development having a sevenfold nature, it must follow that our immediate present—the fifth post-Atlantean cultural epoch—must be influenced by the fifth of the mysteries, *evil*. This does not apply in its entirety, but only as a partial truth belonging to the future, because the more comprehensive principle is the fourth mystery, which still prevails and holds sway throughout the whole of Earth evolution. The fifth mystery will be revealed in a far more powerful way during the fifth planetary stage of the Earth than it is today, during the fifth cultural epoch. In the fifth epoch, it will attain its full strength once the Earth has developed into the Jupiter stage of consciousness (Munich, Jan. 16, 1908, CW 245).

The letter to Günther Wagner tells us that theosophy (the aspect of theosophy one might find in Blavatsky's *Secret Doctrine* and its esotericism) consists of the sum of partial truths from the fifth mystery. We are inclined to ask: *What does evil have to do with theosophy?* This question is answered partially by the view of spiritual science toward good and evil. Accordingly, knowledge of good and evil during our cultural epoch is connected with knowledge of the spiritual impulses behind human and cosmic evolution (Dornach, Sept. 28, 1918, CW 273). Evil appears when people, whether individually or collectively, deviate from conformity to progressive cosmic impulses. There is not *evil* as such; evil is not an absolute reality but arises when something good in some aspects is used improperly in the world. As a result, something good is turned into something evil (Munich, Aug. 25, 1913, CW 147).

Another view of evil was the determining factor in the previous cultural epoch—the Greco–Latin age. As the fourth epoch, it was ruled by the fourth mystery, that of birth and death. This can be seen from the following modification of the seven steps to initiation.

The Christian–Gnostic way of initiation that was customary for the fourth epoch had the following seven steps: 1) the Washing of the Feet; 2) the Scourging; 3) the Crowning with Thorns; 4) the Crucifixion; 5) the Mystic Death; 6) the Laying in the Grave; and 7) the Ascension. The Christian–Rosicrucian way of initiation appropriate to the fifth cultural epoch has the following seven steps: 1) study toward true self-knowledge; 2) imagination; 3) learning of the occult script, or inspired knowledge; 4) creating rhythm in life (preparation of the Philosopher's Stone); 5) correspondence of microcosm and macrocosm (knowledge of the connection between human being and the universe); 6) resting or immersing oneself in the macrocosm; and 7) godliness. Now the experience of evil in both ways of initiation certainly lies at the fifth step, but in the Christian–Gnostic way of the fourth epoch it was connected with the experience of the Mystic Death as the "Descent into Hell." In the way of initiation of our fifth epoch, however, we become acquainted with the true good in the correspondence of the microcosm to the macrocosm, and evil as the deviation from this correspondence in either direction. Since the way of initiation appropriate to a particular epoch is always bound up with the powers that epoch must develop in connection with the seven life secrets, Anthroposophy must, therefore, necessarily become the science of correspondence—or even the non-correspondence of microcosm to macrocosm. The question regarding good and evil, according to that, must be solved today by means of knowing the proper correspondence.

Seen in this light, the passage from the letter of December 24, 1903 stating that Theosophy is the sum of the partial truths of the fifth mystery is explained, in that this statement refers only to the double aspect of the fifth step in the modern way of initiation: the correspondence between microcosm and macrocosm on the one hand, and on the other hand, the deviation from this expressed as evil. Through this, knowledge of good and evil that shows a more fixed character (more "spatial," so to speak) during the fourth epoch will receive a more "flowing" quality during the fifth epoch. It becomes increasingly a question of knowing the true impulse of the age or, expressed differently, knowing the true impulses behind cosmic evolutionary history. There is a certain law and order about this step from the more "spatial" to a more "temporal" knowledge, which Rudolf Steiner once pointed to when he spoke about the relationship of the first four cultural epochs to the three following ones: "When what has spatial nature changes into something temporal, the process comes about through the relationship of four to seven, and fourfoldness extends to become sevenfoldness.... The relationship of four to seven depends on a certain law" (Berlin, Oct. 28, 1904).

It is also clear from the following notebook entry[24] that the stand toward the question of good and evil must be very different from what was right during the previous epoch:

> The masters are not a rampart against evil, but the leaders in absorbing evil. We should not cast out evil, but just take it up and use it in the service of the good. The rage of the lion remains evil only as long as it is used by the lion in an egoistic way; if some conqueror could use the rage of the lion to accomplish social service, then it would be beneficial. Therefore, what is evil can be recognized as unreal. There is no evil. Evil is only a misplaced good. Only when one recognizes this fact is spiritual alchemy possible.

In connection with the seven great mysteries of life and in the sense H. P. Blavatsky expresses, "Every new root race [great epoch] has to receive its mystery and its revealer of mysteries at the beginning of a new round of evolution," we can infer only that Rudolf Steiner (as revealed in his work) is the first revealer of the fifth esoteric root truth, the fifth of the great life mysteries, and that, indeed, in its double sense, on the one hand, that of the correspondence of macrocosm to microcosm, and on the other, that of its deviation expressing itself as evil.

---

24 1906, Archive-no. B 105; Compare CW 264.

Research into Occult History

In the collection of notes referring to the early years of Steiner's lecturing activity on behalf of Spiritual Science, the truth about the mystery of evil is only hinted at, but it is nevertheless touched upon in its full depth. For instance, in the report[25] of what Rudolf Steiner said at the first General Meeting of the German Section of the Theosophical Society states that one of the most important of the many reasons leading to the founding of the theosophic movement as a "powerful occult necessity" is that every race (epoch) is given a "mystery" and that we, as representatives of the fifth epoch, had arrived at the stage of the fifth mystery, which could not, however, be revealed yet in the present day. It then proceeds as follows:

> We are, however, at the point when we will gradually move toward it. Its nature is hinted at by Saint Paul, who was an initiate. It will be revealed to us only during the course of the epoch. A premature speculation about this mystery through purely intellectual ability would pose an indescribable danger to humanity. Because speculation of this kind has already nearly succeeded twice [26] and is about to happen again soon, the great teachers of humanity have brought the theosophic movement into being. Humanity is to be prepared for the great truth. Theosophy is working toward a particular moment in time. A core group of people is to be prepared; they will understand this mystery when the time is right for its revelation. A core of people who understand it correctly will use it for good and not allow it to become a curse on humanity. Earlier epochs formed such a core of people from those already appointed, as well as from specifically chosen suitable individuals and families. The manu led them into suitably remote areas. Because of the universal spread of human movement over the whole globe, this method is no longer appropriate and no longer necessary. Instead, education through the worldwide international Theosophical Society is intended to form this core of people. (Berlin, Oct. 18, 1903)

---

25 Report in "Der Vahan," Nov. 1903.
26 No further details are known about this.

If at that time the fifth mystery of life was described in a more general way, it was later described more concretely as the unjustified use of the sacred forces of transmutation.

> Profound insight into the secret of existence arises when we understand the root of injustice, evil, crime, and sin in the world. These happen because the best and most holy powers that exist in humankind (the powers of transformation) are improperly applied. There would be no evil in the world if there were not also these *most holy powers of transformation* (Dornach, Oct. 5, 1914, CW 156).

Rudolf Steiner spoke with ever-greater emphasis and clarity about the dominance of evil and, above all, its prominence in history as retrogression from the progressive stream of evolution, especially after the outbreak of World War I. The great importance attached to knowledge of evil as the root mystery of our epoch helps us understand why the visible sign of the anthroposophic movement—the Goetheanum building—was connected with this. At the laying of the Foundation Stone,[27] Steiner spoke for the first time from "esoteric obligation" about the Fifth Gospel, the Gospel of Knowledge, the central message of which was the macrocosmic Lord's Prayer:

> AUM, Amen
> The Evils hold
> Witness of Egoity becoming free
> Selfhood's guilt incurred through others
> Experienced in Daily Bread
> Wherein the Will of the Heavens does not rule,
> In that we severed ourselves from Your Kingdom
> And forgot Your Names
> You Fathers in the Heavens.

During the following ten years of intensive work on the building, in cooperation with many voluntary helpers, the central motif,

---

27 *Inner Reading and Inner Hearing*, lect. 3 (CW 156), Dornach, Sept. 20, 1913; *Guidance in Esoteric Training;* also in *Esoteric Lessons*, CW 266/1.

the carved group, *The Representative of Humanity between Lucifer and Ahriman,* was created as visible artistic expression of the double nature of the fifth life secret. *The Representative of Humanity* (or Christ, acknowledged by Rudolf Steiner as the Master of all Masters) personifies the full correspondence of microcosm to macrocosm and gained the mastery, through his radiating love, over Lucifer and Ahriman, the powers of opposition, or evil. When the nearly completed building was destroyed by fire on New Year's Eve, 1922/23, only this wooden carving was saved—a legacy and a warning by its creator to remind us to be aware of the deepest life secret belonging to our fifth epoch.

Supplement to Chapter 3

To Günther Wagner in Lugano

Günther Wagner wrote the following to Rudolf Steiner on November 14, 1903:

> *Esteemed Doctor:*
> ...It was a great pleasure to me to have made your acquaintance at the Annual Meeting, and I hope that we shall long continue in our joint work and will continue to support one another.
> It would give me great pleasure if you would care to supply me with a particular piece of information. The allusion to a riddle that each Race [epoch] has to solve was quite new to me; I could not find anything about it in the *Secret Doctrine.* Can you name the four riddles, which the first four epochs have (apparently) solved? I would also like to read H. P. Blavatsky's indications about it. Perhaps you could give me the exact reference.
> In the meantime I remain yours most respectfully,
> *Günther Wagner*

Rudolf Steiner replied:

Berlin, December 24, 1903, *very confidential!*

Dear esteemed Mr. Wagner:

On page 42, volume 1 of the facsimile edition of *The Secret Doctrine*, in an explanation of the sixth stanza of the *Book of Dzyan*, stand the words: "Of the Seven Truths or Revelations only four are manifested, because we are still in the Fourth Round." I have indicated—while you were in Berlin—that, in the sense of a particular esoteric tradition, the fourth of the previously mentioned Seven Truths is derived from seven *esoteric root truth*s, and that of these seven partial truths (the fourth being considered as complete), one is divulged (as a rule) to each "race" [epoch]. The fifth will manifest fully once the fifth race has reached the goal of its development. Now, I would like to answer your question as well as I can. At the moment the matter stands thus, that the four partial truths are the subject of meditation sentences for the aspirants in the mysteries, and that nothing else can be given apart from these (symbolic) meditation sentences. Something of a higher nature emanates from them, by esoteric paths, to the one who meditates. I therefore set down these four meditation sentences, transmitted from the symbolic sign language, as follows:

1. *Consider*: how the point becomes the sphere and still remains itself. If you have understood how the infinite sphere is, after all, merely a point, then return, for then the infinite will appear as finite within you.
2. *Consider*: how the grain becomes an ear [of rye] and then return, for then you will have understood how what is living exists in number.
3. *Consider*: how light desires the dark, heat the cold, how the male desires the female, then return, for then you will have understood which aspect the great Dragon of the Threshold will turn toward you.
4. *Consider*: how one enjoys hospitality in someone else's house, then return, for then you will have understood what awaits one who sees the midnight sun.

The fifth secret then arises, if the meditation was successful, from the other four. Let me state, provisionally, only this much, that Theosophy—the fragment of Theosophy that could be found in *The Secret Doctrine* and its esotericism—is made up of partial truths contained in the fifth secret. An indication of how one can get beyond this point is to be found in the letter from the Master KH [Kut Hoomi] published by Sinnett, beginning with the following words: "I have to read each word" (A.P. Sinnett, *The Occult World*).[28]

I can only give you the assurance that in the sentence by Kut Hoomi: "When science will have learned how it is that impressions of leaves can appear on stones...," practically the whole of the fifth secret lies hidden. That is all that I am able to tell you at present with regard to your question. Perhaps I will be able to enlarge on it when more questions are forthcoming.

The above four sentences are what one calls *living* sentences, that is to say, they begin to sprout during meditation and send forth shoots of knowledge.

With joyful Christmas greetings.
Yours faithfully, Rudolf Steiner
Berlin W., Motzstrasse 17

---

28 The exact rendering of Kut Hoomi's words is given by A.P. Sinnett as follows: "Of course I have to read every word you write, otherwise I would make a fine mess of it. And whether it is through my physical or spiritual eyes, the time required for it is practically the same. As much may be said of my replies; for whether I precipitate or dictate them or write my answers myself, the difference in time saved is very minute. I have to think it over, to photograph every word and sentence carefully in my brain, before it can be repeated by precipitation. As fixing on chemically prepared surfaces of the images formed by the camera requires a previous arrangement within the focus of the object to be represented, for otherwise—as often found in bad photographs—the legs of the sitter might appear out of all proportion with the head, and so on—so we have to first arrange our sentences and impress every letter to appear on paper in our minds before it becomes fit to be read. For the present it is all I can tell you. When science will have learned more about the mystery of the *lithophyl* (or *lithobiblion*), and how the impress of leaves comes originally to take place on stones, then I will be able to make you better understand the process. But you must know and remember one thing—we but follow and servilely copy Nature in her works."

4

RUDOLF STEINER ON THE FIRST SECTION OF THE ESOTERIC SCHOOL, 1904–1914

FROM HIS AUTOBIOGRAPHY, CHAPTER 65

In the monthly periodical I was able for the first time to publish the material that became the foundation for anthroposophic activity. Published there for the first time was what I had to say about the inner effort needed to attain suprasensory knowledge through one's own inner perception. I wrote monthly installments of "How to Know Higher Worlds." I also wrote a series of articles called "From the Akashic Record" (*Cosmic Memory*, CW 11), the basis for an anthroposophic cosmology.

The anthroposophic movement grew from this foundation, not from anything borrowed from the Theosophical Society. When I wrote on spiritual knowledge, if I considered what was generally taught in the society, it was simply to present correctly what seemed to me to be errors in that teaching.

In relation to this, I must discuss an issue that is always raised by opponents, usually those fogged by misunderstandings. Inner reasons would not require me to speak of this, because it has no influence at all on my path of development or on my public activities. It has remained entirely private in contrast to much of what I have described here. It is the matter of my acceptance into the Esoteric School of the Theosophical Society. The Esoteric School dated back to H. P. Blavatsky. Within the society she instituted a small inner circle in which she communicated matters she did not wish to speak of to the general society. Like others with insight into the spirit world, she maintained that it was impossible to impart certain, more profound teachings to the general public.

All this was connected with how H. P. Blavatsky attained her teachings. There has always been a tradition concerning such teachings that goes back to the ancient mystery schools. This tradition is nurtured in all kinds of societies that strictly guard the teaching from reaching the outside world.

However, from some source it was deemed proper to impart such knowledge to H. P. Blavatsky. She combined what she attained in this way with revelations that arose within herself. She was an individual with peculiar atavistic powers. Spirit worked through her in a dreamlike state of consciousness, just as in ancient times it had acted through leaders of the mysteries—unlike our modern consciousness, which is illumined by the consciousness soul. Thus in "Blavatsky the human being" something recurred that was innate within the mysteries during primordial times.

Today, one can determine with certainty the spiritual perceptions that can be imparted appropriately to larger circles. Spiritual investigators can convey anything that can be clothed in ideas appropriate to the consciousness soul—in character, the kinds of ideas used in conventional science.

It is different, however, when spiritual knowledge is not alive in the consciousness soul but lives more in subconscious soul forces. *Those* soul forces are not sufficiently independent of the body's active forces. Consequently, it may be dangerous to communicate teachings derived from such subconscious regions. Such teachings can be taken in again only by those subconscious regions. Consequently, both teacher and student move in a sphere where one must be very careful to distinguish between what is wholesome and what is harmful for a human being. This is not an issue for Anthroposophy, however, because what it communicates is raised entirely into the realm of full consciousness.

Blavatsky's inner circle continued as the Esoteric School. Because I had introduced my anthroposophic activity into the Theosophical Society, I had to keep informed of everything taking place within the society. That is why I became a member of the Esoteric School, and because I also thought that a closer circle was necessary for advanced students of anthroposophic, spiritual knowledge. But the group I had in mind was intended to serve a different purpose than that of the school. It would be a higher section, a higher class for those who had absorbed enough basic knowledge of Anthroposophy.

I always wanted to link whatever I did with what already exists historically. I wanted to do this in the Esoteric School, just as I had done in relation to the Theosophical Society. Thus my more intimate circle first arose as well in connection with the School. But the connection was related only to the *external arrangements,* not to the suprasensory knowledge I imparted. Thus, in the early years my smaller circle was seen as a section of Mrs. Besant's Esoteric School, yet according to its inner nature it was completely unrelated to that School. In 1907, when Mrs. Besant attended our theosophical conference in Munich, even that outer connection was severed completely by mutual agreement.

There is no possibility that I received any special knowledge in Mrs. Besant's Esoteric School, simply because I never participated in the School's activities, except for a few times when I merely wanted to know what was taking place. In any case, at the time the only real substance in that school came from H. P. Blavatsky, and that could be obtained in print.[1] Moreover, for developing spiritual knowledge Mrs. Besant gave various types of Indian practices, which I rejected. Thus, as for the external arrangements before 1907, my restricted circle was connected with that of Mrs. Besant.

---

1   *Esotericism* (Blavatsky, *Secret Doctrine,* vol. 3), published from her estate by Annie Besant (1897).

5

THE STRUCTURE OF THE ESOTERIC SCHOOL

I always wanted to link whatever I did with what already existed and was present historically. (Autobiography p. 219)

The Esoteric School of Theosophy, abbreviated as EST or ES, was founded in 1888 by H. P. Blavatsky, and remained under her sole leadership until her death in 1891. Her pupil Annie Besant then took over the leadership, at first with William Q. Judge and, from 1895 on, alone. The few German theosophists who sought esoteric instruction were affiliated to this London ES. A German Esoteric School was founded for the first time by Rudolf Steiner along with the German Society.

It has been possible to reconstruct the following details about the successive stages of building up the First Circle, which had been attached originally to the ES. The German Section of the Theosophical Society, centered in Berlin, was officially founded Oct. 20, 1902, with Rudolf Steiner as general secretary and Marie von Sivers as secretary. Annie Besant, who was then one of the most active representatives of the Theosophical Society and leader of the Esoteric School, came to Berlin with the foundation charter. At this occasion Rudolf Steiner allowed her to enroll him as a member of the ES.[1] He reported about this in chapter 65 of his *Autobiography.*

---

1 Oct. 23, 1902. Marie von Sivers had already become a member of the ES in the spring of 1902 in Bologna.

The collected letters of the first part of *From the History and Contents of the First Section of the Esoteric School* (CW 264) record that Rudolf Steiner was asked for esoteric instruction immediately after the founding of the German Section, that is, even before he was officially nominated as the first arch-warden (*Landesleiter*) of the Esoteric School in 1904. The institution of the restricted Circle, which he regarded as so essential, and was so much desired by his first pupils, is touched upon in the letter to Marie von Sivers of April 16, 1903: "Without a body of true theosophists to improve the karma of the present by hard-working meditation, theosophical teachings would be expounded merely to half-deaf ears" (*Correspondence and Documents,* CW 262, and letter of May 1, 1903, CW 264).

This is exemplified, too, by the answer given to a corresponding question by Mathilde Scholl: "It would be really wonderful if the newer members of the German ES could somehow come closer together. This is just what is needed in Germany, for the ES must become the heart of the Theosophical Society" (May 1, 1903, CW 264).

A year after this statement, in May 1904, Rudolf Steiner stayed for a week in London with Marie von Sivers, to discuss his functions in the ES with Annie Besant. Marie von Sivers was always present during his personal discussions with Besant to act as interpreter. In an open letter of May 10, 1904, to all members of the ES in Germany and Austria, Besant proclaimed that Steiner was authorized as her representative in Switzerland and Hungary. According to Steiner, he was also responsible for the German–Swiss. Annie Besant's circular read:

> To all members of the ES in Germany and Austria:
> I hereby appoint Dr. Rudolf Steiner as arch-warden of the ES in Germany and the Austrian Empire, with full authority as my representative to call meetings of the school, organize groups and appoint wardens, and do all else needed for the welfare of the school, remaining in direct communication with me.
>
> *Annie Besant*

The Structure of the Esoteric School

From London, Rudolf Steiner returned to Berlin and began working to build up his Esoteric School, alongside his other activities of spreading Spiritual Science and developing the Society. Since from the very beginning the main emphasis of his work was on his public work, he started to propagate the ideas of the Christian–Rosicrucian path of development (of great importance for the West) in a series of articles that appeared in the publicly available theosophic periodical *Lucifer–Gnosis*, which he founded and published. Those articles appeared from June 1904 to 1908 as "How to Know Higher Worlds," published as a book in 1909 (CW 10).

June 1904 is also notable as the first recorded date that he functioned as Arch-Warden in the ceremonies of the ES, during the Theosophical Congress in Amsterdam, which took place from June 18 to 21. Apart from Rudolf Steiner and Marie von Sivers, other German theosophists also took part, among them Mathilde Scholl from Cologne; Sophie Stinde and Pauline von Kalckreuth from Munich; Günther Wagner from Lugano; and his sister Amalie Wagner from Hamburg. Mathilde Scholl recounts that Amalie Wagner was admitted into the ES on that occasion and that Rudolf Steiner performed this act in her hotel room. But that can only refer to a kind of preliminary event, as the official ES work was only begun in Berlin after the Amsterdam Congress. There the first esoteric lessons took place on July 9 and 14 of 1904 (CW 266/1)—at least those are the first recorded dates of esoteric lessons in Berlin, and from the available records it is to be assumed that the work of the ES first took place in Berlin at that time. But these lessons must also be reckoned as merely a preliminary proceeding, which basically continued into the autumn of 1905. For only when the Second and Third Sections were added was the School fully complete.

During the holiday month of August 1904, Steiner sent personal letters to several members living at a distance whom he thereby either admitted to membership of the School or invited to join. Another ES gathering was planned for the beginning of September (according to a letter of Aug. 29, 1904, to Günther Wagner), however, it is not known if this actually took place.

In the second half of September 1904, Steiner accompanied Annie Besant on her lecture tour of several German cities and presented an account in German of her public lectures given in English. At the last place they called, in Cologne, both stayed at the home of Mathilde Scholl, who reported that a gathering of ES members occurred: "Mrs. Besant, Dr. Steiner, Fräulein von Sivers, Miss Esther Bright, Mr. Keightley, Mathilde Scholl, in Mrs. Besant's room. Before we left the room Mrs. Besant spoke to Dr. Steiner about the study material for pupils of the ES. Mrs. Besant recommended Leadbeater's 'Christian Creed.' Politely but firmly Dr. Steiner answered that he could not make use of this book for his pupils." A few esoteric lessons then took place until May 1905 in Berlin. But the first official communication through the "long-prepared circular to the German ES members" containing rules appeared only at the beginning of June 1905.

At the General Meeting in October 1905, the School was extended to include the *Cognitive Ritual* (that is, the second and third sections), and members, at the specific request of Rudolf Steiner, flocked in greater numbers to Berlin, where several ES lessons occurred. The contents of the lesson of October 24, 1905, were written personally by Rudolf Steiner for Anna Wagner, the wife of Günther Wagner, who was unable to take part for health reasons. Apart from the short summing-up of the lesson of October 4, 1904, for Adolf Kolbe in Hamburg, this is the only version of an esoteric lesson given in Rudolf Steiner's own handwriting. Otherwise, all that has been preserved of the contents of such lessons were written afterward from memory by those present, who were not allowed to make notes during the lessons.

Increasingly, esoteric lessons took place from autumn 1905 on, not only in Berlin but also in other German cities, and later in other countries, too, where Rudolf Steiner's pupils were working in this way. After the start of World War I during summer 1914, the esoteric activity came to an end because work in strictly closed circles could have aroused suspicion, but also because it would have been impossible to undertake any esoteric activity at a time charged with such strong emotions. It was ten years before an Esoteric School could again be inaugurated, this time in connection with the reestablishment of the Anthroposopical Society.

General Rules of the School

The relevant documents reveal that during the initial stages of the first esoteric study circles, "rules" were given, modeled on those of the E.S.T. The latter are said to have been originally very strict, but were in many respects modified over time. At the time Rudolf Steiner joined, one could apply for membership after two years in the Theosophical Society. The School was divided into degrees, acquired according to four different paths, or methods of discipline: a general discipline, a discipline related to yoga, a Christian–Gnostic discipline, and a Pythagorean one. But before admittance to the training proper one had to have belonged to the probationary or hearer degree (the Shrâvaka degree of India) for at least one year, and later two. At the time of admittance a written "promise" had to be submitted, affirming that the papers received would be handled in confidence and returned on demand. After the predetermined trial period one could be accepted into the actual first degree upon giving a written statement that Theosophy would be made the all-determining factor of one's life.

Because Rudolf Steiner's first esoteric study circle was joined outwardly to the probationary degree of the EST, and actually came within the general discipline, his pupils were obliged to make the compulsory "promise," which is evidenced by various letters. Meanwhile, he led his study circle independently. For example, there was no choice of discipline, even though in a letter to Anna and Günther Wagner on January 2, 1905, the four disciplines were mentioned. At the time, however, everything was in a transition, and before long it was taken for granted that everything should be determined according to Rudolf Steiner's intentions. Thus on January 23, 1905, he received a letter from Mathilde Scholl who, through his intercession, had been admitted by Annie Besant into the first degree of the EST in London, in May 1904, but had not yet received its instructions: "For me personally, it is not a matter of importance whether Mrs. Mead[2] sends the writings or not, for all that I need is given me by you, and will continue to be given me; and that is in such profusion that I can only look forward with respectful astonishment to all that is to come." Something similar is expressed in a letter from Günther Wagner, April 3, 1905:

> Some months ago I already received a printed article in English from Mrs. Oakley that gave information about the four ways that were practiced in the ES, and which you mention in your valued and kind letter to my wife. My wife and I have decided on the "Christian" path, and we would now ask if we may also begin on the first of April in Germany, as described in the article printed in English. Is a German set of instructions going to be made available? This will most probably be the case, because you will be unable to provide written instructions to all ES members who live at a distance. I would also like to know if pupils of the first degree (old order) should receive other instructions than those from the article printed in English, or whether these now apply to all pupils. You prescribed for my wife on January 2 that she should carry out the exercises from January 6 for about four weeks. She has done so and is continuing with them, but she requests new instructions from you.

These questions were answered in the first ES circular letter of June 5, 1905, and were further elaborated in later instructions.

---

[2] Mrs. Laura Mead, the wife of G.R.S. Mead, was the secretary of the ES in London.

Nothing more can be reconstructed of the gradual development of the First Circle. The question of how the EST's "promise" was dealt with remains open; Rudolf Steiner's pupils did not enter the degrees of the EST, and yet some of those "promises" that remain extant originated in 1906, insofar as they are dated. It is not known whether the promises were given on admission to the first degree of the cognitive–ritual section or in some other connection. At any rate, Rudolf Steiner wrote to an esoteric pupil in the same year, 1906: "Please do not regard the keeping secret as a strict injunction, but as a temporary one, owing to the present confused circumstances in the ES and TS…. I would also be pleased if this were unnecessary." This statement agrees with the fact that nothing has come down to us—even though the circle of pupils had already grown—to say that after the separation from the EST in May 1907 written "promises" were still asked for by Rudolf Steiner. In fact, at the reestablishment of the Esoteric School in 1924, the obligation to treat the lesson material confidentially was left to the individual's consciousness of responsibility.

In this sense Marie Steiner wrote after Rudolf Steiner's death: "It was not his opinion that esotericism could still be practiced in the greatest seclusion and with strictly binding vows as in former times. That could not have been reconciled with the feeling of individual freedom. The soul must stand before its own higher self and recognize what it owes to this higher self and the spiritual world in the way of respectful silence."[3]

Lesson Material

The instruction was, as it were, divided into three parts: the rules and exercises that applied to all equally; the personal exercises; and

---

3   Foreword to the first edition of *Karmic Relationships of the Anthroposophic Movement*, (German edition, Dornach 1926). Newly printed in German in *Beiträge zur Rudolf Steiner Gesamtausgabe* (Contributions to the Rudolf Steiner collected works), no. 23, Christmas 1968.

the esoteric lessons, which mainly dealt with intimate aspects of the path of development and directed the consciousness toward the Masters of Wisdom and of the Harmony of Sensations and Feelings, as the true leaders of the School. The ideal aim of the instructions lay, after all, in the gradual attainment of personal access to the Masters through the higher consciousness developed through the exercises.

The descriptions of the nature and activity of the Masters given in the esoteric lessons were meant as a guide along this path. The little thereof that has been handed down to us is summarized in the section dealing with the Masters. However, as Rudolf Steiner has spoken about them not only in esoteric lessons, but also in lectures to Society members, and even in public, they can be adequately grasped from the picture presented there.

Knowledge of the Masters had been of basic importance in the Theosophical Society and its Esoteric School since their founding (see chapter 3). For Rudolf Steiner the existence of the Masters had been a personally experienced reality decades before his connection with the Theosophical Society, as he testified many times.[4] Also, that it was his own Master who convinced him of the necessity of spreading the truth of esotericism in the world is vouched for by his own testimony: "...had the Master not convinced me that, in spite of all this [unpreparedness of the time for higher truths of esotericism], Theosophy is necessary for our age, I would have written only philosophical books and lectured on literature and philosophy, even after 1901."[5] He joined the Society only after having recognized "at the culmination of many years of inner development" that "the spiritual powers that I serve are to be found within the Theosophical Society."[6]

---

[4] See the notes for Édouard Schuré and letters to Marie Steiner-von Sivers, both in *Correspondence and Documents* (CW 262); see also *Self-education: Autobiographical Reflections 1861–1893* (CW 25); and the autobiographical lecture of Feb. 4, 1913, in *"Contributions...,"* nos. 83/84, 1984.

[5] Letter to Marie von Sivers, Jan. 9, 1905, *Correspondence and Documents*, CW 262.

[6] From the rough draft of a first circular to the German theosophic lodges in the summer of 1902, before the founding of the German Section. In

Whereas the Masters were referred to only as the "Masters of Wisdom" in the Theosophical Society, Rudolf Steiner nonetheless spoke of them as "The Masters of Wisdom and of the Harmony of Sensations and Feelings," or sometimes "of the Feeling Life of Humanity," because they possessed not only a high degree of wisdom, but also a "limitless source of human love" (letter to Amalie Wagner, Aug. 2, 1904, CW 264). This aspect points, as everything of his does, to the central theme of his spiritual knowledge—the unique significance of the Christ principle for the whole of the development of humanity and Earth. For him Christ was the Master of all Masters, and the "Masters of Wisdom and of the Harmony of Sensations and Feelings" were those who "stand in direct relationship to the forces of the higher hierarchies" (Düsseldorf, June 15, 1915, CW 159), and who have comprehended the fact that "the progress of humanity depends upon the understanding of the great significance of the event of Golgotha" (Berlin, Mar. 22, 1909, CW 107).

What Dr. Steiner said in one of his earliest public lecture cycles, given in Berlin, may be considered the most revealing statement of his personal relationship to the Masters. Referring to those highly developed individualities as described in Sinnett's *Esoteric Buddhism*, he attempted to show that for the European way of thinking the concept of the Masters did not necessarily bear any great significance when we consider that on the ladder of development—from the less advanced to, for instance, a Goethe, or beyond—there are an infinite number of possible stages. And then follow the words of such significance for himself:

> The so-called Masters are great inspirers—nothing more than that—great inspirers on the spiritual level. To be sure, their development extends far beyond the measure offered by our present-day culture. They are our great inspirers. They do not, however, demand belief in any kind of authority, or in any dogma. They make a demand only of the individual's human

Correspondence and Documents, CW 262.

understanding and give instruction, through certain methods for developing the powers and abilities dormant in every human being, which leads upward to the higher domains of existence. (Berlin, Oct. 13, 1904, CW 53)

In his next lecture he characterized the Masters in a way that makes clear that they respected human freedom to the highest degree, so that no kind of dependence could arise. No one, for instance, can suffer any harm from the rules given in *How to Know Higher Worlds*, in contrast to many other similar books that certain people recommend. Because so much is recommended that is without value but can instead be harmful, "the Masters have given permission for the publication of these rules" (Berlin, Dec. 15, 1904, CW 53).

If one looks at the various statements about the Masters, they appear at first glance to be contradictory. In particular, what is quoted above from the lecture of October 13, 1904, in Berlin appears to contradict what can be read in letters to esoteric pupils:

> I am able and allowed to be your leader only insofar as the exalted Master by whom I myself am guided gives me instruction" (letter, Aug. 11, 1904, CW 264); or also where it states that the theosophical doctrines refer back to the Masters: We affirm quite rightly that Theosophy did not come into the world through this or that book, through this or that set of dogmas. Theosophy springs from those high individuals, whom we call the Masters of Wisdom and of the Harmony of Sensations and Feelings, for they have uncovered the sources of the spiritual life that can henceforth flow into humanity. (Berlin, June 21, 1909)[7]
>
> Spiritual life can be traced back to those sources, which are found in the individuals we call the Masters of Wisdom and of the Harmony of Sensations and Feelings. Through them we can find the impulses if we truly search; they help us work through the epochs from age to age. (Berlin, Dec. 26, 1909)

---

7   *News for Members of the German Section*, published by Mathilda Scholl, no. 10, Jan. 1910.

If, however, one looks more closely at these statements, then the apparent discrepancy between them is resolved. It becomes clear that Rudolf Steiner himself belongs to those initiates who receive the impulses of the Masters through their free powers of reasoning and whose task is to elaborate those impulses for the progress of humanity. The world of the suprasensory, and also of the Masters, has its own language. It is revealed through signs and symbols that can be studied and deciphered only by means of a special training. How the esoteric language of revelation is interpreted and used depends entirely on the extent to which the capacity of understanding penetrates, and also on the moral awareness of responsibility of the one who uses it. Rudolf Steiner's achievement on behalf of cultural progress quite obviously rests on his ability to convert the symbolic language of the creative–spiritual basis underlying all existence into a conceptual language appropriate to the modern consciousness, which is expressed in Anthroposophy. He had to stand by this personal deed in the eyes of the world without relying on the authority of the Masters. His manner of teaching was quite personal. Perhaps this helps to explain why he ceased to speak in the same intimate fashion about the Masters as he did in earlier times, the more he developed the scientific character of Anthroposophy. This is especially the case during the years following World War I.

Instruction in the Esoteric School

Whereas, in the preceding sense, Rudolf Steiner took personal responsibility for the suprasensory knowledge he gave in public, this did not apply in the same way to the Esoteric School. He stated that the School stood under the direct guidance of the Masters and that therefore all that flowed through it must emanate only from the Masters of Wisdom and of the Harmony of Sensations and Feelings, and from no other source. The chief obligation of the pupils of the School was to apply all the common sense they had to what was taught them and to ask themselves if it was a reasonable path to follow (Esoteric lesson, Düsseldorf, Apr. 19, 1909).

Clearly, it was not always the case, but in certain of Steiner's esoteric lessons, or at certain moments during his esoteric lessons, he spoke as the direct spokesperson of the Masters. A participant in the Düsseldorf lesson of April 19, 1909, reported that this particular lesson commenced with the following words: "My dear Sisters and Brothers, this esoteric lesson is one in which the responsibility does not rest with the one who is speaking!" Those words were spoken because, in the following description of how Zarathustra had once received initiation from the Sun Spirit, Rudolf Steiner himself was Zarathustra at that moment. It must have come as a grand experience that "our great teacher, who had shared the results of his investigations with us, could now demonstrate through his own person how an ancient leader of humanity revealed himself by means of inspiration"—that is, how Steiner, as the first of the modern age, could transform himself through his own strict inner discipline into a serviceable tool through which spiritual beings could work, not as a medium but as a fully conscious spiritual investigator.[8]

There are very few accounts of this particular feature of Rudolf Steiner's activity in the esoteric lessons, where he could be experienced as the messenger of the Masters. The following account is from memory:

> I remember exactly how Rudolf Steiner entered the room. It was he and it was not he. When he came to the esoteric lesson he did not look like Rudolf Steiner, but only like his outer sheath. "Through me are speaking the Masters of Wisdom and of the Harmony of Sensations and Feelings," he began. It was always a solemn occasion. One is quite unable to forget it—the expression of his countenance.[9]

---

[8] Lecture by Elisabeth Vreede in Stuttgart on July 9, 1930. See Elisabeth Vreede and T. H. Meyer, *The Bodhisattva Question*.

[9] Jenny Schirmer-Bey in *What Is Happening in the Anthroposophical Society: News for Members*, Sept. 1, 1974.

The Structure of the Esoteric School

Another person wrote of the deep impression he had when first attending an esoteric lesson:

> Everyone sat in silence. When Rudolf Steiner entered the room, it seemed to me that a supra-earthly radiance still shone upon his features out of the realm from which he had come to us—it not only appeared this way; it was so. As though with direct knowledge and understanding, he spoke of the great Masters who guide our life and our endeavors from above: Kut Hoomi, Morya, Jesus, and Christian Rosenkreutz—the "Masters of Wisdom and of the Harmony of Sensations and Feelings."
>
> This much can be said: that the sanctity of this hour was indescribably beautiful. Rudolf Steiner appeared at this moment entirely as the messenger of a higher realm. The impression is unforgettable.[10]

In greatest detail and in the most delicate phrasing, the Russian poet Andrei Belyi described in his memoirs *Verwandeln des Lebens* (transforming life, 1975) how he experienced it as his task in the "probationary degree" to train his attention more on the *how* than on the *what*. There was no outer distinction between the esoteric lectures and the other lectures, for all of them had an esoteric nuance. The more they were given in popular form, the subtler the wording. What, however, could be experienced in concentrated form in the esoteric lessons was precisely that the how had become the what, and outshone everything else.

---

10 Ludwig Kleeberg, *Wege und Worte* (Ways and words), Stuttgart, 1961.

6

The Movement, the Esoteric School, and the Society

> *The Masters do not establish any outer organization or society, nor do they administer such an order.... It is different for the Esoteric School.*[1]

During the formative years of the Society and the Esoteric School Rudolf Steiner indicated repeatedly that we must be aware of the difference in character between the movement and the society, and also between the Esoteric School and the Society.

The *movement* signified for him the new spiritual revelation that the "Masters of Wisdom and of the Harmony of Sensations and Feelings" and their earthly messengers could impart to humanity since the last third of the nineteenth century. He once characterized the relationship between the messengers and the Masters in the following way:

> Initiates have the duty to instruct humanity; they, in their turn, have received their instruction from the higher beings who have already progressed beyond human development—that is from the Masters of Wisdom and of the Harmony of Sensations and Feelings, the exalted beings who truly influence every spiritual current that exists on the Earth, and who gradually infiltrate their wisdom little by little as human beings rise higher and higher in their development. (Vienna, June 14, 1909)

---

1   Letter to Anna Wagner on Jan. 2, 1905, CW 264.

Rudolf Steiner named H. P. Blavatsky as the first messenger of the theosophical movement (in a letter, Jan. 2, 1905, CW 264). The second messenger he named was Annie Besant (letter to Mathilde Scholl, Aug. 29, 1905, CW 264); however, this was meant in a limited sense, as he expressed two years later, since it was a short episode in which she had been drawn into the current of the initiators because of her pure and elevated mentality (in a written statement to Édouard Schuré in 1907). The third messenger, looked at historically, was Rudolf Steiner, who was, in fact, the first one who could establish and elaborate the science of the spirit, as demanded by the consciousness of the age. With the method of training described in *How to Know Higher Worlds*, he made it possible for everyone to follow the path to suprasensory knowledge through their own spiritual responsibility, so that all aspirant might meet their master in their own time. Steiner described how he understood this initial act of "leading the aspirant to the path of progress," and how an inaugural act or appointment to the office of spiritual teacher requires a sense of vocation equal to that of a corresponding post in public life. In the introduction to his first book on suprasensory knowledge of the world and human destiny (*Theosophy*, CW 9), he wrote:

> To be a "teacher" in these higher regions of existence, however, having acquired the faculty for perceiving them is not enough. Systematic knowledge belongs here as much as it does to the profession of teaching on the level of ordinary reality. "Higher seeing" does not make a person a "knower" in the spirit any more than healthy senses make a "scholar" in sense-perceptible reality. But in truth, all reality is one; since the lower reality and the higher spiritual reality are merely two sides of one and the same fundamental unity of being, a person who is ignorant with regard to lower knowledge will probably remain similarly ignorant of higher things. This basic fact calls up a feeling of boundless responsibility in those who, through a spiritual calling, feel obliged to speak out about spiritual regions of existence.

As a spiritual teacher, what Rudolf Steiner had to give the world in public, and through the Society and Esoteric School, was recognized as the theosophical movement. He considered the movement and the Esoteric School (as its most direct organ) to be an endowment of the Masters, which could be accountable only to those into whose care it was entrusted; the democratically organized society, on the other hand, was a foundation created by human beings, to whom it was accountable, and who administered its affairs. Through this the latter became the first institution concerned with occult matters that "worked to combine organization with freedom."[2] It was destined, as it were, to act as a bridge connecting occultism proper with what was fully public. At the same time it provided the opportunity, when communities were threatened with greater and greater division, for people working toward similar intellectual ends to meet together in brotherhood. This attitude of brotherliness was expressed during the founding of the Theosophical Society in the following three principles: 1) to form a nucleus of the universal human brotherhood, without distinction of race, creed, sex, caste, or color; 2) to encourage the study of comparative religion, philosophy, and science; and 3) to investigate unexplained laws of nature and the powers latent in human beings. Rudolf Steiner always adhered to these principles, and they were part of the rules of the Anthroposophical Society. It is in this spirit that humankind is to prepare the universal Christian Brotherhood consciousness of our succeeding cultural epoch. He alluded to this as early as 1904:

> In occult schools, three words describe the coming epoch, the epoch of a later human race: brotherly love, *pneumatosophy* [Spiritual Science], and freedom to rely on one's own authority in religious matters. (Berlin, Oct. 10, 1904)

This brotherhood ideal at the foundation of the society was strongly emphasized by Rudolf Steiner not just during the years when the Society was being built up, but he expressed

---

[2] From a handwritten note to the address given at the General Meeting of the German Section in Berlin, Oct. 21, 1906.

the fact that this came about at the instigation of the Masters. (Berlin, Jan. 2, 1905)

A new direction in accordance with this ideal was necessary then, because it could not occur through the Theosophical Society; for soon after the founding of the Society, the more restricted interest in ancient Eastern teachings began to take precedence over the spirit of universal and, therefore, truly Christian occultism. Light is shed on the background of this development by what Steiner wrote as personal guidance for Édouard Schuré on September 9, a few weeks after having reached agreement with Annie Besant at the Munich Congress in May 1907 about the separation of the Esoteric School. This communication therefore appears under the heading: "For information only—cannot be communicated directly in this form at this time."

In 1875, H. P. Blavatsky and H. S. Olcott established the Theosophical Society in New York. This first formation had an expressly Western character. Also the book *Isis Unveiled*, where Blavatsky published a great many occult truths, possesses such a Western character. Concerning this writing, however, it must be said that the great truths that were granted to her were reproduced in a very distorted, often caricatured form. It is as though a harmonious countenance were to be completely distorted in a convex mirror. Things that are spoken of in *Isis* are true, but the way they are discussed is an irregular reflection of the truth. This occurs because the truths themselves are inspired by the *great initiates of the West*, who are at the same time the initiators of Rosicrucian wisdom. The distortion arises because of the inadequate way that they are taken up by H. P. Blavatsky's *soul*; for those who are educated, this fact should have proved the exalted source of these truths. For no one who reproduced these truths in such a distorted way could have arrived at them *of their own accord*. Because the Western initiators saw what little possibility they had of insinuating into humankind in this way the flow of spiritual knowledge, they decided to drop the whole thing completely for the time being *in this form*.

The gateway was now open, however: Blavatsky's soul had been so prepared that the spiritual truths could pour into her. Eastern initiators were able to control her. These Eastern initiators had the best of intentions. They were able to perceive how humankind was being driven by Anglo-Americanism into the most dreadful danger of acquiring a thoroughly materialistic way of seeing things. They—the Eastern initiators—wanted to inject into the Western world their form of spiritual insight, which had been preserved from ancient times. Under the influence of this current, the Theosophical Society acquired an Eastern character; and, under this same influence, inspired Sinnett's *Esoteric Buddhism* and Blavatsky's *Secret Doctrine*. But again, these were both distortions of the truth. Sinnett's work distorted the exalted message of the initiators by introducing an inadequate philosophical intellectuality and Blavatsky's *Secret Doctrine* was distorted by her own chaotic soul.

The result of this was that the initiators withdrew their influence increasingly from the official Theosophical Society, and this became an arena for all kinds of occult powers to distort its high purpose. A short episode was inserted here when Annie Besant entered the stream of initiators, owing to her pure and elevated mentality. But this short episode came to an end when she came to be influenced by certain Indians who had developed a grotesque intellectualism inspired, in particular, by a German philosophical system that they had misinterpreted. This was the situation when I was faced with the necessity of joining the Theosophical Society. Initially, true initiators stood behind it, and because of *that*, it is *presently* an instrument for the spiritual life of today, even though later events gave it a certain imperfection. Its favorable progress in Western countries depends entirely on how well it can adopt the principle of Western initiation into its sphere of influence. For the Eastern initiations must necessarily ignore the *Christ principle* as the central *cosmic* factor of evolution. Without this principle, however, the theosophical movement will remain without any deciding influence on Western cultures, which have as their starting point the life of Christ. The revelations of Eastern initiation would have to set themselves up independently *alongside* the living culture in the West. They do not have a hope of success in evolution unless they can eradicate the Christ principle from Western culture. But this would be identical with eradicating the *true meaning of Earth*, which consists in the recognition and realization of the intentions of the *living Christ*. To reveal this in all its wisdom, beauty, and effectiveness is, however, the most profound aim of Rosicrucianism.

With regard to the value of Eastern wisdom as an object of study, the only opinion that can be held is that it is of immense importance because the people of the West have lost their comprehension of what esotericism is; the Eastern people, on the other hand, have preserved this knowledge. But as for introducing the right esotericism to the West, the only conclusion to be drawn is that this must be the Rosicrucian–Christian one, for *this* has sprung from the Western way of life, and to lose this would be for humankind to deny the sense and destiny of Earth. Only in this kind of esotericism can the harmony between science and religion come to fruition, whereas any other kind of amalgam of Western knowledge with Eastern esotericism produces only such unfruitful, spurious products as Sinnett's *Esoteric Buddhism*, for instance. The following diagram illustrates how it should be:

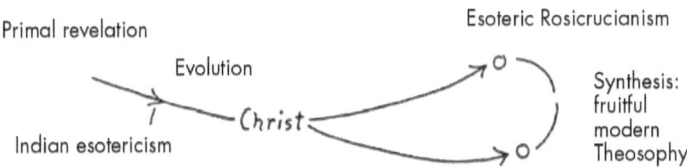

Sinnett's *Esoteric Buddhism* and Blavatsky's *Secret Doctrine* are examples of the following wrong solution:

```
Primal revelation
              Evolution
                           The part of evolution not participated in
  Indian esotericism       by the East
                                                    Modern materialistic
                                                    science
                    Synthesis: Sinnett, Blavatsky
```

Annie Besant, having declared at the Munich Congress in May 1907 that she was not competent to deal with the subject of Christianity and that she therefore relinquished to Rudolf Steiner any part in the movement insofar as Christianity was concerned, came up with a Christ doctrine very soon afterward that contradicted completely the teachings of Rudolf Steiner. Whereas he always taught that, since the event of Golgotha, Christ had become the leading spirit of the Earth and had only once appeared in a physical body, Annie Besant taught that Christ was a teacher of humankind in the same sense as Buddha and other great spirits, and that his reappearance in the flesh was imminent. That was lurking in the background during the next Theosophical Congress in Budapest in 1909. The foregoing is given greatly added weight by Rudolf Steiner's statements, made about that same time, about a law of occult investigation that makes clear the necessity of fostering our spiritual heritage within the community:

> Why should we really bother ourselves about theosophical ideas and theories before we can have experiences in the spiritual worlds ourselves? Some people will say: "We are made aware of the results of spiritual investigation; however, I still cannot see into these worlds. Wouldn't it be better for us simply to be given instructions on how to become clairvoyant ourselves, rather than to be told about the results of clairvoyant investigation? In this way, everyone could accomplish further development themselves." Anyone not involved in occult

investigation may believe it would be good if one were not told in advance about such things. But in the spiritual world a very definite law exists, and its significance can be made clear by an example.

Let us suppose that, in a certain year, a genuine, trained occultist chosen at random made some observation in the spiritual world. Now imagine that ten or twenty years later another occultist, equally experienced, made the same observation without having heard the results reached by the first. If you were to believe that this could happen, you would be greatly mistaken because, in actuality, once an investigator or occult group has discovered a fact of the spiritual world, one can never investigate it a second time without being aware that it has already been researched. Therefore, if an occultist investigated a fact in 1900, and another occultist has progressed far enough by 1950 to ascertain the same fact, this second investigator can do so only after becoming aware that someone else had already researched it.

Thus it is that known spiritual facts can be observed only if one first understands that such communications have already been investigated. That rule establishes universal brotherhood in the spiritual world for all time. It is impossible to enter any realm whatsoever without first uniting oneself with what has already been probed and looked into by the elders of humankind. Provision has been made in the spirit realms to prevent those from becoming a law unto themselves who would say, "I'm not bothering with what is there already; I am going to make discoveries on my own." All the facts that Theosophy disseminates today would never have been observed by anyone, regardless of how learned and advanced, unless these facts had been known previously. The theosophical movement was established as it was because of that—because one is obliged to link up with what has already been investigated.

In a relatively short time, many people will have clairvoyant faculties; they would see only unreality and not the truth of the spiritual world unless they had heard of what was already investigated. First of all, one has to learn the truths that Theosophy provides; only then can one observe them. Thus, even occultists must first become acquainted with what has already been investigated, and then, after conscientious study, they can observe the facts themselves. One can say, "Divine beings fructify a human soul only once for its initial faculty of insight; if this unique virginal fertilization has taken place, then it becomes necessary for others to direct their attention to what this first soul has achieved in order to acquire the right to a similar achievement and to see what the first soul has seen. This rule establishes a universal brotherhood in the innermost depths, a truly human brotherliness. From one epoch to the next, the store of wisdom has been handed on through the mystery schools, and the Masters have faithfully guarded it. And we must also help to maintain this treasure and remain united in brotherhood with those who have already achieved something if we want to make our way into the higher realms of the spiritual world. What has to be worked for as a moral law on the physical plane constitutes a law of nature in the spiritual world. (Budapest, June 4, 1909)

This exposition makes it comprehensible why the link with the Theosophical Society was necessary. In the first place, the fact that it finally separated was not the result of opinion that differed with Annie Besant about an acknowledgment of the Christ, but of the untruthfulness about actual occurrences connected to running the Society.

7

Separation of the Esoteric School from the Theosophical Society

Truthfulness and Continuity (CW 264)

The Coulomb affair of 1884/85 led to Mme. Blavatsky's permanent return to Europe and the establishment of the Esoteric School. Then, 1894/95 saw the Olcott–Besant campaign to have W. Q. Judge, the General Secretary of the American Section, expelled from the Theosophical Society. This introduced manifold splits in the Theosophical Society. And finally, in 1907 the new alleged Masters K., H., and M. appeared at Olcott's deathbed, supposedly to express their preference that he should name Annie Besant as his successor. The fact that Annie Besant used this appearance to support her candidacy for president led to the dismissal of Rudolf Steiner's Esoteric School from the English Esoteric School of Theosophy and to its eventual separation from the Theosophical Society. What follows is a brief overview of this development.

The Coulomb affair began in spring 1884, after HPB (as H. P. Blavatsky was generally called) as the founder and president, Henry Steel Olcott, traveled from India to Europe. The Coulombs (the married couple who took care of Madam Blavatsky's household in Adyar) were dissatisfied with their modest position in the Theosophical Society. They felt discriminated against and organized a deception, both as an attempt at extortion and to seek revenge. The two took sole possession of HPB's home and built secret passageway doors there. They had forged letters from HPB to Mme. Coulomb that, had they been real, would have shown that she (HPB) had conspired with her (Coulomb) to fabricate the letter from the Masters, which "precipitated" the whole matter in a less-than-ideal way. The conflict between the Coulombs and the business management of the Theosophical Society in India had been smoldering the whole time during the absence of the Council instituted by the founder (the German Dr. Franz Hartmann, a member of the Council), leading to a crisis in May, requiring the Coulombs to vacate the residence of the Theosophical Society in Adyar. The still-incomplete renovation of HPB's rooms were discovered. A nearby "Christian" mission station took the Coulombs in and cared for them. In September, the station published their assertions in its periodical, *The Christian College Magazine*. HPB immediately demanded that the libel be countered in court so that the Masters could remain connected with the Theosophical Society. If she had to leave the Society, the Masters would leave with her. Olcott, however, let her down. In December he foiled the libel charges, and this lack of defense was judged by the public as an unspoken declaration of guilt.

Independent of these events, in May 1884 the Society of Psychical Research (S.P.R.) in London had hoped to profit from the presence of HPB at the time and instituted a commission to study the occult phenomena connected with her. After the disclosures by the Coulombs became known, the commission sent Richard Hodgson (then just twenty-three years old) to Adyar in December to explore those difficult issues. A year later, he published his report on behalf of the S.P.R., openly asserting that HPB was a fraud. This was a direct result of the missing defense. Olcott's argument against taking legal action was that a positive court judgment would not help. Those who held occult phenomena to be illusion would continue to do so with or without such a judgment. Those, however, who were convinced of HPB's sincerity and uprightness would nevertheless hold fast, even if no one countered the accusations; a negative judgment,

Separation of the Esoteric School from the Theosophical Society

however, might make them doubt her. This argument, in itself, is right; despite that, Hodgson's report proved how wrong it was. It became a judgment without the accused party being able to defend herself, which burdened the Theosophical Society for decades.

The Coulomb affair nearly ruined the Theosophical Society. Many members left the Society. Madam Blavatsky, who saw her entire work in danger, became ill at the beginning of 1885 and only through a miracle escaped death. At the end of March she gave up her honorary position as "corresponding secretary" and traveled to Europe. She never returned to India.

When she arrived in Europe, her friends gathered around her in support. The patient was nursed and cared for, first in Naples, then in Würzburg, and finally in Ostend (off the Belgian Coast). In May 1887, she was brought to England. During the summer, she finally recovered after a two-and-a-half-year illness.

In London, new life flourished for Madam Blavatsky. Her friends had established the "Blavatsky Lodge," where she gathered the members around her. On September 15, 1887, the first issue of *Lucifer* was published, founded and managed by her so she could write unhindered by Olcott, which she considered a necessity. The following year, in 1888, she founded the "Esoteric Section of the Theosophical Society" (E.S.T.), which changed a year later to the "Eastern School of Theosophy." This assembly of the Masters and HPB's loyal and devoted esoteric pupils came under her sole leadership, completely independent of the exoteric Society, except for the fact that only members of the Theosophical Society were admitted.

After two wrong decisions by Olcott concerning Paris lodge, the European members demanded in 1890 that Olcott surrender his presidential powers to HPB. This led to the formation of the European Section under her sole authority. All of these developments in London—the direct consequences of the failure of the Society—took place despite fierce opposition from Olcott. It is important for understanding the history of the Theosophical Society to realize Olcott's relationship to HPB. Olcott cared wholeheartedly for the organization of the Theosophical Society and his position in it, and less for Theosophy itself. He was interested in hypnotism and mesmerism; he attempted to join the various Buddhist movements from Ceylon to Japan. He also tried to distance the Theosophical Society from HPB during the Coulomb affair to spare the Theosophical Society from blame. HPB repeatedly had to stand against his intentions for the sake of the issue, and thus she became a real troublemaker in his eyes.

The second scandal was the "Judge case." H. P. Blavatsky died on May 8, 1891. At a conference on May 27, 1891, the council she had installed for the Esoteric School decided that the Esoteric School of Theosophy leadership should pass to Annie Besant and William Quan Judge. This decision was based on their official positions in the Esoteric School of Theosophy. Indeed, Annie Besant had been a member of the Theosophical Society for only two years, but she was well known in England as a speaker in non-theosophical settings and was already president of the "Blavatsky lodge." Five weeks before her death, HPB had appointed her "chief officer of the inner group of the Esoteric Section." Judge was cofounder of the Theosophical Society in 1875; Vice-president of the Theosophical Society; General Secretary of the American Section; a close friend of HPB; and appointed by HPB in 1888 as her sole representative in the E.S.T. in America, which comprised two-thirds of its total membership. Following the death of HPB, the first "letter from the Masters" came during the meeting of the council. Others followed, and the relief was great; evidently the connection with the Masters remained unbroken.

Because the letters concerning Judge were connected with the earlier ones connected with HPB and because Olcott had hoped to be rid of HPB's disturbing influence of his organization (Judge would be a successor for whom Theosophy was more important than the Society), but now found that Olcott sought allies in an attempt to get rid of this influence. At the beginning of 1894, Annie

Separation of the Esoteric School from the Theosophical Society

Besant and Olcott went privately to Judge and accused him of falsifying the new letters from the Masters. They threatened to bring it to an investigative committee and demanded his resignation as the price for their silence. Judge, however, immediately published their accusations in a circular to all the members of the Theosophical Society and protested resolutely against them.

In July 1894 the investigative committee met in London with Olcott, Besant, and Judge present. Judge declared that he was prepared to prove he was in contact with the Masters. After this, the investigation ended with the explanation that such proof would rely on the members' belief in the existence of the Masters, which, according to the Constitution of the Theosophical Society, shall not be required. A year later, Annie Besant repeated her demand for the expulsion of Judge, and the American Section declared at its General Meeting that it would separate from the Theosophical Society and declare its autonomy as the "Theosophical Society in America." A third of the members in England joined this protest and established a corresponding "Theosophical Society in England." Moreover, in Germany, Dr. Franz Hartman (previously mentioned) founded the "Theosophical Society in Germany."

A short while later, however, on March 21, 1896, W. Q. Judge died, and this part of the theosophical movement was unable to develop. As a leader of the American Society, Catherine Tingley assumed the role of making such decisions. She was an ordinary medium who relied on the communications from the Masters, as well as from HPB and Judge from the other side. The members who disagreed with such nonsense left and established their own Theosophical Society in America. In Germany, too, the Hartmann Society distanced itself from Mrs. Tingley. In 1896, Mrs. Tingley undertook an effective "crusade" to Europe and founded lodges in Germany that were sympathetic to her approach.

This was the situation when Rudolf Steiner began to build up the German Section in 1902. In various cities there were Adyar lodges and Tingley lodges, as well as Hartmann lodges based in Leipzig called the *Leipziger*. Just before the Section was founded in 1902 several attempts were made to unite all of the theosophists in Germany, resistance to which played a great role in the minds of some older members during the early years of the German Section.

In 1907, Rudolf Steiner explained to Édouard Schuré why he was prepared to work in this Theosophical Society, despite the fact that it was already in ruins when he was called:

> Such was the situation when I saw myself placed before the necessity to join the Theosophical Society. True initiates had stood at its cradle and *because of this* it is, even though the events that followed have given it a certain imperfection, *for the time being*, an instrument for present spiritual life.

Apparently, he was convinced that he could work in connection with this original source, as he expressed in 1923: "Until 1905 or 1906, some hope was certainly justified that the content of Anthroposophy might become the meaning and purpose of the Theosophical Society's existence" (Dornach, June 15, 1923, CW 258).

In the beginning, his activity in the Theosophical Society was welcomed not only in Germany, but also prominent leaders such as Annie Besant, Bertram Keightley, and George Mead (in their individual ways) approached him in positive ways. Looking back, at the time there was the promising prospect of bringing the Theosophical Society worldwide together on a healthy spiritual foundation to become the cultural factor that was so necessary. However, it would happen differently. The old spiritist inheritance that had driven the Theosophical Society proved to be stronger in the leading personalities. This led to the third scandal, also in connection with the Masters.

In London during May 1906, Charles Webster Leadbeater was accused before a Theosophical Society investigative committee of certain moral transgressions and had to leave the Society. Because of his own clairvoyant researches, Leadbeater, who, was a prominent theosophical author, originally belonged to Sinnett's "London lodge" and was engaged there with mediumistic, occult examinations. In a letter to Annie Besant in July 1906, Rudolf Steiner took an absolute position in the Leadbeater affair:

> I *have* to see the cause of all this misfortune in the peculiarity of Mr. Leadbeater's occult methods. In certain cases, such occult methods necessarily lead to this or other mistakes similar to those indicated in Mr. Leadbeater's case, because such methods are no longer appropriate to the current stage of Western humanity. (CW 264)

Six months later, at the beginning of January 1907, Olcott sent two circulars to the general secretaries. Rudolf Steiner's copies bore the notation on them: "to be published in *Lucifer*." Thus they were to be communicated to all the members. In the first circular, Olcott reported that his doctor expected his death soon, and that both Master KH and Master M appeared before witnesses at his sickbed to say that he should name Annie Besant as his successor. In the second circular, titled "A Conversation with the Mahatmas," Olcott reported that those same Masters had appeared to him several times. In particular, they supposedly assured him that the convicted Leadbeater worked under their leadership. That circular was the beginning of Annie Besant's drive to accept Leadbeater's readmittance into the Society.

Olcott died soon thereafter, on February 2, 1907. Rudolf Steiner wanted those appearances of the Masters to be considered Olcott's private matter. Completely against his wishes, the news of the visits spread throughout the membership and even out to the public. There were endless discussions about their genuineness and meaning, and views were split. Some considered it a simple deception. Others took them in complete earnestness. Annie Besant belonged to the second group. She defended her candidacy for the presidency in several circulars as being the "orders of the Masters." Still others, mostly the English, took the view that the appearances were not what they claimed to be.

This last view might be the correct one. Rudolf Steiner did not want to give any further definitive explanation of the appearances during the election for president, so that the members would not be influenced by those occult issues. Nonetheless, in a letter to the members of the Executive Council of the German Section, he indicated, "It is incorrect, as many seem to believe, that these revelations either emanate from the Masters, whom one must obey, or are an illusion. There is, as every occultist should know, a third possibility. But as I said before, because I am not allowed to speak about these revelations, it must remain only an indication" (CW 264). He did not go beyond offering only indications at the time. However, he said in a 1912 lecture to Russian theosophists gathered in Helsinki:

> The moment a special interest enters occultism in place of universal human interests, the possibility of real errors are present.... Through the way that England is karmically connected with India in the world, the possibility was presented simply that the sublime powers that stand at the beginning of the theosophical movement were falsified. It is an ordinary process in occultism that those powers wishing to follow their own special interests assume the form of those who have already given the true impulse. (Helsinki, Apr. 11, 1912, CW 158)

From this history we can see the truth of Rudolf Steiner's comment to Schuré—that the Theosophical Society had "become a hotbed for all kinds of powers that distort the higher cause" (see chapter 6 in this volume). Occult phenomena (letters that suddenly appear where nothing was before) and people who appear without having entered or exited can be traced to the most varied origins. Such appearances might have had meaning or individuals who have encountered these phenomena and were able to sense the quality of the origin. When passed on to others and used as an argument, they sidestep levelheadedness—never mind the possibility of desired deception. There is a very fine line between truth and charlatanism in occultism (Helsinki, Apr. 11, 1912, CW 158). Insofar as these occult influences were limited to the teachers, individual members retained, in principle, the possibility of making their own judgment. When they attempted to intervene in the management of the Society and made Mrs. Besant their own, however, the situation became impossible.

Even before these events, in a letter to Anna Wagner on January 2, 1905, Rudolf Steiner characterized the relationship of the true Masters to the exoteric Society and how it should be understood:

> It is incumbent on me now to speak to you about the nature and significance of the School. You know that behind the whole theosophical movement stand highly developed beings, whom we call "masters" or "mahatmas."... They work on the physical plane through their appointed "messengers," the first of whom is H. P. Blavatsky—that is, the first insofar as the theosophical movement is concerned. The Masters do not establish any outer organization or society, nor do they administer such orders. It is true that the Theosophical Society was established by its founders (Blavatsky and Olcott among others) to advance the work of the Masters on the physical plane, but the Masters have nonetheless *never* exerted any influence themselves over the Society itself. In its nature and leadership it is purely the work of human beings on the physical plane.
>
> It is different for the "Esoteric School," which was founded by the Masters themselves and exists under their guidance. All that flows into the theosophical movement as knowledge and power flows into it from this School. (CW 264)

In his circular of March 12, 1907, to the members of the German Section, he also explained the care with which the esoteric must be separated from the exoteric:

> As soon as we adopt the right esoteric attitude in attributing our teachings to suprasensory sources, we should also carefully guard against bringing a matter that concerns only the Society

(the election of a president, for example) into any connection with suprasensory powers. To introduce the subject of the suprasensory into the discussions one has during a presidential election would contradict all esoteric principles. (CW 264)

Under HPB and Olcott, the esoteric was kept absolutely separate from the management of the Society. According to Rudolf Steiner, the fact that Olcott supported his "appointment" of a successor on the appearances of the Masters can "be attributed to the weakness of his last extreme illness" (CW 264).

In January 1907, when Annie Besant, as her first act as designated president and with Leadbeater's support, proclaimed those appearances of the "Masters" authentic, it became clear to theosophists that certain powers that distort the high cause attempted to interfere in the Society's leadership. Everything that could be asserted against the candidacy of Annie Besant came out from the leaders in England. They claimed those appearances could not be genuine because the real Masters would never make decisions for the members concerning the fulfillment of their duties; such lack of discrimination would disqualify her as a leader of the Theosophical Society. Above all, as leader of the Esoteric School of Theosophy, she could not also become president of the Society, since she was all-powerful in the Esoteric School of Theosophy and could thus, through its membership, develop "psychic tyranny" over the Society. Those arguments were all correct, though clouded by the fact that the English were in fact fighting for Bertram Keightley to become president. Rudolf Steiner had written to Marie von Sivers in 1905 about Keightley, who until 1907 was generally expected to become Olcott's successor:

> Because the theosophical attitude itself is so elevated, those who are not fully imbued with it will become the worst materialists. Theosophists will cause us to experience much worse things than those who have never been influenced by theosophic teachings. It is precisely theosophical teaching, assimilated as

dogma instead of *life*, that could lead to the depths of materialism. We have to understand such matters. Consider Keightley; without Theosophy he would have been simple and untalented, but probably an obedient scholar. Through Theosophy he is becoming an arrogant, envious, and niggling striver. (Jan. 1, 1905, CW 262)

Rudolf Steiner handled the events in a masterful and reserved way. He did his best to keep the discussions out of the German Section. Olcott's circulars published in *Lucifer* and the various arguments from England and Annie Besant were not sent out to the branches. In spite of this, the things from outside came into the German Section, especially after G. R. S. Mead sent his anti-Besant document to all the branches at the beginning of March. Because this made it necessary for Rudolf Steiner to address the events, he did so very carefully in an article in *Lucifer* at the beginning of April (CW 264). He was clearer in relation to his esoteric pupils. In a letter to Anna Minsloff on March 26, 1907, he wrote:

> Now the important thing at the moment is not *who* should be chosen; the main thing is not to connect the sacred affairs of the Masters with something like voting. Whether Mrs. Besant is voted for or not is unimportant; the important thing is that she fails to find it wrong to connect voting with the exalted Masters. This will create the greatest imaginable confusion, and in the future might lead to breaking the last remaining link between the Masters and the Society. It's possible that the Masters would no longer bother with a Society that assigns them a role such as that presently upheld by Adyar.
>
> Far more important than whether Mrs. Besant is chosen or not is that she herself is brought back to the right course. If no particular complications arise, then Mrs. Besant must be chosen. Of all the older members of the Society, she appears to be the most suitable for now. (CW 264)

On April 28, 1907, Steiner explained in a circular to the members of the Executive Council of the German Section:

Now I have to state immediately and openly that because of matters that, to my distress, have to do with Besant's attitude toward occult matters, and with other things connected with her, I can foresee difficulties because of her that might affect our work in the German Section. Therefore, I do not make a secret of the fact that I, too, have great misgivings. Moreover, few people know how difficult it is for me to speak of such things here.... Nevertheless, the matter is this: We do not have to agree with Mrs. Besant's particular spiritual bent, but we can nevertheless acknowledge that, given the present circumstances, she is the only candidate being considered for the presidency. We need to consider that Mrs. Besant's personality is not the cause of such opposition, but those who have turned against her are also turning against spiritual life in general. They will certainly not acknowledge this without argument, but it is true nevertheless. There is a current within the Society that, if it succeeds in its aims, will gradually extinguish the spiritual life. Through it, this Society could become an association for comparative religion, philosophical musings, ethical culture, or the like. It would not continue as a spiritual brotherhood. We may therefore adopt the attitude that we cannot go along with Mrs. Besant's spiritual tendency; we do want, however, to preserve the spirituality as such of the Society; thus we are obliged to vote for Mrs. Besant under present circumstances, even though it might lead later to spiritual conflict regarding her spiritual pathway. We simply have to accept this fact as conditional on the circumstances within the Society. (CW 264).

In the Besant–Keightley alternative (between Besant's spirituality and Keightley's intellectual erudition), Rudolf Steiner decided for the lesser evil, hoping that Annie Besant would still get "on the right track." The degree to which he foresaw the end of the Theosophical Society (not as an organization but as the bearer of a spiritual impulse) is shown in his letter to Marie von Sivers, quoted at the beginning: "No matter what happens, everything will be disastrous for the Theosophical Society but not for the spiritual movement. We must not fear even the collapse of the Theosophical Society as such."

For the sake of continuity, it was no longer possible, with all that had happened, to maintain the connection (which had existed until then, if only loosely) to Annie Besant's E.S.T. In his letter to George Mead at the beginning of March he had written: "I would like to add a personal comment to one of the points in your circular—that I consider it inappropriate for a president of our Society to be the head of an esoteric school" (letter, Mar. 6, 1907, CW 264).

8

THE SECOND SECTION OF THE ESOTERIC SCHOOL, 1904–1914

From Rudolf Steiner's Autobiography, *chapter 68*

Strictly speaking, an arrangement established within the Anthroposophical Society and originally intended to have no connection with the public does not belong within the framework of this account. Nevertheless, I will describe it because this, too, has caused attacks against me.

Some years after Marie von Sivers and I became active in the Theosophical Society, we were invited to lead a society like those still existing that preserve the ancient wisdom in symbols and religious ceremonies. I had no intention at all to work in the way of such a society. All that Anthroposophy represents *must* arise from its own source of knowledge and truth. There could not be the slightest deviation from this goal. But I have always respected what has arisen in the course of history; it reveals the spirit living in human evolution. Consequently, I favored linking, whenever possible, the new with the historical. And so I accepted the certificate offered me by the society referred to, which belonged to the stream represented by Yarker. It took the form of Freemasonry of the "high degree." I took over nothing, absolutely nothing from this Society except the merely formal right to establish, in historical succession, my own symbolic ritual activity.

The Second Section of the Esoteric School, 1904–1914

Historically, all of this activity was completely *independent* of any tradition whatever. Although I possessed the formal certificate, *nothing* was cultivated that did not provide a picture of anthroposophic knowledge. This was intended to accommodate a need that arose among the members. In addition to developing the ideas that clothed spiritual knowledge, there was a need for something that spoke directly to the heart and mind. I wanted to meet those needs. If that society had not made the offer, I would have instituted a symbolic ritual with no historic connection.

However, this was *not* intended to create a "secret society." It was made clear to those who wished to participate that they were not joining an "order" but that they would experience, as participants in a ceremony, a kind of illustration, or demonstration, of spiritual knowledge. It was not a ceremony of an "order," even though some of it assumed a form similar to the ceremonies of existing orders when their members were accepted or promoted to higher grades. It was a visual, pictorial demonstration of the path a human soul follows when ascending spiritually. There was no question of performing or transmitting anything the way existing orders were doing. This is shown by the fact that members of many different orders participated in the ceremonial activities I arranged, and they found aspects that were *completely different* from anything in their orders.[1]

Once, a person who participated in our activity for the first time came to see me immediately afterward. He had reached a high rank within an order. But his experience of what had just occurred made him want to hand over to me his insignia of that order. He felt that, since he had now experienced true spiritual meaning, he could no longer participate in something stuck in mere formality. I set it right. Anthroposophy may not tear people from their life connections; rather, it should add something to those connections, not take

---

[1] It was always a matter here of people who were connected with Rudolf Steiner's Spiritual Science.

away from them. So he remained with his order and continued to participate in our symbolic ceremonies.²

It is certainly reasonable that misunderstandings arise when arrangements such as those described become public knowledge. There are many to whom the external fact of being associated with something is more important than any meaning they gain. And so many of the participants themselves spoke about this matter as though they belonged to an order. They were unable to discern that what we demonstrated was *free of any connection to an order*, and that otherwise it would be given only within an *order*.

The fact is that, in this sphere as well, we broke with old traditions. Everything was done as it must be when investigating spiritual reality in an original way as required for a fully conscious soul experience.

Marie von Sivers and I signed certain certificates when, for the sake of historic continuity, we joined the Yarker institution. The fact that those certificates later became the source of all sorts of slander indicates that people had to treat the ludicrous with earnest scowls in order to create slander. We gave our signatures as a formality. The usual practice was maintained. As we signed, I made a point of saying clearly that it was a mere formality, and that what I wanted to establish would retain nothing from the Yarker arrangement.

Of course, it is easy later on to observe that it would have been more "intelligent" not to have connected at all with something that provided opportunities for later slander. But I may say in all modesty that during that period of my life I was still one of those who assume uprightness rather than crookedness in those with whom they deal. Spiritual perception did not in the least alter that faith in human beings. Spiritual perception should not be misused to investigate the inner intentions of other people unless they themselves

---

2 This would be Herman Joachim, who died 1917 in Berlin, the son of the well-known violinist Joseph Joachim and godson of Herman Grimm. He held one of the highest offices in the Great National Freemasonry Lodge of Germany. See Steiner's memorial for him in *Our Dead*, CW 261.

request it. Otherwise, to investigate the inner life of others is forbidden to a spiritual investigator, just as opening a letter without authorization is forbidden. Thus one's relation to others is the same as for those who have no spiritual cognition. There is a difference, though; either one must assume people to be honorable until proven otherwise, or one must distrust the whole world, in which case it becomes impossible to work socially with others, because this must be built on a foundation of mutual trust, not on mistrust.

Within the Anthroposophical Society, the instituted ritual symbolism having spiritual meaning proved greatly beneficial to many members. As in every other sphere of anthroposophic work, in this area everything was excluded that did not fit into the framework of full consciousness; there was no question of using unjustified magic, suggestive influences, and so on. Members received something that spoke to their ideation, yet in a way that their power of feeling could also penetrate the meaning with direct perception. And this helped many toward a deeper understanding. The possibility of continuing this activity ceased when the war began. Although there was certainly nothing like a secret society, it was assumed to be one. And so this symbolic–ritual section within the anthroposophic movement closed in the middle of 1914.

The fact is that those who participated in it became slanderous accusers of that section, to which no one who considered the matter with good will and a sense of truth could object. This is an example of the strange human behavior that can arise when people who are not inwardly sincere enter a movement that has genuine spiritual meaning. Such people expect something to satisfy their trivial soul life, and when they naturally do not find that they turn against the very thing they had looked for in the first place—although with unconscious insincerity.

A society such as the one belonging to Anthroposophy could be formed only from the soul needs of its members. An abstract program that declares this or that action be taken in the Anthroposophical

Society could not be instituted; instead, it has to work with reality.[3] But the reality is simply the soul needs of its members. Anthroposophy, as the content of life, was formed from its own sources. It stepped before the contemporary world as a spiritual creation. Many who were inwardly drawn to Anthroposophy sought to work with others. Thus the Society was configured by people—some who wanted a more religious character, while others wished for something more scientific and still others for an artistic element. And it had to be able to be what was sought.

Because the work was based on the real soul needs of its members, private material had to be assessed on a very different basis from what was fully public to begin with. The private material was intended to be given orally, not printed. What was discussed came from listening to the members' soul needs as they arose in the course of time.

The substance of the public writings corresponds to the demands of Anthroposophy as such, whereas the soul configuration of the whole society, as indicated, played a part in the way the privately printed material came into existence.

---

3   Cf. Steiner's lectures of Jan. 19–Feb. 10, 1924, *Anthroposophy and the Inner Life* (CW 234), especially part 2; also *Anthroposophical Leading Thoughts* (CW 26); Carl Unger, *The Language of the Consciousness Soul*.

9

ESTABLISHING THE COGNITIVE–RITUAL SECTION

> *Recently I was obliged to embark on something in my esoteric work that, with certain assumptions, could be said to lie in the direction of esoteric Freemasonry.*[1]

Just as the book *From the History and Contents of the First Section of the Esoteric School 1904–1914* (CW 264) records the fact of and reason that Rudolf Steiner began by connecting the First Section of the Esoteric School to the existing School of the Theosophical Society to preserve continuity, *"Freemasonry" and Ritual Work* (CW 265) records the reason for and the way in which the historical continuity of its Second and Third Section (the Cognitive–Ritual Working Group) is preserved through its link with the existing connection of working with ritual symbolism.

Once it became known that this was concerned with the so-called "Egyptian Freemasonry," he was labeled a "Freemason" in a derogatory sense by some people. Rudolf Steiner himself expressed his opinion about this on two occasions, once shortly after he had formally joined the Freemasons, in a letter written on August 15, 1906 (see addendum), to A. W. Sellin, a theosophist and Freemason, and again in a note that he added one week before his death to chapter 68 in his *Autobiography*. The attacks made on him after his death by those on the side of the National Socialist Movement were countered by Marie Steiner-von Sivers, the cofounder and administrator

---

1   This letter is printed in the addendum.

of the study group, with an article entitled: "Was Rudolf Steiner a Freemason?"[2] All of these and other documents are collected chronologically in the first part of *"Freemasonry" and Ritual Work*....

The form of the question Marie Steiner-von Sivers used as the title of her essay indicates a problem inherent in the subject. This question can be answered in both the affirmative and the negative— affirmatively if we consider only the outer fact of the union and ignore Rudolf Steiner's motivation for forming the link, or negatively if we consider that, despite the formal union, he never considered himself as a Freemason in the usual sense of the term. He had no connection with the ordinary Freemasonry (Egyptian Masonry was considered irregular anyway) and was never thought of as a Freemason. To elucidate this seeming contradiction and to explain this link to Freemasonry only the question of choosing Egyptian Masonry will be dealt with to begin with.

Why Make a Connection to Egyptian Masonry

> We can look at the whole of modern civilization: it presents itself to us as a memory of Ancient Egypt.... This can be seen even in the principle of initiation.[3]

According to its legendary source, Egyptian Freemasonry traces its origin back to the mythical first king of Egypt, Menes—Hebrew Misraim—the son of Ham, who was the son of the biblical Noah. Menes occupied the land of Egypt and gave it his name (*Misraim*, the ancient name of Egypt) and instituted the mysteries of Isis and Osiris. At the beginning of the Christian era the Egyptian priest–sage Ormus,

---

2   Included in this volume as Chapter 3.

3   Stuttgart, Aug. 16, 1908, CW 105. The same thought is expressed in Rudolf Steiner's *Four Mystery Dramas* in both initiation scenes (7 and 8 of the third play, *The Souls' Awakening*), in which the karmic connection of a group of modern pupils of Spiritual Science is traced to their initiation in a mystery temple of ancient Egypt. See also *How Can Mankind Find the Christ Again?* lect. 4, CW 187.

who was converted to Christianity by Saint Mark, united the Egyptian mysteries with those of the New Covenant. Since that time they have been preserved as the Ancient Egyptian Freemasonry. In this sense those who brought the Misraim Rite from Italy to France at the beginning of the nineteenth century as "the root and origin of all Freemasonry rites" described them.[4] According to Rudolf Steiner, King Misraim, after having conquered Egypt, was initiated into the then existing Egyptian mysteries, which contained secrets from ancient Atlantis. A continuous tradition has existed since that time. Modern Freemasonry is only a continuation of what was initiated in Egypt at that time (Berlin, Dec. 16, 1904, *The Temple Legend*, CW 93).

Along with the secrets of the ancient mysteries goes the experience of the immortality of the human spirit[5] and esoteric Freemasonry also wished to awaken this experience. It is in this direction that the deeper meaning of Rudolf Steiner's words may be explained when he says that he linked up with the Memphis–Misraim Order, because the latter "presumed" to work in the direction of esoteric Freemasonry.[6] Its manifesto of 1904 asserts that it received the means from the ancient mysteries to acquire "proof of pure immortality" in this earthly life.[7]

---

4   Lennhoff and Posner, *International Dictionary of Freemasonry*, "Misraim-Rite." Compare also Rudolf Steiner's exposition, Berlin, Dec. 16, 1911, in CW 265. Also, the Freemason Joseph Schauberg testifies to the correctness of the Egyptian origin of the Masonic symbols in his main work: *Vergleichendes Handbuch der Symbolik der Freimaurerei mit besonderer Rücksicht auf die Mythologien und Mysterien des Altertums* (Comparative handbook of the symbolism of Freemasonry with consideration of the mythology and ancient mysteries), Schaffhausen, 1861.

5   In this connection it is interesting to note that in Rudolf Steiner's opinion it is just *The Book of the Dead* that is an almost complete record of ancient Egyptian mystery wisdom. This statement was transmitted by the Egyptologist Gregoire Kolpaktchy who translated *The Book of the Dead* at the instigation of Steiner. Only a person holding the key to both the hieroglyphs and esoteric knowledge is able to make such a translation. See *The Book of the Dead* (tr. E. A. W. Budge).

6   In the letter mention, of Aug. 15, 1906, to A.W. Sellin.

7   See lecture given in Berlin, Dec. 9, 1904, (CW 93), in which the "Manifesto of the Grand Orient," of the United Scottish, Memphis and

Following the esoteric duty of preserving continuity, when Rudolf Steiner linked to this current, he did not contemplate for a moment working in it in the usual way. He was from the very beginning most decidedly of the opinion that people of the modern age should search for a new wisdom suited to their needs, which would have its source in the Mystery of Golgotha, and that real knowledge of immortality can be attained nowadays only through a deep understanding of the Mystery of Golgotha (Berlin, May 6, 1909, CW 57). He explained the need for this new wisdom in one of his descriptions of ancient Egyptian knowledge in the following way:

> Our age must give birth not merely to an ancient wisdom, but to a new wisdom, a wisdom that points not only to the past, but that must work prophetically—apocalyptically—into the future. In the mysteries of past ages of civilization we see an ancient wisdom preserved, but our wisdom must be an apocalyptic wisdom, the seed for which must be sown in us. Once again we have need of a principle of initiation so that the primeval connection with the spiritual worlds may be renewed. The task of the anthroposophic world movement is to supply this principle. (Stuttgart, Aug. 5, 1908, CW 105)

Another illuminating matter is the findings of spiritual–scientific research, which show that secret connections exist between what happened in the third post-Atlantean cultural epoch (the Egypto–Chaldean epoch) and our own fifth post-Atlantean epoch.

> Taking the whole of modern culture, we have to see in it a memory of ancient Egyptian culture; Egyptian thought is reflected in it from its beginning.... This can be seen even in the principle of initiation, and as modern life is to receive a principle of initiation in Rosicrucianism let us ask what it is?... This wondrous harmony between the Egyptian remembrance is wisdom and the Christian impulse of power (CW 105).

Misraim–Masonry Rites were discussed in connection with the idea of immortality.

On another occasion, Anthroposophy is alluded to directly as the new Isis wisdom for the new era. Even a new Isis legend has been developed, and in connection with it a rumor arose that behind the wooden sculpture, *The Representative of Humanity between Lucifer and Ahriman* (originally intended to occupy the central position in the first Goetheanum and to reveal the central impulse of Anthroposophy to visitors through a work of art), was another, invisible sculpture—*The New Isis, or Isis for a New Era* (Dornach, Jan. 6, 1918, CW 180). Again, a deep connection was established between the Isis Mystery and the Grail Mystery, the latter being a Christianized revival of the Egyptian mysteries, just as the Parzival figure acts as "a model for our spiritual movement" (Dornach, Jan. 6, 1918, CW 180; Berlin, Feb. 6, 1913, CW 62; Berlin, Jan. 6, 1914, CW 148).

Another reason for this link only to the Egyptian Masonry arises from the results of spiritual investigation, showing us that people of today are in a position opposite to people of ancient Egyptian times. For just as the spiritually directed ancient Egyptian once prepared humankind for intellectual, brain-bound thinking of the intellect by preserving the human form by mummification, so must a person today acquire spirituality alongside intellectuality by a process analogous to mummification, namely through the use of the ancient ritual forms. These latter are analogous to Egyptian mummies because, in contradistinction to ancient times when it was possible to attract real spiritual substance into ritualistic deeds, this is no longer the case either in the lodges or in the churches. In these ritualistic enactments today there is no more spiritual life than there was life in the Egyptian whose body had been mummified. Nevertheless, something was preserved in these mummified rites that can and will be awakened into life when people have discovered how to bring into all their deeds the power that streams from the Mystery of Golgotha (Dornach, Sept. 29, 1922, CW 216).

These few results of spiritual investigation are sufficient to explain why Rudolf Steiner chose Egyptian Masonry alone to elaborate his cognitive–ritual work.

The "Outer" Prehistory of the Cognitive–Ritual Section

> *I want the step I have taken to be judged simply from the perspective of esoteric loyalty.*[8]

The year 1902 was notable for three events related to the Theosophical Society. Rudolf Steiner and Marie von Sivers assumed leadership of the nascent German Section of the Theosophical Society, founded in 1875 by H. P. Blavatsky, among others. Annie Besant, Blavatsky's successor as leader of the Esoteric School of Theosophy (though not President of the Theosophical Society at that time) was admitted to the "mixed" Freemasonry Order. John Yarker, honorary member of the Theosophical Society and General Grand Master of the Egyptian Freemasonry of the Order of Ancient Freemasons of the Memphis and Misraim Rite of Great Britain and Ireland, presented Theodor Reuss, Heinrich Klein, and Franz Hartmann (who belonged to both the Freemasonry Order and the Theosophical Society in England) with a deed for establishing this teaching in Germany.

When it is stated in Rudolf Steiner's *Autobiography* that soon after the founding of the German Section in 1902, he and Marie von Sivers were offered the leadership of a society of the kind still in existence that preserves the ancient wisdom embodied in symbolism and religious ceremonies, this does not imply that the offer was made, as is generally supposed, by the chief representative of the German Memphis–Misraim Society, Theodor Reuss, but, as Marie Steiner states in her essay "Was Rudolf Steiner a

---

8 Letter to Sellin, Aug. 15, 1906.

Freemason?" by a person who held the opinion about Rudolf Steiner that he understood more about spiritual matters than any Freemason. She added to this in private that it concerned a certain Czech. The fact that this person must have been connected with the Memphis–Misraim Freemasonry can be inferred from the remark in the *Autobiography*: "I would have instituted a symbolic ritual without a historic connection had I not been approached by the previously mentioned society."

This offer may have been made around 1903/04, for since May 1904 a symbolic–ritual way of working had been prepared by a series of corresponding lectures. On September 15, 1904, Rudolf Steiner held a lecture in Hamburg, where he first became acquainted with the Freemason A. W. Sellin. He must have asked Sellin about the Memphis–Misraim Order, as is evident from the report of December 12, 1904. But even before this report by Sellin appeared, Rudolf Steiner had already paid a visit to Reuss. And in his Berlin lecture, on December 9, 1904 (CW 93), in which he spoke about the multiple degrees and the Memphis–Misraim Order, he quoted from its official publication, the *Oriflamme,* whereas Sellin was still enquiring about it. Rudolf Steiner's first conversation with Reuss must therefore have taken place between September 15 and December 9, 1904. The further conversations cannot be dated. On November 24, 1905, Rudolf Steiner and Marie von Sivers joined the Memphis–Misraim Order. The discussions about the conditions under which the charter could be operated for the independent running of a study group dragged on, however, until the beginning of 1906. The contract was signed January 3, 1906.

The fact that Rudolf Steiner does not mention Reuss's name in his *Autobiography,* but only the name of Yarker, is often interpreted by opponents to signify that he wished to cover up his connection to Reuss, because the latter soon afterward came into disrepute in Freemasonry circles as an occultist. This, however, cannot be the real reason because at the time his autobiography was written it had long become publicly known that Reuss was the one who had issued Steiner's certificate. Much more likely was the fact that here too the motive of historical continuity was the decisive factor. As for Yarker, mentioned by Rudolf Steiner in his lecture of December 16, 1904 (CW 93), as a "significant person" and an "excellent Freemason," he was already at that time an authoritative representative of Egyptian Freemasonry in Europe and a central figure in the Theosophical Society. He was its honorary member, evidently on account of the fact that he had been crucially involved in its founding in the year 1875. As it is reported in the account by the Italian Vincenzo Soro in his *La Chiesa del Paracleta* (Todi, 1922, p. 334), a book in Rudolf Steiner's own library: "At the founding of the Theosophical Society the most celebrated heads of International Freemasonry participated, among whom John Yarker was especially prominent, the most intimate friend of Garibaldi and Mazzini."[9]

The Theosophical Society, which was of a decidedly Western trend to begin with, was to have become the pioneer for the necessary popularization of suprasensory truths in modern times. Through *Isis Unveiled* (1877), the first great work of the Theosophical Society founder, H. P. Blavatsky, an abundance of knowledge from ancient Western esotericism had been made public. For this Blavatsky was presented by Yarker with the highest adoption degree of Egyptian Freemasonry.[10] Both also conferred with each other in the inauguration of a ritual for the Theosophical Society.[11] This plan, however, was not realized at that time. When Annie

---

9 According to Robert Ambelain: *Cérémonies et rituels de la maçonnerie symbolique* (Ceremonies and rituals of the freemasonry symbolism), Paris, 1978, the Italian freedom-fighter Guiseppe Garibaldi (1802–1882) became the Grand Master of Italian Memphis–Misraim Freemasonry in 1881, followed by Guiseppe Mazzini (1805–1872). See Steiner's lecture in Stuttgart, Apr. 9, 1924, *Karmic Relationships*, vol. 7.

10 Nov. 24, 1877. Perhaps it was pure coincidence that Steiner and Marie von Sivers joined the Misraim current on the same day of the year, but in 1905.

11 Josephine Ransom, *A Short History of the Theosophical Society*.

Besant, Blavatsky's successor, started to work with the symbolic–ritual stream, this was within a different Masonic current.[12]

Rudolf Steiner had ample reason, therefore, to mention only the name of Yarker in his Autobiography, for it was Yarker who represented everything that was of decisive value to the promotion of Rudolf Steiner's intentions—not Reuss who, as merely the representative of the Freemasonry Order in Germany, represented something with which Rudolf Steiner could not work.

The "Inner" Prehistory of the Cognitive–Ritual Section

It is no reward, but a heavy task.[13]

Confirmation that Rudolf Steiner acted in accordance to the situation in which he was placed is provided in his letter to Marie von Sivers on November 30, 1905, a few days after joining the Memphis–Misraim Order. From that we conclude that he did not act from a personal sense of "doing good," but in conformity with the esoteric powers, that is to say with the spiritual world, and that—because "at present it seems valueless to all esoteric powers" to link his not-yet formed work group to this order—he was still unable to say whether the thing could be done or not.

This problem seems to have been solved for him during the last weeks of the year, for on January 2, 1906, the constitution of the group was given form when he lectured for the first time to a mixed audience of men and women on the theme of "royal art in a new form." "Although we see Freemasonry today as a mere caricature of the great Royal Art, we must nevertheless not lose heart in our attempt to reawaken its slumbering forces, a task that is incumbent upon us and runs in a parallel direction to the theosophical

---

12 In connection with the Great Lodge of Paris, "Le droit humaine," after she was rejected by the Memphis–Misraim Order.

13 Personal statement by Rudolf Steiner, recorded by Marie Steiner-von Sivers and Clara Walther.

movement." This statement receives further backing from a lecture about Freemasonry given a short while later in Bremen on April 9, 1906. According to that lecture there is an inner connection between Theosophy and Freemasonry, insofar as Theosophy presents the more ideal and studious side of esoteric endeavor and the Masonic ritual the more practical side. But whereas in the Masonic world the ceremonies and effectiveness of the rituals are no longer understood, Theosophy is able to speak about the inner truth of these ceremonies and about the spirit that underlies the ceremonies and symbols.[14]

Further confirmation of the fact that Rudolf Steiner did not act arbitrarily follows from his oral statement that his task to save the Misraim Service for posterity had grown for him from his previous esoteric investigations into rainbows; "One has no reward, but a heavy task." He seems to have never explained where the heaviness of the task lay. It could, however, be thought to exist in connection with the important statement made in his preparatory lecture (for men only) given in Berlin on October 23, 1905 (CW 93): "I have reserved to myself the achieving of a unification between those of Abel's race and those of the Cain race." This intention—of overcoming through the Christ impulse the primordial polarization of humankind into two oppositely striving main currents—did not lie only with his cognitive–ritual work, but with his whole endeavor.

The statement that his task arose from his esoteric research into the rainbow is in a certain way borne out by the reference made to it in lectures given at the time that the Cognitive–Ritual Working Group was in preparation. There it is stated, "The rainbow has a special significance in esoteric wisdom. You are aware of the rainbow that has appeared since the time of the Flood. We now find this symbol appearing again in northern mythology (a rainbow leads from Valhalla over to the Earth).

This signifies the transition from Atlantean to post-Atlantean times. In Atlantean times the air was much denser and the water was

---

14 From telegram-style notes by Marie Steiner-von Sivers.

much less dense than they are today; a rainbow could not have been formed at that time. Atlantis was actually a land of mists, a home of fog, Niflheim. In the North, humankind evolved from clouds of mist. From this region of fogs, the water masses arose that engulfed and submerged the continent of Atlantis. There was no rainbow in Atlantis. Esoteric research has investigated what this explanation signifies (Berlin, May 5, 1905, CW 53). In response to a request (following a lecture eighteen months later) for more information about Noah and the flood, he replied:

> The question of Noah belongs to what I have just been researching. You will not find anything in *Lucifer* that I did not know at the time of writing the article.[15] But now I know a little more. Now I am able to picture the climatic conditions clearly and vividly. I have understood something that I would have included in my account had I known it when I wrote the article. Initially, I took the account of Noah to be allegorical; it was a picture of deep inner significance to me. Now I know, however, that the rainbow mentioned in the Bible corresponds with an actual fact. In ancient Atlantis, other climatic conditions prevailed. The distribution of air and water was different...; we find in ancient Atlantis that a rainbow could not have formed. Such conditions could arise only after Atlantis had been submerged and new continents appeared. Now, it is suggested [in the Bible] that the rainbow emerged from the flood.[16]

If we ask ourselves what has the task of preserving the Misraim Service to do with research into the rainbow, an answer will be provided if the characterization of the Misraim Service as "bringing about a union of Earth and Heaven, the visible and invisible," is transformed into the picture of a bridge. Then the connection between his rainbow research and Misraim Service will become

---

15 *Lucifer* is the magazine that was afterward known as *Lucifer–Gnosis*, and the article contained therein: "Aus der Akasha-Chronik" (from the akashic record); cf. Rudolf Steiner, *Cosmic Memory*.

16 Berlin, Oct. 22, 1905, "Questions and Answers," in *What Is Happening in the Anthroposophical Society: News for the Members*, 1945, nos. 34–35.

clear. On the one hand the rainbow has always symbolized a bridge between the visible and the invisible;[17] on the other, it was always Steiner's intention to build such bridges in all walks of life.

How bridge-building in the realm of art should be put into practice in connection with the Misraim Service is expressed in a letter he wrote to Marie von Sivers on November 25, 1905,[18] in which he says concerning the union with the ancient Misraim current that had taken place the previous day: "The present task would be to rescue masonic life from its externalized forms and to recreate it...to turn religious spirit into a form of sense-perceptible beauty."

The first opportunity to do so came soon after at Pentecost 1907, when the task of organizing the yearly Congress of the Federation of the European Sections of the Theosophical Society fell to the German Section; by using Rudolf Steiner's models, sketches, and written contributions, a harmonious scientific–artistic–religious experience could be conveyed. The rainbow too was included among Rudolf Steiner's sketches for the Apocalyptic Seals, and this appeared as a new element in contrast to its traditional portrayal. And with the performance of the *Sacred Drama of Eleusis*, which signifies a new birth of the dramatic art in the history of civilization, a link was forged, in however weak a form, to the essence of the ancient mysteries.[19] This latter statement gains nuance through the additional information that the Misraim Rite was intended to be a renewal of the Eleusinian mysteries.[20] For the Greeks, the Goddess Demeter, founder of these well-known mysteries, personified what Isis meant for the Egyptians.

A few years after the German Section hosted the Munich Congress at Pentecost 1907, Rudolf Steiner's first mystery drama was

---

17 Instructional lesson, Berlin, Dec. 16, 1911, CW 265.
18 See letter in addendum.
19 See *Rosicrucianism Renewed*, CW 284.
20 Compare Karl Heise in *Entente-Freimaurerei und Weltkrieg* (Entente-freemasonry and world war), Basel, 1919.

performed and work began on the construction of the building. Having quickly created an abundance of new artistic forms, these, too, including Spiritual Science itself, were characterized as a "synthesis between heavenly and earthly understanding"[21]—thus a bridge, too, speaking figuratively. Later he even used the term *bridge-building* himself to describe how art is the best means of building a bridge between the invisible and the visible, since it reveals what would otherwise remain hidden. In retrospect, he said of the twenty years he spent with Marie Steiner-von Sivers, endeavoring to "channel the esoteric current into art" literally: "All that arose in this way within the Anthroposophical Society arose from the impulse to build a bridge from the spiritual to the physical" (Torquay, Aug. 20, 1924, CW 243). If, therefore, the intention behind Anthroposophy as a science of the spirit and the artistic language of the form derived from it was to build a bridge from the invisible to the visible, the intention behind the endeavor to build a social life upon the basis of new insight had the same aim. This can be seen if one takes account of what is written into the constitution of the new Misraim Service.

The Constitution of the New Misraim Service

> *What I have founded has no connection therefore with what previously gave itself out to be the Memphis–Misraim Degree in Germany.*[22]

The founding of the constitution took place quite apart from the transactions carried out with Reuss concerning the legal authorization of the completely independent leadership of the Working Group. If the negotiations had come to nothing, Rudolf Steiner

---

21 Dornach, Sept. 20, 1916, in *Bauformen als Kultur- und Weltempfindungsgedanken* (Building forms as cultural and world feeling-thoughts), Dornach, 1934.
22 Letter to Sellin on Aug. 15, 1906.

would have instituted his Working Group even without regard to historical continuity. He had already begun the preparation for this a short while before the start of negotiations—directly after settling the outer affairs of the First Section of his Esoteric School with Annie Besant in London in mid-May 1904—through a series of lectures, which took place from May 23, 1904, until January 2, 1906,[23] and a course of esoteric instruction, which was given in 31 lectures between September and November 1905.[24]

There are no records concerning the time or manner in which Rudolf Steiner informed members of the German Section about his intention to found the cognitive-ritual way of working. Only from a letter of February 17, 1905, from a Leipzig member[25] can it be gathered that he had said "that he would try to introduce the esoteric teachings of Theosophy into Freemasonry in the near future," wherewith, of course, Freemasonry was alluded to as a "thing," not as an organization. He had already expressed in his Berlin lecture of December 16, 1904: "If you hear anything about the German Memphis–Misraim way, you must not think that this is of any importance for the future. It is merely a framework into which a good picture might be placed at some time."

Another record has been preserved that informs us that at the end of his lecture to the Berlin Branch on October 16, 1905,[26] he announced that he intended to speak about matters connected with Freemasonry at the General Meeting of the German Section fixed for October 22, and that therefore one should invite as many people as possible also from outlying districts. He then announced at the General Meeting that next day, according to an old tradition, which must be superseded by theosophical ideology, he would speak to men and women separately about esoteric

---

23 *The Temple Legend*, CW 93.
24 *Foundations of Esotericism*, CW 93a.
25 Rudolf Jahn, Chairman of the Leipzig Branch between 1905 and 1908.
26 Unpublished.

questions in connection with Freemasonry. Following that he spoke about the fundamental relationships of the Theosophical Society to esotericism, thus preparing the theme for the next day's lectures. On the following morning (Oct. 23, 1905, CW 93) a lecture, first to men and then to women, was held on the subject: "Freemasonry and the Evolution of Humanity."

Two days later, on October 26, 1905, in a public lecture, he spoke for the first time—not, it is true, in outer connection, but all the more so in inner connection with the intentions of the cognitive–ritual work—on the subject of the "main social rule of the future": that labor must on the one hand be freed from its commodity character by separating it from payment, and on the other hand must be sanctified by becoming the sacrifice of the individual for the good of all. In future, work must be carried out for the sake of others because they are in need of what we produce.[27] The connection between the public acknowledgment of this "main social rule of the future" and the start of the cognitive–ritual work arises on the one hand from the significance of visual thinking for the social life and on the other hand from the motive inherent in the cognitive–ritual work to stimulate selfless social activity out of one's own feeling of moral responsibility, as at one time the rules for moral behavior proceeded from the mysteries. Thus, in the sense of Goethe's words—*"Nothing is within, nothing without; for what is within, that is without"*—the establishment of the new Misraim Service and the simultaneous proclamation of the "main social rule of the future" prove to be the two poles of one and the same impulse. The aim of bridge-building is evident here.

With the lecture, "The Royal Art in a New Form" (Jan. 2, 1906, CW 93), given to a mixed audience of men and women, the

---

27 Lecture given in Berlin, Oct. 26, 1905, "The Social Question and Theosophy," published in *Beiträge zur Steiner Gesamtausgabe*, (Contributions to Rudolf Steiner's collected works), no. 88. In the essay starting with the Oct. number of *Lucifer–Gnosis*, the "main social rule" was first mentioned in the third installment, which only came out in Sept. 1906.

constituting was brought to a close. On the next day there followed the written agreement with Reuss, whereby Rudolf Steiner became entitled to establish an independent working group. Marie von Sivers was authorized to admit women into the group, but from the very beginning both men and women had always enjoyed equal rights within Rudolf Steiner's group. The following illuminating remark was found in notes made by Marie von Sivers to a lecture about Freemasonry held in Bremen on April 9, 1906:[28] "Because the Freemason wished to see his womenfolk banished to the family, he expelled them from the lodge. Something happened on the higher planes that made it necessary for women to be included in all cultural activities. The future meaning of Freemasonry lies in the cooperation between men and women. The excesses of the male culture have to be tempered by the esoteric powers of the female."[29]

From the beginning of 1906 onward, wherever there were esoteric pupils of Rudolf Steiner, cognitive–ritual work was carried on. The first lodges to be inaugurated were in Berlin, Cologne, Leipzig, Munich and Stuttgart. After the admittance of the hundredth member at the end of May 1907, the leadership of the Misraim Rite in Germany became vested in Rudolf Steiner, as had been agreed. From that time on he was the sole spiritual and legally historical representative of the Misraim Service, until with the outbreak of World War I in the summer of 1914 he declared the Rite dissolved. By that time about six hundred members had been admitted.

---

28 Unpublished notes.

29 In an undated letter from Paula Moudra, a Bohemian author who had spoken to Rudolf Steiner in Prague in Nov. 1907 about her admittance and was asked by him to present a written application, there occurs the following: "You pointed to an important happening in the astral world in Nov. 1879, since women have now been accepted for inauguration. I consider it to be very significant that my approach to you and my application for admittance took place just in Nov. 1907."

SUSPENSION OF THE COGNITIVE–RITUAL WORK

> *What was to have served humankind, irrespective of race and differences of interest, acquired a malevolent quality with the outbreak of World War I and the opposition it aroused against Freemasonry.*

In the description of the cognitive–ritual section that Rudolf Steiner gives in his *Autobiography* he states that it "fell asleep" at the outbreak of war in the summer of 1914, because, although it was in no way a secret society, it could have been taken for such. Marie Steiner reports in her essay "Was Rudolf Steiner a Freemason?" that he regarded the whole thing as finished, and to demonstrate this he tore up the relevant document.[30] This was evidently done because it had become plain to him, as a result of the war, that through certain Western secret societies Freemasonry—originally a good and necessary institution serving all humankind equally—had been placed in the service of national egoism and the selfish interests of particular groups of people.[31]

It was to this misuse for political ends that he attributed and strongly condemned the catastrophic development that began with World War I. This has been thoroughly explained by him in lectures given during the war years 1914/18.[32] He found it tremendously important at that time to discover all he could about its esoteric background, especially to be able to contribute to a clear exposition of the question of who was to blame for starting the war. That is why he wrote a preface for *Entente-Freimaurerei und der Weltkrieg* (understanding freemasonry and the World War) by Karl Heise

---

30 Not to be confused with the "Contract and the Brotherly Agreement."

31 From Rudolf Steiner's foreword to Karl Heise's book: *Entente-Freimaurerei und der Weltkrieg* (Entent freemasonry and the world war), Basel, 1919.

32 See the 7-volume lectures series, *Kosmische und Menschliche Geschichte* (Cosmic and Human History); *The Karma of Untruthfulness*, vols. 1 and 2 (CW 173 and 174); *Mitteleuropa zwischen Ost und West* (Central Europe between East and West) (CW 174a); and *Die geistige Hintergründe des Ersten Weltkrieges* (The Spiritual Background of World War I, CW 174b).

when asked by him to do so. However good or bad the book is, it was at any rate the first attempt to give documentary evidence of the tendencies that Rudolf Steiner had exposed.

The rigorous condemnation of the private political aims of certain Western secret societies was not directed, of course, against Freemasonry as such. This was confirmed, for instance, when, shortly after the end of the war, Johannes Geyer advised a member of his quiescent Symbolic–Ritual Organization to join the Freemasons. This followed from his letter of February 25, 1919, to Rudolf Steiner, in which he writes:

> On February 13, following your advice, I joined the Order of the Freemasons. Indeed, I joined the Unit of the Grand National Mother Lodge in the State of Prussia called "To the Three Globes," belonging to the St. John's Lodge "From the Cliffs to the Sea." It is the same lodge to which our friends A. W. Sellin and Kurt Walther belong, as does Häckländer from Wandsbeck. I hope that, over time, I shall be allowed to awake an interest in the anthroposophically inclined esotericism in this group and to keep it alive. I took this step through that motivation. May the restitution of the meetings in our own esoteric Brotherhood also soon take place!"[33]

Rudolf Steiner's tolerance toward Freemasonry was demonstrated some years later when in 1923 at the founding of the English Society the question arose as to whether the man nominated for the chairmanship of the Society was eligible for the post, as he was a Freemason. Rudolf Steiner replied as follows:

> I always said, where it concerns coming to the anthroposophic movement from any other movement (Freemasonry was meant

---

33 Johannes Geyer, a pastor in Hamburg at the time, and after 1919 a teacher at the Free Waldorf School in Stuttgart. From 1912 on he belonged to Rudolf Steiner's Esoteric School. According to "Der Lehrerkreis um Rudolf Steiner in der ersten Waldorfschule" (The circle of teachers around Rudolf Steiner in the first Waldorf school), Geyer gave many lectures in a Freemason context on the origin of Freemason symbols in the light of Rudolf Steiner's Anthroposophy, thereby winning great acclaim.

in this case), and it is really not a matter of what one is by virtue of belonging to another movement, the question is whether when one comes into the anthroposophic movement one is a good anthroposophist. It really does not matter, therefore if, apart from this, one belongs, let us say, to a shoemakers' or a locksmiths' guild. I am not making a comparison, just stating the principle: the fact that a person belongs to a shoemakers' or a locksmiths' guild does not in any way interfere with being an anthroposophist. Being a good anthroposophist is what matters to the anthroposophic movement. Apart from that, whether one is a good, bad, or indifferent Freemason is irrelevant to the Anthroposophical Society.... It would be a foolish conclusion to reach if eligibility to become a member of the Anthroposophical Society were judged by whether one was a Freemason or not.

I said [earlier] that a number of just the oldest and most valuable members are Freemasons. I cannot imagine how an impediment to joining the Anthroposophical Society could arise from any kind of Freemasonry. I cannot imagine it. I would say that the anthroposophic movement should be something on its own account. It would not be a creative world movement if it were not able to be creative from its own pro-creative powers, would it! That is the crux of the matter, what the positive result is. How it appears when compared to the one or other thing is not important. If I buy myself a suit what matters is that it is to my taste and what I choose. What has that to do with the opinion of someone else who comes and says: That suit is not the same as that worn by someone else. It really is quite irrelevant to think that one ought to put on another person's suit. One puts on one's own suit. One does not put on Freemasonry when one becomes an anthroposophist. Thus it is quite impossible to hold such a view.

But there is, of course, more to it than that. There is, in my opinion—if you will excuse me for saying so—not always enough esteem paid to Anthroposophy by its members. There is a tendency nowadays to pay higher regard to what is older, what creates more stir, what assumes an air of mystery and so on, and to undervalue what is open and sincere according to the amount of sensation it arouses and its rather indistinct reputation. It is a kind of denigration of the anthroposophic movement when one says of it that it can be harmed by the fact that this or that member comes to it from one or the other movement. It would have to be terribly weak to be harmed by such things as that. (London, Sept. 2, 1923)

Rudolf Steiner's Resistance to Calling His Cognitive–Ritual Work a "Secret Society"

A secret society was not made through that.[34]

It was not so much the principle of secrecy in Rudolf Steiner's case, but rather of the basic difference between his method of symbolic ritual activity and that of the so-called secret societies. He regarded it as his main task to make what is expressed in Symbols, Signs, Handclasp, and Word understandable by explanations corresponding to them gained through spiritual insight. But with the word "understandable" he did not mean, "this symbol means this and that symbol means that," for in that case everything could be made to mean anything. No; instruction must be arranged so that to begin with "one finds a solution to the secrets in the course of the development of Earth and humanity and allows the symbols to evolve from that"; in other words, one must first have comprehended what can be grasped by understanding the content of Anthroposophy.

Over against that the mere gazing at symbols, as it is usually practiced in esoteric societies today, is an unauthorized extension of a practice that was fully justified in days gone by. For at that time human beings had a greater sensitivity of the etheric body at their disposal, by which means they were able to arrive at a corresponding inner experience.

To people of the modern age of the consciousness soul—for whom the sensitivity toward the etheric body has been largely replaced by

---

34 *Autobiography*, CW 28.

an understanding connected to the physical brain—symbols, signs, handclasps, and words have necessarily become external things; they cannot be connected to the consciousness soul. Despite the fact that they affect the etheric body (that is, the unconscious). To work directly on the etheric without first engaging consciousness is not permitted today, since the consequence would be

> ...that one can make other people into ready tools for any kind of plan, if one so desires. This is obvious; if you were to influence other people's etheric body without them being aware of it, you would eliminate the forces that they would otherwise have in their understanding—that is, if you do not provide the intellect with something such as Spiritual Science is to become. You eliminate that and turn such brotherhoods into a tool for those who want to carry out their own private plans and objectives. In such a case, one would be in a position to make use of such brotherhoods for any sort of political aims, or one could postulate a dogma: "Alcyone" is the outer physical vessel of Jesus Christ.[35] Those who have been conditioned in this way make themselves into instruments to carry that out into the world. One must then only be correspondingly insincere and dishonest, and all sorts of things can be achieved by making tools in this way.

And now—it all follows from real insight, does it not—whoever knows how the fifth post-Atlantean epoch differs from the fourth post-Atlantean epoch—and that is reiterated again and again in our circles—will know why a knowledge of Spiritual Science must first be present, and only then can

---

35 Alcyone = the official name of Jeddu Krishnamurti (1895–1986) for whom the Order of the Star of the East was created by Annie Besant and C. W. Leadbeater in 1911. At a young age Krishnamurti was proclaimed as the intended bearer of the expected reborn Christ, the future World Teacher. The Order soon spread over the whole theosophic world. Rudolf Steiner was the only one to reject this vigorously as occult nonsense. For that reason, the German Section led by him was officially excluded from the Theosophical Society in 1913. Krishnamurti then disbanded the Order of the Star of the East in 1929 and publicly distanced himself from the role allotted to him. He also dropped his connection to the Theosophical Society because in his view every kind of organization is a hindrance to spiritual development.

an introduction to Symbolism be given. Wherever a spiritual-scientific movement is honestly striven for, this course will naturally be held to. For whoever has got to know what, for instance, is contained in my *Theosophy* or *Outline of Esoteric Science* and has tried to understand it, will never be harmed by any tradition or symbols. (Berlin, Apr. 4, 1916)

The hidden cause of the aversion to secret societies at the present time might lie in the instinctive but justified feeling that it is not proper to employ ceremonial acts for personal ends. Rudolf Steiner always condemned this rigorously, but at the same time he always emphasized that this did not apply to all esoteric societies, but only to certain ones.

On the basis of what has just been stated and the fact that everything in his symbolic–ritual work was done for the good of all in general and to permeate the ritual symbols with consciousness—thus *Cognitive Ritual*—it becomes understandable why, despite the obligation to observe secrecy, he did not wish his circle to be considered a "secret society."

THE NAME OF THE STUDY CIRCLE

It was a "Cognitive Ritual"

For inner reasons Rudolf Steiner had no actual name for the study circle.[36] It was therefore abbreviated in one instance to "FM" (Freemasonry), in another to "ME" (Mystica aeterna), and later, at the express wish of Rudolf Steiner, to "MD" (Misraim service). For the present work the designation *Cognitive Ritual,* later used by Rudolf Steiner, was chosen because its most essential feature was thereby expressed best. It was in the year 1923, in response to a question by a priest of The Christian Community concerning the relationship of the Cognitive Ritual to the earlier esoteric ritual, that he answered:

---

36 Explicit in CW 265.

The earlier ritual was purely demonstrative. It was a Cognitive Ritual with degrees. The first degree brought knowledge of earthly humanity. It showed human development from Lemurian times until the present in imagination. The second degree demonstrated the connection to the spiritual world. The third revealed the secrets of the threshold of death and so on. This ritual was beyond time, interdenominational, and interreligious; only one specific degree bore a Christian character. The use of this ritual had to be abandoned because its demonstrative character could no longer be made clear to the outer world.[37]

Rudolf Steiner also spoke about this in a lecture to the priests of The Christian Community (Stuttgart, July, 12, 1923, CW 345):

The knowledge movement is the anthroposophic movement.... When there was no religious movement, people who were in the anthroposophic movement sought a replacement for it in all kinds of esoteric circles. These were, however, so formed that they were essentially knowledge circles, and what was similar to a ritual served knowledge only. Therefore, also nothing could be taken from these circles over into the movement for religious renewal [The Christian Community]. And if one had not penetrated the things that were of a ritual-like of nature, that could be done at that time, with the knowledge impulse, they would have been interpreted in an outward manner. In light of their inherent nature, this must not be.

Rudolf Steiner also pointed to the importance that knowledge plays in rituals in a lecture to the members of the Anthroposophical Society in Dornach, December 30, 1922, with the words: "For everything connected with ritual must eventually disappear if the backbone of knowledge is lacking."

Based on this, the term *Cognitive Ritual* was chosen because it expresses best its essential intent.

---

37   Reported by Emil Bock to the priests of The Christian Community.

Addendum: Extracts from Letters

Rudolf Steiner to Marie von Sivers in Berlin

1. Nuremberg, November 25, 1905

You yourself saw yesterday what little remains of the esoteric institutions of the past, which were once a physiognomic expression of higher worlds. In reality the three symbolic degrees of apprentice, journeyman, and master expressed the three stages in which human beings find themselves in the spirit, i.e., find their self within humanity. And the higher grades were meant to indicate the gradual growth through which the human being builds the temple of humankind. And in the same way that the existing human organism—i.e., the astral, etheric, and physical organism, is a microcosm of the past world, so the temple to be constructed by the Masons in wisdom, beauty, and strength is to be the macrocosmic image of an inner microcosmic wisdom, beauty, and strength of soul. With materialism, humankind has lost the living awareness of these things and the outer form has largely been passed to people who have no access to the inner life.

The task now should be to reclaim Masonic life from its externalized forms and give it a new birth; and, of course, this reborn life would have to create new forms as well. That should be our ideal: to create forms that express the inner life. For an era that cannot see forms, and in seeing create them, must of necessity cause the spirit to vanish into an abstraction without substance, and reality is subsequently forced to mirror this abstract spirit as aggregate matter devoid of spirit. If human beings are capable of comprehending forms, e.g., the birth of the soul from the etheric clouds in the Sistine Madonna, then spiritless matter will soon cease to exist for them. And because the masses need the medium of religion to comprehend forms, which are spiritualized, future work must be directed toward developing spirit with an aesthetic form. But that requires a deepening of the content. Theosophy has to bring this deepening in the first instance. If human beings have no inkling that spirits live in fire, air, water, and earth, neither will they have an art that reflects this wisdom in outer form.

2. Karlsruhe, November 30, 1905

Let us deal with the Freemasonry matter steadily and without haste. Reuss is not a person on whom we can rely. We must be clear that caution is an urgent necessity. We are dealing with a "framework," not with greater reality. At the moment there is nothing behind the matter. The spiritual forces have withdrawn completely from it. All I can say just now is that I do not know yet whether or not one day I will be forced to say after all: that must not be done. Please therefore do not discuss anything with them except very provisionally. If we should be forced at some time to say we cannot go along with that, then we do not want to be too deeply involved. Motives partly of a personal nature and partly of vanity are involved, and the spiritual powers flee both. Certainly, all the spiritual powers see no value in our doing such things at the moment. But I cannot say anything certain about it today either. If we notice that something is not right in the next talk with Reuss, then we can still take appropriate action....

Rudolf Steiner to A. W. Sellin

Motzstraße 17, Berlin W 30
August 15, 1906

Dear Director!

At last I am able to write my long-announced letter to you. In the first place I beg of you—I refer to one or two sentences in your last letter—never to assume that I can ever be offended by anything. Please delete that word from the dictionary of our correspondence.[38]

---

38 Sellin had asked for an explanation of the Misraim affairs (see his letter to Marie Steiner of Apr. 9, 1925). The above-mentioned letter from Sellin to Rudolf Steiner is not available.

Without further ado, I will come to the point. The doubt you voiced in connection with a section of my esoteric investigations rests on erroneous suppositions.

Equally erroneous are the things you have heard from others. Let us speak quite plainly: recently I was obliged to embark on something in my esoteric work that, with certain assumptions, could be said to lie in the direction of occult Freemasonry. I would ask you now to accept my every word and every turn of phrase quite exactly. I do not use these turns of expression in a rigid or legal sense, but in order to describe exactly the real facts of the case.

In Germany there was a "Memphis and Misraim Order," which gave itself out to work in that direction. This Order called itself a Freemasonry organization. And it worked "degrees" of which the first three corresponded to the recognized Freemasonry.[39] My esoteric endeavors have, to begin with, nothing whatever to do with this "recognized" Freemasonry. They cannot and do not wish to invade its territory. Freemasonry does not have the slightest reason to engage in these endeavors of mine in any way.

When I was about to start work in the aforesaid direction I was obliged to introduce a ritual for certain happenings on a higher plane for the people who were looking for such a thing. This ritual can be nothing else than a mirror image of what is a fact on the higher plane. This ritual is just the same as what occultism has acknowledged for the past 2,300 years and that was adapted for European conditions by the Masters of Rosicrucianism. If in this ritual something is discovered that has been transmitted from the three St. John degrees that only goes to prove that these St. John degrees have accepted something from occultism. My source is only that of esotericism and the "Masters."[40]

Now I had two ways open to me: either ignore completely the so-called order or come to terms with it. The first would have been

---

39 The three St. John degrees.
40 See chap. 3 in this volume.

Establishing the Cognitive-Ritual Section

possible only if the Order had rejected my application. Under any other circumstances it would have been disloyal in the sense of certain historical concessions that esotericism has to make.

I will tell you what I have done under the assumption that you will not let it go further. The general grand master of the Order was a certain Theodor Reuss. Anything the latter otherwise did has nothing to do with the present discussion; it could be anything whatsoever. What comes into consideration here is only the fact that he was the grand master of the Order that gave itself out to work in the aforesaid way; I had to come to terms with that fact. To this end, I had to visit the aforementioned Theodor Reuss, whom I had never met and about whose circumstances I had never been informed in any way whatsoever. It would have been easy, of course, for me to have made enquiries about him, but it was of no concern to me.

Then I said to Mr. Reuss something like this: I want to have nothing—nothing at all—from your Order. But I will work along the same lines as this Order alleges that it works. What is important is that the Order recognizes on its own behalf, not for my sake, that I am working with the degrees that it lays claim to for itself. I make it a condition that the Order does not impart anything of its rituals to me. No one will be able to say that I have received anything from this Order. I want my step to be judged only from this point of view of esoteric loyalty. And nobody should have the right to interpret it otherwise.

Reuss responded rather abruptly that he could not do that, for it would put him in an impossible situation as regards his Order. Initially, I withdrew. What actually happened and will continue to do so, happened then and will go on happening whether with or without the aforesaid Order. After a few days Reuss summoned me to further discussions. He made no demands, except that I should recognize his right, purely as a business proposition, to receive a normal fee from all who liked to work in the way that the Order saw as its own. All further arrangements concerned mere formalities. I established formally everything that had to be thus established without Mr. Reuss ever having been present. On his part, Mr. Reuss recognized all that I did. I virtually ignored the Order completely. Mr. Reuss gave me the diplomas and rituals, he said, so as not to offend the rules of the Order. That is to say, he brought them to my house. To have bought all these things would have been the greatest folly, even if for no other reason than that there was nothing contained in all that stuff that could not have been obtained for very little expense from any antiquarian dealer. The fact that Reuss simply received a fee from every member to which he is legally entitled is merely a loyal recognition of his entitlement, no matter what fault one might otherwise find in him.

What now takes place within the "lodges" that have been formed can, of course, be learned only by someone who is a member.[41] I can say only very little about it myself. But this is objectively quite enough. *First*, the name *Reuss* is never mentioned in those lodges. *Second*, no one I have admitted can show a diploma issued by Reuss. *Third*, nothing has ever taken place that harms in any way the loyalty owed to Freemasonry. *Fourth*, everyone has been informed about its relationship to Freemasonry. *Fifth*, and to conclude, only *theosophists* are included in our "lodges." If former members of the aforesaid Order wish to join us, they must attest to the fact not only that they hold the degrees legally (having paid the fee) and have the relevant diploma, but also that they have them "at heart."

What I have established, therefore, has nothing to do with what formerly pretended to hold "Memphis and Misraim degrees." And what goes on around the Order of Reuss and his associates is of absolutely no concern to me. There have even been naïve people coming to visit me in order to bargain with me about what they know of Reuss, or even to "warn" me about him. But actually that does not affect me in the least. It also does not worry me that people

---

41 Sellin apparently only became a member later.

Establishing the Cognitive-Ritual Section

who have formerly received "degrees" from Reuss feel they have been duped and are now angry about it. I understand their being angry; but it would be disloyal of me to get involved in any way in such matters.

You see, esteemed Doctor, how all is in order on my part. I have given you an answer because you asked me in a loyal fashion. What to do about people who try to blame me for things that have been said by those who know nothing about it only the future can show....

> With hearty greetings
> Your Dr. Rudolf Steiner

Following Rudolf Steiner's death, this letter was given into Marie Steiner's care by the recipient A. W. Sellin. In a letter of April, 9, 1925, that accompanied it he writes, "I am impelled to place at your disposal two letters of our dear departed one, which might be of importance in future for the history of the Anthroposophical Society. In any case, they will be preserved better in your keeping than in mine."[42]

The first letter, written to me on August 15, 1906, concerns the history of the Mystica aeterna[43] when it was first incepted and is the answer to the question I directed to the doctor on this subject.[44] This question was all the more important to me, standing at that time amid the German lodge activity, because Reuss had been so indiscreet as to publish, in the first edition of the fifth year of his magazine, *Oriflamme,* the text of his permission granted for the founding of a chapter and of a grand council for the Adoption Lodge under the name *Mystica aeterna* and to name Dr. Steiner as the deputy grand master and you as the grand secretary of this new

---

42 The second letter is addressed to somebody else and concerns other matters.
43 One of the names of the Cognitive-Ritual Working Group.
44 A written inquiry is not available; the question could have been an oral one.

association.⁴⁵ This indiscretion of Reuss, who had sent the said number of his magazine to many of the Freemason lodges, caused me much annoyance later in the Freemasonry unions, which I overcame only gradually as a result of the explanation given in the enclosed letter from the doctor.

---

45   Compare CW 265.

10

RITUAL IN RUDOLF STEINER'S ESOTERIC WORK

THE SPIRITUAL–SCIENTIFIC MEANING OF RITUAL

We understand through anthroposophic knowledge that human beings times were endowed in ancient with instinctive clairvoyant consciousness and that both human beings and all of nature were motivated, formed, and supported by the creative powers of a divine–spiritual world. This consciousness grew ever fainter in the course of time until it disappeared completely when reasoned thinking directed solely toward the laws of the physical world was developed. This was necessary because it was only thus that humankind could become spiritually independent of the creative powers of the universe and so be able to gain inner freedom from them. We are now faced with the task of developing a new connection to the spiritual world through our free and independent intellect.

It was this fact that made it the main goal of Rudolf Steiner's life to prepare modern intellectual thinking to become an instrument for comprehending the spirit. That is why the opening sentence of his *Anthroposophical Leading Thoughts* begins, "Anthroposophy is a path of knowledge to guide the spiritual in the human being to the spiritual in the Universe."[1] The concrete steps for following this path are set out in the whole body of Rudolf Steiner's work, but foremost in his basic works: *The Philosophy of Freedom* and *How to Know Higher Worlds*.

---

1 *Anthroposophical Leading Thoughts*, CW 26.

Self-evident as it was for people of the ancient civilizations to make use of symbols and to practice rituals in order to give form to their social life, with the fading of their connection to the divine spiritual world the understanding of the meaning of their rituals also disappeared. And so for modern abstract intellectual understanding, which has become increasingly the all-powerful, world-embracing influence during the course of the twentieth century, the surviving ritual traditions now stand for little more than incomprehensible relics of a bygone age. Nevertheless, present ritual needs do not arise from the intellect but from other layers of the human soul.

With that, the question arises about what induced Rudolf Steiner, as a thoroughly modern thinker, to cultivate ritual forms in his Esoteric School and to use them later in other contexts. To give appropriate consideration to this question, the whole depth and expanse of his spiritual–scientific views on the essence and the task of ritual in human and earthly development would have to be made clear. As this is beyond the scope of the present work we can only refer to a few important aspects pertaining thereto.

UNDERSTANDING RITUAL IS BASED ON SPIRITUAL INSIGHT

> *We need harmony among knowledge, art, religion, and morality... for our complicated social life, which threatens to spread chaos throughout the world.*[2]

Rudolf Steiner's basic conception of ritual was founded on his spiritual insight trained according to modern methods of acquiring spiritual knowledge. In this the spiritual content of the world is revealed as "the basis and underlying principle of all existence,"[3] and by its

---

2   Ilkley, Aug. 5, 1923.

3   "The world of ideas is the basis and underlying principle of all existence"; beginning of *The Creed: The One and All*, in *Wahrspruchworte* (*Truth-Wrought-Words*), German edition, CW 40.

nature instills an experience that is at the same time conscious, artistically sensitive and pious. As long as humanity lived in a condition of instinctive clairvoyance civilization was supported by a uniform scientific, artistic and religious spiritual insight. "What was known to human beings was incorporated by them into the material world; they turned their wisdom into something artistically creative. And while the pupils of the mysteries vividly experienced what they thus learned as the divine–spiritual pulsing through the world, they offered up their religious rites, a sacred art, as it were, transformed into a ritual" (Berlin, March 5, 1922).

For the advancement of humanity it was necessary that this unified experience should become split up into three separate currents, those of art, science, and religion. During the course of further evolution these three sides of human nature moved ever further apart and have lost all connection with their common origin. The result of this has been that cultural and social life has become ever more chaotic. In order for new forces of direction to become active again the three "ancient sacred ideals" of art, science, and religion must be born again from the modern knowledge of the spirit. Rudolf Steiner regarded this as the primary concern of Anthroposophy, and he used to refer to it, especially on important occasions within the anthroposophic movement, as for instance before the first performance in the Goetheanum. In the sense of the words spoken on that occasion: "Those who begin to decipher nature's open secrets through clairvoyant insight so that they have the urge to express them in ideas and shape them in artistic forms will also feel the need to venerate them from the innermost depths of their heart through religion. For them religion becomes the handmaiden of science and art."[4]

Rudolf Steiner had always felt the need to elaborate the results of his spiritual vision, not only by means of science, but also through art and depicting spiritual truths. "Pictures lie behind everything

---

[4] Rudolf Steiner's report of his address on Sept. 26, 1920, at the opening of the first high school course at the Goetheanum. *Waldorf News Letter*, March 1921.

surrounding us; these pictures are indicated when people speak of spiritual primal causes" (Berlin, July 6, 1915, CW 157). Because it seemed important to him, just on account of the social life, to foreshadow the spiritual not only in scientific terms, but also in visible form, for that reason everything that characterizes the anthroposophic view of life had to be embodied in the representative piece of work, the Goetheanum building.[5] After we had been bereft of the Goetheanum on New Year's Eve 1922, Rudolf Steiner expressed what he had intended it to show to the world in the following rather concise formula: "The Goetheanum was perceived as a bodily symbol for what the three main interests of humanity seek to build up in the depths of the soul. These three are the morally religious, artistic and scientific interests."[6]

The work carried out in the cognitive and artistic fields of interest are plain to see, but how is it in the case of religion? Though this is not so evident it can nevertheless be characterized on the one hand as a keenness of soul for the spirit lying behind what is material (Mannheim, Jan. 5, 1911, CW 127), on the other hand, it can be epitomized by the oft-recurring statement that the inherently religious–moral influence of Anthroposophy cannot contribute to religion in a confessional sense; that spiritual–scientific endeavors are not a substitute for religious practice and a religious life; and that one should not make Anthroposophy into a religion although it can be in the highest degree a supportive base for religious life (Berlin, Feb. 20, 1917, CW 175). Anthroposophy as a science of the suprasensory and the Anthroposophical Society as its physical base should not be bound to any particular religious confession, for in its essence it is interreligious by nature. Its most central piece of knowledge, that of the significance of the Christ spirit for human and earthly evolution, does not rest on the doctrine of the Church but

---

5   Dornach, Jan. 23, 1920; in *Architecture, Sculpture, and Painting of the First Goetheanum* (CW 288), Dornach 1972 and 1982.

6   In an outline for an article about the first Goetheanum after it was destroyed by fire on New Year's Eve 1922.

is based on initiation science from which all religions have sprung. It was in this sense that Rudolf Steiner once characterized the task of spiritual–scientific investigation as that of identifying the thread of truth common to all religions, thereby bringing about the mutual understanding among the various religious currents throughout the world (Berlin, Apr. 23, 1912, CW 133).[7] From this it follows logically that from an anthroposophic view practical religious exercises carried out within a confessional context must remain a private concern of the individual. That was also to be found laid down in the statutes of the Society from the beginning.[8]

THE IDEAL OF APPROACHING ALL OF LIFE AS A SACRAMENT

> *Sacramentalism is an expression of human dealings fired by sanctity.*[9]
>
> *What formerly took place only at the Church altar must become the prerogative of all humanity.*[10]

The capacity of being able to experience how spirit becomes visible in ritual practices had to disappear, for it is an evolutionary principle that faculties must cease before they can be newly won on a different level. For that reason every development occurs in a sevenfold rhythmic process, evolving during the first four stages and regressing during the last three. The result of this is that the third, second and first stages are passed through a second time, but now with the addition of what was newly acquired up to the fourth stage. For

---

7 This is also one of the aims of the Theosophical Society. (The second of the three principles runs thus: "Through investigation of the central truths of religions, sciences, and the worldviews of all ages and peoples to lead humankind to a higher understanding.")

8 Already in the Statutes of the Theosophical Society, and then also in those of the Anthroposophical Society, it is laid down from the start that the membership is not dependent upon a religious confession.

9 Cologne, Dec. 27, 1907, CW 101.

10 Dornach, Nov. 27, 1916, CW 172.

earthly humanity what is newly acquired is the "I" or individuality, which develops during the evolutionary phase through birth and death, and in the regressive phase becoming spiritualized toward freedom and love. The latter, however, necessitates the sacrifice of egoism, which was a consequence of developing individuality and the sense of freedom. Many references to this micro–macrocosmic development are to be found throughout Rudolf Steiner's work. This is made particularly clear by the following because they are in the form of the following diagrams and meditations (pages 155, 156)

Handwritten entry in a notebook from 1903 (archive no. 427):

> Striding you move through the power of thought on the flow of separate existence and follow seven guiding powers under the leadership of truth: earthly desire drags you down, putting the guiding powers under the dominance of disbelief; the spirit uplifts you, raising the seven to the reverberating Sun.

1. In separateness discover the law; the law wove the first of the seven into the material.
2. In movement discover life; life cast the second of the seven into the material.
3. In desire discover the person; the person stamps the third of the seven into the material.
4. In thought discover your Self; the fourth of the seven gave its Self to your "I."
5. In your desire discover renunciation; through renunciation the fifth of the seven sacrificed its Self so that you might exist.
6. In your movement discover heavenly peace; heavenly peace was sacrificed by the sixth of the seven so that you might be animated as an individual.
7. In your separation, discover your eternal law; as eternal law, the seventh of the seven created your Self and will lead it as eternal law through separateness.

Notebook page, archive no. 593

Translation of written notes:

Spirit
/ \
Soul   Matter

Evolution is expansion of the Spirit outside of the Material
Involution is the contraction of the Spirit in the inner aspect of Soul
Evolution is impossible without a corresponding Involution
Involution is impossible without a corresponding Evolution

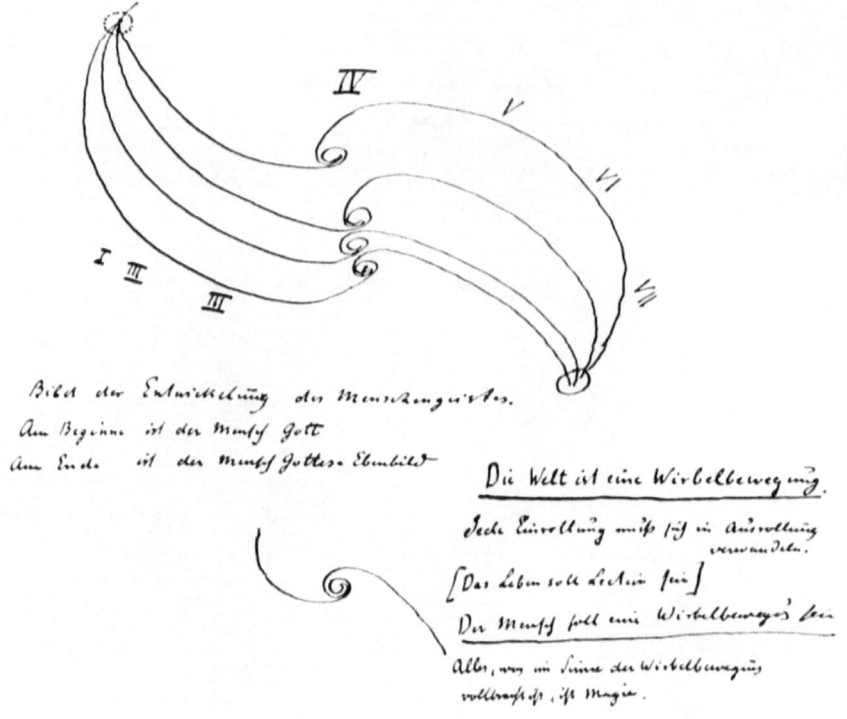

Notebook page, archive no. 712
Translation of handwritten notes:

Picture of the evolving human spirit
At the beginning the human being is God
At the end the human being is God's likeness

<u>The world is a spiral movement.</u>
Every inward spiraling must become an outward spiraling
[Life must be a lesson]

<u>The human being must be a spiraling movement</u>
Everything performed in the sense of a spiral movement is magic

The power of involution was born in humankind when Christ, who brought about the cosmic/human–evolution/involution process in the world, appeared historically and became the leading spirit of the Earth through his great sacrifice on Golgotha:

> The fact that human beings can regress to a consciousness of their spiritual connection [to the cosmos], is to be attributed to the Mystery of Golgotha. But what one owes to the Mystery of Golgotha must be searched for through one's own free inner impulse. Christianity presupposes freedom.[11]

Since the regression of consciousness must come about from the present day onward, it becomes necessary for ritual and the sacraments to be introduced into the element of freedom within Christianity. That is to say that increasingly toward the future it will not be a case of the one making a sacrifice for others, but of all humanity collectively going through the experience of becoming similar to Christ, to Him who descended to the Earth as a being from the Sun (Dornach, Dec. 23, 1922, CW 219). Freedom, individualism in religious matters and in sacramentalism does not signify for Spiritual Science that everybody should have their own religion—that would lead to a total fragmentation of humanity into single individuals—but that through acceptance of anthroposophic knowledge a time will come, "however distant it might be," in which humankind will become ever more deeply stirred by a knowledge of the inner world of truth. And thereby "in spite of all individuality, in spite of the fact that everyone will be able to find the truth within themselves, agreement will prevail"; amidst strict maintenance of freedom and individuality one will be able to work together in free association (Berlin, June 1, 1908, CW 102).

In this sense, reference was continually made to the fact that what had hitherto only been performed at the Church altar must be embraced by all humankind, that all human activity must become an expression of the suprasensory. Especially since World War I, it

---

11 The date for this was given as Feb. 11, 1920, but is an error. The exact date has not been found.

was increasingly strongly emphasized how important it is for the whole of society to regain a harmonious relationship to the cosmos lest humankind be condemned "to develop ever greater disharmony in social life and to spread ever more war materials over the Earth." One will not acquire improved cultural powers as long as one only serves human egoism, especially in the fields of technology and science, alongside a segregated religion, and so long as experiments at the laboratory table are not carried out in deep reverence for the great "world principle." "The laboratory table must become an altar" is a statement that we hear ever again.[12]

It is abundantly evident from the following statements that it will be a long path on which tolerance will need to be practiced, by both those who need to cultivate the old tasks and those preparing for the new ones: "True as it is that with regard to spiritual life a totally new age is about to dawn, so it is also true that the way to Christ, which for many centuries has been the right one, will continue to be that for centuries to come. Things merge only gradually into one another. But what used to be right will gradually change into something else when humankind is ripe for it to happen (Karlsruhe, Oct. 13, 1911, CW 131).

Those who think that through the deep understanding that their innermost soul has of Christ—the Spirit of Golgotha—they can hold direct intercourse with the Christ, must look with understanding upon those who need the positive declarations of a confession of faith, and who need a minister of Christ to give them comfort with the words "Thy sins are forgiven thee." On the other hand, there should be tolerance on the part of those who see that there are people who can be independent. This may be all an ideal in the Earth existence, but the anthroposophist, in all events, may look up to such an ideal (Norrköping, July 16, 1914, CW 115).

---

12   Heidenheim, Apr. 29, 1918. See also *The Spiritual Guidance of the Individual and Humanity*, CW 15; Dornach, Nov. 27, 1916, CW 172; Zurich, Oct. 9, 1918, CW 182; Dornach, Dec. 30, 1922, CW 219.

However, it was not just in connection with the individual human being that the importance of ritual was mentioned, but also in connection with all of humanity's and Earth's evolution. In lectures given when the movement for religious renewal (The Christian Community) was established, this remark arose: "The mysteries are hidden in the ritual and will not be revealed in their true significance until sometime in the future"—the "mysteries of the Future." On that occasion it was said that a time will come when the Earth no longer exists; all the substances in the universe that presently comprise the kingdoms of nature and our human bodies will be turned to dust. All mechanical processes will belong to the past. However, because the proper rituals have been enacted, having arisen from a "true understanding of the spiritual world," elemental spirit beings connected with earthly progress can be summoned to the aid of these degenerative processes in nature and cultural life, enabling the Earth to rise anew from destruction (Dornach, Sept. 29, 1922, CW 216).

Further confirmation of the far-reaching implications for all of human and cosmic evolution that support the statement—that future mysteries lie with ritual—is provided by the results of spiritual research, which reveals that in the future the divine–spiritual of the cosmos will experience a profound change by working with the free human being endowed with self-awareness: "It will be no longer the same being as before when it shines forth from humankind. The divine–spiritual, in passing through humankind, will experience a being that had not previously been revealed."[13] For this new way of revealing the cosmic spirit being, the relevant forms of culture will not be created until the future, for the essence of a true ritual consists of the fact that "it is a copy of events in the spiritual world" (Dornach, June 27, 1924, CW 236).

---

13 See "The Future of Humanity and Michael's Deeds," in *Anthroposophical Leading Thoughts*, CW 26.

The spiritualization of thinking is a prerequisite to all of this. Until we make this our starting point we be unable to turn all our deeds into acts of sacrament. By knowing spiritual realities the ancient ceremonies will change, because symbols are unnecessary for reality (Karlsruhe, Oct. 13, 1911, in *From Jesus to Christ*, and the lecture to the workers at the Goetheanum, Sept. 11, 1923, CW 350).

The change in the ceremonies mentioned here is in the Christian sacraments that, according to the traditional view, enshrine the meaning of Christianity, but really originate in the ancient mysteries. The Latin *Sacramentum* did not replace the Greek *mysterion* until the Council of Trent in 1546, when the Vulgate Bible was pronounced the sole authentic translation; "sacrament" as a concept was already contained in ecclesiastical parlance since the time of the Church Father Tertullian in the second century. In terms of number, significance, and effect, this interpretation varied until the Roman Catholic Church fixed the number of sacraments to seven at the Council of Ferrara–Florence in 1439 (Baptism, Communion, Confession, Confirmation, Marriage, Ordination and the Last Anointing), proclaiming as dogma that the sacraments, initiated by Christ, are rituals consisting of a visible element (*materia*) and a formation of words (*forma*) through which to confer sacramental grace.

When, on the other hand, the Evangelical Church recognized only two sacraments (Baptism and Communion), this arose from (as Rudolf Steiner explained in a lecture in Dornach, October 2, 1921, CW 343) awareness of the inner numerical constitution of the world by the time of the Reformation. For the idea of the seven sacraments sprang originally from the ancient knowledge of the evolutionary and involutionary processes controlling the whole of existence. With the seven sacraments, therefore, the seven stages of life through which one passes, including the social life, in which one develops partly evolutionary and partly involutionary values, should have the corresponding opposite values added to them. The seven stages of human life are: birth, strength (maturity), nourishment, procreation, recovery, speech, and transformation. They can be characterized as follows: the involution within the birth forces is the process of death, which comes into play when birth takes place: it is to be sanctified by the sacrament of Baptism. The whole process of becoming mature, including puberty, is to be sanctified by the sacrament of Confirmation. The process specified here as nourishment is the embodiment of the soul–spiritual into the bodily–physical, that is to say, between the soul–spiritual and the bodily–physical the right rhythm has to be established so that the soul–spiritual does not sink to the level of the animal but also does not lose itself in other-worldliness. The involution, which is part of the evolutionary process, is to be sanctified by the sacrament of Holy Communion. Along with this process of rhythmic vacillation between the soul–spiritual and the bodily–physical is the possibility of always being able to go back in time through the power of memory. For development to be complete there must be a recollection of the previous events that one has experienced. The involution belonging to the power of memory that evolved from our inner being is to be sanctified by the sacrament of Confession, which includes the searching of conscience, repentance, and the resolve to atone for past sins by undertaking penance, either self-imposed or laid down by a priest, in order that the act of memory becomes Christianized and simultaneously raised into the moral sphere.

With the four processes characterized here, the events of evolution since humanity's birth have been exhausted. The act of memory represents a strong intensification; evolution and involution are already drawing nearer to one another. Death is a natural involutionary event. The corresponding sacrament is the Last Anointing. As formerly the natural events of life stimulated the physical–bodily nature, so now the soul–spiritual life must be stimulated by the Last Anointing, which was regarded by the old nature wisdom as an ensouling process. "Expressed through rhythm the physical–bodily nature disappears at death; the soul–spiritual regains its form." That is what is understood by transformation.

As at death our individual life comes to an end, the two missing stages and sacraments must relate to something that is not of an individual nature. An interchangeable relationship between humanity and the divine–spiritual world, which is unconscious to ourselves, exists in every human being. If that were not the case we would never be able to find our way back again. But there exists a deeply hidden involuntary process within us, "much more hidden than what takes place inwardly when with one's organism one passes through death." It is a process that never comes into our consciousness during the course of an individual life. The evolutionary process that is equivalent to this involuntary one is to be seen in the sacrament of Ordination, which corresponds to what is called "speech."

What is represented by the seventh sacrament is a picture of the soul–spiritual within the physical–bodily nature as it comes to expression in man and woman: "One would have to say that the descent to Earth is circumscribed by a certain boundary. A woman does not completely reach this boundary; a man, however, overshoots the mark. Therein lies the real contrast on the physical–bodily side." Because each possesses a certain imperfection there is a naturally occurring state of tension present. "When we look for the sacrament equivalent to this, we find it in the marriage ceremony."

This basic idea of Christian esotericism in connection with the sacraments—that we enter life as an imperfect being, that we acquire evolving qualities on the one hand, involutionary ones on the other, to which, in order to perfect our development, opposite qualities are added by means of the sacraments—is no longer understood. Today, however, it is very necessary for us to acquire involutionary qualities.

Spiritual Thinking as Spiritual Communion: The Proper Beginning of a Cosmic Ritual for Today

> *The first beginning of what must come to pass if Anthroposophy is to fulfil its mission in the world is that our whole relationship to the world must be recognized to be one of cosmic ritual or cultus.*[14]

Rudolf Steiner starts with Communion when he tackles the spiritualizing of the form of the sacraments, which is justified from the point of view of the law of evolution by the fact that in the sacrament of Communion we have the involutionary opposite force to incorporation of the soul–spiritual in our physical being. As the last stage in the process of incorporation is the binding of the thinking to the physical brain, so in the regressive, spiritualizing process intellectuality has to be introduced into this thinking, which is now physical.

Rudolf Steiner starts from this point already in the first of his publications: *A Theory of Knowledge Based on Goethe's World Conception* (1886). Here he demonstrates the fact that pure thinking, that is thinking not based on the senses, unites with world spirituality, which he then, one year later, describes as Communion.

> Whoever accredits thinking with the capacity of grasping what goes beyond sense perceptible objects must also of necessity acknowledge the existence of such objects. But the objects of thinking are ideas. When thinking grasps an idea it merges with the primal ground of existence; what works outwardly enters the human spirit; it identifies completely with objective reality. The becoming aware of an idea in its reality is the true communion of humankind. Thinking has the same significance for ideas as the eye has for light and the ear for sound. It is an organ of comprehension.[15]

---

14 Dornach, Dec. 31, 1922, CW 219.

15 Introduction to second volume of *Goethe's Natural Scientific Writings* in the Kürschner edition, annotated and published by Rudolf Steiner, preface to vol. 2 (1887), CW 1b; for Steiner's introductions, see CW 1.

Because the content of Anthroposophy is nothing other than what can be investigated in this way from the world of ideas (i.e., the world of spiritual reality) and is naturally of a moral–religious nature, it is unsurprising that even in the early years it was said that by its teachings the whole of life right down into its everyday details would be sanctified and become a sacrament, and that this was even the deeper meaning of its existence (Berlin, July 8, 1904, unpublished). It also becomes clear why it is said in the lectures *Man and the World of Stars* (CW 219), which are so important for our present theme, that the spiritual Communion experienced through spiritualized thinking is the "first beginning of what must come to pass if Anthroposophy is to fulfill its mission in the world" (Dornach, Dec. 31, 1922, CW 219).

How the sacrament of Communion can become reality through the symbol of the Last Supper is described in the lecture given in Kassel, July 7, 1909 (CW 112): "Humanity is at only the beginning of Christian development. Its future lies in the recognition that the Earth is the body of Christ. For through the Mystery of Golgotha a new center of light was created in the Earth; it was filled with new life right into the structure of the atoms. That is why Christ could say as he broke the bread made of the grain from the Earth: 'This is my body.' And what he could say to them as he gave them the juice of the grape—the sap of a plant, 'This is my blood.'" It continues, "Because he had become the soul of the Earth he could say of the solid substance, 'This is my body'; and of the plant's fluid, 'This is my blood'—just as you say about your body: This is my body, and about your blood: This is my blood. Those who are able to grasp the true meaning of these words of Christ create thought images for themselves that attract the body and the blood of Christ into the bread and the wine, and they unite with the Christ Spirit. *In this way our symbol of the Lord's Supper becomes reality.*"

Nevertheless, it thus continues: "Lacking in our hearts the thought that unites us with Christ we cannot engender the force of attraction that draws the Christ Spirit to us at Holy Communion; but by means of such a thought form the attraction is generated. For those, then, who need the outer symbol in order to perform the spiritual act—that is, to unite with the Christ—Communion will be the way until such time as their inner strength will have grown and they are so permeated by the Christ that they can dispense with the outer physical agency. The sacrament of Communion is the preparation for the mystical union with the Christ, the preparatory schooling. That is the light in which we must see these things. Just as everything evolves up toward spirit from matter through Christian influence, likewise those things that existed primarily as a bridge must grow and develop under the influence of Christ. The sacrament of Communion must rise from the physical to the spiritual plane if it is to lead to a true union with the Christ. One can do no more than hint at such matters, for only if they are received with a full sense of their sacred nature will they be rightly understood."

In the same sense, from the lecture given in Karlsruhe on October 13, 1911 (CW 131), we learn that: "By means of meditations, concentration exercises, and all that we can acquire as knowledge of higher worlds, we become ripe in our being to experience not merely thought worlds, not merely worlds of abstract feelings and perceptions, but to permeate ourselves inwardly with the element of spirit, whereby thoughts, meditative thoughts, will be able to live in us. They will even be the very same, only from within outward, as the symbol of the Holy Communion, the consecrated bread, has been from without inward." Friedrich Rittelmeyer recounted in his memoir (*Rudolf Steiner Enters My Life*) that Rudolf Steiner was asked, "Isn't it possible only in meditation to receive the Sacrament without bread and wine?" He responded, "It is possible. It is the same from the back of the tongue on."

The lecture in Dornach, December 31, 1922, starts with the words, "Spiritual knowledge is a veritable communion, the beginning of a cosmic ritual that is right and fitting for the person of today," a ritual "that can also grow." This suggests that the Communion with the World Spirit can be deepened further. In other connections it is also suggested that a certain sacrificial offering has to be brought so that one can go beyond the general experience of Spiritual Communion and arrive at truly cosmic knowledge. What has to be sacrificed in this case is indicated by the technical expression "the sacrifice of the intellect." But under this heading it is not in any way meant that one should forego thinking as such, but rather that one should renounce egoism and self-will in thinking, which consists of the arbitrary linking of thoughts. Explanations about this are contained in two lectures from 1904 and two lectures from 1923 and 1924.

The two lectures from 1904 are, to be sure, preserved only as imperfect copies and thus have not yet been published. For that reason, the part that concerns us here is quoted verbatim. In the lecture of June 1, 1904, Steiner stated that to decipher the akashic record and investigate cosmic evolution, certain preliminary conditions must be met, one of which follows:

> Put one's thoughts at the disposal of this principle, this power, and these beings whom, in theosophic parlance, we call the Masters. Ultimately it is the Masters who have to give us instructions to enable us to read in the akashic record. It is written in symbols and signs, not in words of an existing language or one that has existed. So long as one uses only the power one usually applies to thinking—and all who have not been trained for this purpose use this power—one cannot read the akashic record.
>
> If you ask, *Who is thinking?* you will have to say, *I think.* You connect object and predicate to form a sentence. So long as you yourself connect the single concepts you are not able to read in the akashic record. You are unable to read because you connect your thoughts with your ego. You have to obliterate the ego. You have to renounce all your opinions. You have to merely presented your ideas for the connection to be made by forces outside yourself, by the spirit.

Thus, it is renunciation—not of thinking itself, but of connecting the single thoughts yourself—which is necessary for you to be able to read in the akashic record. Then the Master can come and teach you, with the help of the outer spirit, to surrender your thoughts to the universal world spirit, so that he can show you what happened in history. Then it is not you who judge the facts, but the universal world spirit who speaks to you. And you place your thought substance at his disposal.

Now I have to say something that may awaken prejudices. I have to say what it is that is necessary today before one can eliminate the ego to be able to read in the akashic record. You know that one looks askance today at what the monks practiced in the Middle Ages—namely the "sacrifice of the intellect." The monks did not think in the same way as a modern investigator thinks. The monks had a kind of sacred science, the sacred theology. One did not have to decide about its content. One therefore said that the theologian of the Middle Ages must use his judgment in order to expound and defend the given revelations.[16] Whatever one may think of it today, that was strict schooling in the sacrifice of the intellect for the sake of established content. We will not consider if it is a good thing or a bad thing according to modern ideas.

This "sacrifice of the intellect" performed by a monk of the Middle Ages led to the elimination of personal judgment based on the ego. It enabled him to learn how to place the intellect in the service of something higher. Through reincarnation the effect of his former sacrifice resulted in him becoming a genius of observation. If higher vision were then added to this he should be able to direct his thoughts upon facts observable in the akashic record (Berlin, June 1, 1904, unpublished).

A few weeks later, Steiner said in a lecture:

---

16 Concerning the two sorts of truth in modern Spiritual Science—that based on knowledge and that from revelation—see the lecture given in Liestal, Oct. 16, 1916, in *Philosophie und Anthroposophie* (CW 35); also the study by Hans Erhard Lauer, *Erkenntnis und Offenbarung in der Anthroposophie* (Knowledge and revelation in Anthroposophy), Basel, 1958.

The farther one proceeds along the path of knowledge, the more it becomes necessary to acquire devotion; one becomes increasingly devotional. From this devotion then flows the strength to acquire the very highest knowledge. Those who manage to forego making their own thought combinations will gain the ability to read in the akashic record. One thing, however, is necessary: one eliminates the personal ego to such an extent that it makes no further claim to combine the thoughts itself.

This is not at all easy to understand, for a person claims the right to be allowed to combine the predicate with the subject. As long as one continues to do that, however, it is impossible for one to really study esoteric history. When, unselfishly—but also with clarity and consciousness—one lets thoughts rise up within one, then an event occurs, which, from a certain point of view, is well known to all esotericists—namely, that the ideas, the thoughts, which one previously formed into sentences and opinions according to one's own views, now form themselves from the spiritual world, so that it is not I who forms opinions, but opinions are formed in me. It is then the case that one has offered oneself up so that a higher self speaks from the spirit through one's ideas.

In other words, what was called—esoterically conceived—"sacrifice of the intellect" in the Middle Ages. It signifies the relinquishment of one's own opinions, one's conviction. So long as I make my own thought combinations and do not place my thoughts at the disposal of higher powers who simultaneously inscribe them into the tablet of the intellect, I am unable to study esoteric history (Berlin, July 25, 1904, unpublished).

The concept "sacrifice of the intellect" reappears in two lectures in connection with the results of investigations into the lost manuscript of a dramatic epic poem of the first four centuries of the Christian era (Penmaenmawr, Wales, Aug. 31, 1923, CW 227, and Prague, Apr. 5, 1924, CW 239). This poem was written by the mystery teachers of that time, because they foresaw that people in the future would develop their intellect increasingly. This would bring them freedom, but at the same time would take away their clairvoyance. They would thereby experience a great crisis through the fact that their understanding would no longer extend to those regions from which the actual deeper foundations of human and earthly evolution and the cosmic significance of Christianity could be understood. This foresight aroused in the mystery teachers the greatest anxiety as to whether humankind would be able to gain sufficient maturity to receive what had come into the world through the Mystery of Golgotha. For that reason they clothed their message—"that, to understand the cosmic significance of Christ, a sacrifice of the intellect was necessary"—in a mystery drama,[17] the lost epic drama we mentioned.

In a thrilling way, the scene depicts a young hero who gains clairvoyant insight into the cosmic significance of Christianity by his willingness to sacrifice his intellect. These mystery teachers wished by means of this poem (the greatest poem inspired by the New Testament) to present humankind, in a kind of credo, with the challenge of *sacrificium intellectus*. If humankind is to find the connection with what has come into the world through the Mystery of Golgotha, this *sacrificium* must be practiced by all who strive for a spiritual life to acquire learning. Everyone who aspires to learning and wishes to gain wisdom must develop a sense of ritual and sacrifice. "Sacrifice is a law of the spiritual world" (Berlin, Feb. 16, 1905, CW 93). "There must be sacrifice; without sacrifice there is no 'becoming,' no progress" is what is recorded in notes of a class lesson in Basel, June 1, 1914.

The "sacrifice of the intellect" is shown artistically in Rudolf Steiner's third mystery drama, *The Guardian of the Threshold*. In a spiritually dramatic moment in the play, the spirit pupil Maria—with the help of her spiritual teacher Benedictus, who is dressed characteristically in priestly robes in this scene located in spirit

---

[17] Rudolf Steiner used the designation "mystery drama" in a notebook entry to the lecture in Prague, Apr. 5, 1924 (archive no. 336).

land—makes a sacred vow in front of Lucifer (who represents egoistic forces) to keep all knowledge free of self-love:

> Never from this hour will I
> Allow myself to be possessed by joy
> Such as is felt when thoughts grow ripe within.
> I'll steel my heart to serve as sacrifice
> So that my mind can always only think
> In such a way that through my thoughts I may
> Offer the fruits of Knowledge to the gods.

From the lectures of 1904 mentioned previously, it is clear that the sacrifice that the spirit pupil Maria vows to undertake is similar to what is described there as one's "sacrifice of the intellect."

In addition to the reference to the sacrament of Communion in spiritualized thinking, we also find references to the spiritualization of the sacrament of Baptism. In contrast to Spiritual Communion, which is an individual event taking place within the human being, the latter points to a spiritualizing of outward labor. A beginning can already be made to put this into practice in education and in lessons if all children are looked at from the point of view that in their own personal ways they bring with them into the world the power of the Christ Spirit.[18] In another context comes the following remark: "What was previously enacted in the mysteries as a symbol of the sacrament of Baptism should be carried out today in outer happenings and in outward deeds. Spiritualization of human labor, sacramentalization of outer happenings, that is the true Baptism."[19]

---

18 Dornach, Nov. 27, 1916, CW 172.
19 Notes by Camilla Wandrey from an Esoteric Class, possibly Nov. 28, 1916, or possibly Nov. 28, 1910.

Ritual Forms for the Various Groups

Ritual binds together those who unite in it.[20]

The extent to which ritual unites people in communities was thoroughly discussed in 1923 when, owing to the many new daughter movements that had sprung up since the end of World War I, and also the burning of the Goetheanum, a complete overhaul of the Anthroposophical Society became necessary. The problem of "community-forming" was particularly acute at that time, on the one hand because of the influx into the Society of younger members, which largely came from the "wanderer movement," a youth movement struggling with the ideals of community, and on the other hand because of the founding of The Christian Community, or movement for religious renewal, which took place in autumn 1922, just prior to the Goetheanum fire.

This movement had come into existence through the appeal made to Rudolf Steiner in 1920/21 by a group of young theologians, mostly students, who asked him for advice and help in their particular concern for a renewal of religious life. His reply was that his own task was to bring Spiritual Science into the world, and he could not involve himself in founding a religion; if, however, they could carry out what they had in mind with a group of thirty or forty likeminded people, that would be something of immense importance for humankind as a whole.[21] For he was convinced that for those people who were looking for a path to the spirit through the practice of religion, the renewal of Christian religious life was profoundly important. And, as requested, he gave his most energetic support to this young movement—not as its founder, certainly, but, as he said, as a "private person." In his lectures he gave the fundamental structure

---

20 Dornach, March 3, 1923, CW 257.
21 Emil bock in *Wir erlabten Rudolf Steiner. Erinnerungen seiner Schüler* (We experienced Rudolf Steiner. Recollections by some of his pupils), M. J. Krück von Porturzyn, 1st ed., Stuttgart 1956.

to fit "the needs of a future theology," and first and foremost he gave them "a valid and spiritually effective ritual full of substance;" for the establishment of healthy religious life must depend on the building up of a healthy social order, which, again, can only be given in the form of a ritual (Dornach, Dec. 31, 1922, CW 219, and March 3, 1923, CW 257).

When, after the founding of The Christian Community, some uncertainty arose as to the relationship of the two movements, he felt obliged to speak about community-building and ritual work. Starting from the question as to whether the community-building as achieved in the founding of The Christian Community is the only kind there is at present, or whether there are other possibilities of achieving the same goal in the Anthroposophical Society, he described the two poles of community-building that were made possible through ritual work. Whereas the known pole of a religious service lies in the fact that beings and processes of the higher world are projected by words and ritual acts into the physical world, in the case of the other pole we are dealing with a "reversed ritual," which can be experienced by a group of anthroposophists when, in striving together after suprasensory knowledge, they raise themselves up into the spiritual world.

When people meet together to experience through Anthroposophy what the spiritual world offers them, then "the experience within a group of people is different from that of an individual." If the anthroposophic content is experienced in the right way, a process of awakening to the other person's soul is brought about and the participants are raised up to the Community of Spirit: "When this kind of consciousness is present and groups of anthroposophists are formed in this way, then something of an eminently community-building nature appears in this other pole of the cult—in what I might call the 'reversed ritual,' and from this can grow this specifically anthroposophic way of creating community" (Dornach, March 3, 1923, CW 257).

This possible form of ritual experience, lacking outward ceremony, is obviously one of the ways in which the cosmic–ritual can be experienced. Nevertheless, if Rudolf Steiner had lived longer, he would have also created an outwardly practiced ritual as, so to speak, an effective help along the difficult pathway toward experiencing the cosmic–ritual through purely spiritual search. The goal should always be to experience the cosmic–ritual as a spiritual-mystic union of the human spirit with the universal spirit; however, this can seldom be achieved today anyway. Rudolf Steiner once hinted at this:

> I call to mind one of the great mystics of the Alexandrian school, who confessed in his old age that he had rarely experienced a moment in his life in which his soul had reached a sufficient depth for the Spirit of Eternity to awaken within it, that mystical moment in which God could be experienced within the human breast. Those are midday moments when such things as this are experienced, when the sun of one's existence is at its zenith, and for those who are always at hand with their abstract ideas that lead them to say: "When people develop the right thoughts they will be led to the highest"—For them such "midday moments of life, which one must regard as moments of grace" are "not the hour in which they like to travel."[22] For such theorists, every moment should be one used to solve world's mysteries (Heidelberg, Jan. 21, 1909, CW 109).[23]

The fact that Rudolf Steiner intended to recreate an anthroposophic ritual form in 1923, the year when the Anthroposophical Society was reconstituted, is vouched for by two statements made by him in the spring of that year. The one statement was made when he was describing the "reversed ritual" as a specifically anthroposophic form of community-building. He added, "Many individuals

---

22 A reference to words of the Will-o'-the-Wisps in Goethe's *Green Snake and the Beautiful Lily*.

23 Public lecture in Heidelberg, Jan. 21, 1909. At the time being, only in the special edition of collected interpretations: "Goethe's Secret Revelation in his fairytale *The Green Snake and the Beautiful Lily*" (Dornach, 1998).

are presently entering the Society, seeking Anthroposophy not just in the abstract but in a communal association that satisfies the yearning belonging to the age of the consciousness soul. It might be suggested that the Society, too, should adopt a ritual. It could do this, of course, but that would take it outside its proper sphere" (*Awakening to Community,* Mar. 3, 1923, CW 257).

The second statement was given as the answer to a question asked during a private conversation concerning a ritual for the anthroposophic movement. The questioner, René Maikowski, recorded the conversation and gave permission to publish it:

> I was a member of the committee of the Delegates' Meeting that took place in Stuttgart at the end of February 1923. After this meeting, at Rudolf Steiner's suggestion, the founding of the "Free Anthroposophical Society" took place. During the subsequent building up of the Society in this committee, as elsewhere in the Society, discussion often turned to the relationship between work in the Anthroposophical Society and that of The Christian Community. This was especially noticeable following Rudolf Steiner's lecture on December 30, 1922.
>
> A discussion arose in our group about our tasks and way of working. Some of us asserted that the work of The Christian Community was easier because there the spiritual substance is provided by a ritual that satisfies the needs of those who seek direct contact to the spirit, whereas we others rely mainly on lecturing activity for that purpose. And so some of us raised the question as to whether it would be possible to have a ritual for the Society. Opinions were divided. I turned to Rudolf Steiner with this question—it was in the spring of 1923—as I often accompanied him on his travels. To my surprise he reacted very positively to this question. He explained that a ritual had already existed before the war, but that in future it would have to take a different form.
>
> The ritual of The Christian Community did not come into question for this purpose. Then he characterized the difference in the basic structure of Anthroposophy and The Christian Community. The two movements represent a different

approach and in part they were under the guidance of different Masters. A ritual activity in the anthroposophic movement must proceed from the same spiritual current as the School Services and represent a kind of continuation in form and content of what is given in the School Offering Service. And he intimated that he would return to this question, since he had been asked about it.

This new structure of the anthroposophic cognitive–ritual work was never put into practice however. After Rudolf Steiner's death, Marie Steiner tried to create a kind of substitute for it by the way she organized festivals at the Goetheanum, especially those of the seasons to which she gave an artistic–ritual character.

Retrospectively it can be seen that a variety of ritual texts have arisen from the requests and needs of different circles of people. The first of these were the texts for the interreligious Cognitive Ritual as practiced in the Esoteric School from 1906 until the outbreak of World War I in the summer of 1914.

Shortly before, or directly after the end of the war (1918), he was asked for a new formulation of the Church rituals. This plea came from a Swiss anthroposophic friend, Hugo Schuster, who had been so impressed by Rudolf Steiner's "Christ statue," that it induced him to become a priest. And in the summer of 1918, after having been ordained in the Old Catholic Church—in which the rituals were already said in German—he received from Rudolf Steiner at the turn of the year 1918/19 a burial service and, during the course of the spring of 1919, a new version of the Mass.

Other practicing or retired priests who were anthroposophists received ritual texts on application. Pastor Wilhelm Ruthenberg, who had become a teacher in the Free Waldorf School in Stuttgart, founded in 1919, received a baptism ritual and a marriage ritual in 1921. How this came about was recorded in the following way:

> As early as 1921, anthroposophic friends often asked Pastor Ruthenberg whether he would marry them or baptize their

children. Thereupon he asked Rudolf Steiner for a ritual of baptism. After having received it he felt that the black cassock with the white clerical band was not appropriate anymore, and he asked for a new vestment. Rudolf Steiner drew a picture of the desired object and told him what the colors ought to be. According to Ruthenberg's report the marriage ceremony proceeded as follows: "When a bridegroom once came to me and said he had asked Rudolf Steiner to perform a marriage ceremony for him, but the latter had sent him on to me, I did not want to let the man down, so I performed the ceremony myself. Afterward I went to Dr. Steiner and said to him: "If you send me someone for a marriage ceremony, will you please give me a ritual for it." Some weeks later as I was attending a eurythmy lesson with my class, the door opened, Dr. Steiner came toward me, gave me a few sheets of paper and said: "Here is the marriage ritual that I promised you." I sat down straight away to study it with burning curiosity. After the lesson, in the consulting room, I asked about the vestments for this service. I still had the sketch of the baptismal vestments with me, and Dr. Steiner added the colors for the marriage ceremony. The cut of the garments remained the same.[24]

Previously, another teacher, Johannes Geyer, who had also been a priest at one time, received a ritual of baptism for a child whom an anthroposophic friend had asked him to christen.

So, too, for the free-Christian religious lessons of the Waldorf school, rituals were inaugurated after Rudolf Steiner had been asked if he could arrange Sunday services for the pupils. The answer was that this would then have to take the form of a ritual. In this way the first Sunday service ritual came about, even before New Year 1920. Upon receiving further requests he instituted the other three services: the Christmas service came into being at Christmas 1920; in 1921, the youth service—as the equivalent of

---

24 From the biographical sketch "Wilhelm Ruthenberg" in the collection of the biographies of teachers of the Waldorf School, *Der Lehrerkreis um Rudolf Steiner in derersten Waldorfschule* (The circle of teachers around Rudolf Steiner in the first Waldorf School), Stuttgart, 1977.

the Act of Confirmation of the Church; and in the spring of 1923, the Offering service for the two top classes—as equivalent of the Communion service.

The Offering service was instituted after Rudolf Steiner had been informed during a conference with religious teachers on December 9, 1922, that a girl of the upper school had asked if the class could have a Sunday service that went beyond the youth service. He accepted this suggestion with great seriousness and described it as having broad significance, but wanted to give it further consideration. He did not want to introduce the Communion service into the services of the free religion lessons, but something "of the nature of Communion" could be used. Some few months later, in March 1923, the text of the service was handed over, and on Palm Sunday, March 25, 1923, the Offering service for students of the eleventh class and the teachers was held for the first time.[25]

To the wish expressed at the teachers' conference on November 16, 1921, to have a Sunday service only for teachers, indeed he never responded later.

When, through the involvement of The Christian Community—founded in the autumn of 1922—in the school curriculum, the question arose as to the continued justification for the Free Christian religion lessons and the school services, Rudolf Steiner expressed the definite opinion that both kinds of religious instruction, the free Christian and The Christian Community, possessed their own character and followed their own goals and both had full justification for the future. When some of the parents wanted their children to take part in both kinds of religious instruction he also acquiesced in this, too, provided it would not put a strain on the children themselves. (At that time the religion lessons given by The Christian Community were not held in the school but on their own premises.) The inner unchanging attitude of the greatest possible tolerance in religious

---

25 Maria Röschl-Lehrs in *Zur Religiösen Erziehung. Wortlaute Rudolf Steiners für Waldorfpädagogen* (Concerning religious education. Words of Rudolf Steiner to Waldorf teachers), Stuttgart, 1985.

matters is exemplified by the way he characterized the different aims of the two kinds of religious instruction: "The inner meaning of our youth service is that a person is regarded as a member of humankind as a whole, not a member of any one religious sect; The Christian Community, however, places a person into a particular religious community. Yet [he emphasized this repeatedly] a discrepancy between the two regarding their inner content cannot actually occur."[26] And when, from the side of The Christian Community, the ritual of the youth service had also been offered to them for their use (Confirmation service) the question was asked if it should not be altered for their sacramental purposes, he replied in no uncertain terms that it was "educational" to use the same ritual "as the expression of different earthly connections."[27]

He expressed similar views with regard to the Offering service. Maria Röschl-Lehrs records in what has been cited, how after the Service had first been performed, fellow teachers came to Rudolf Steiner with the wish to have it repeated for the teachers alone. Because the service holders tended to hold the opinion that the service should be performed only for pupils and with the participation of teachers and parents, they were asked to question Steiner on this point:

> I formulated my question in such a way that it was obvious that I thought it was not possible to hold the Offering service for any other people than for pupils. But Rudolf Steiner looked at me with wide-open eyes (I knew this gesture as an expression of surprised, slightly disapproving astonishment) and said: "Why not? This service can be held anywhere, wherever there are people who want it!"

To the range of tasks to be undertaken by The Christian Community, apart from the Communion Service (The Act of Consecration

---

[26] See Erich Gabert's introduction in *Faculty Meetings with Rudolf Steiner*, vol. 1 (CW 300a).

[27] When asked the same question later, he acceded to the desired changes (reported by Emil Bock, a priest of The Christian Community).

of Man) and the earlier established rituals, which had already been given, others were added bit by bit. The last one to be inaugurated was that for the ordination of arch high priests. It was introduced not long before Rudolf Steiner's death.

The manifoldness of rituals thus devised is all the more remarkable owing to the fact that Rudolf Steiner once remarked himself that it is difficult to form a ritual: "You can see how difficult it is to initiate something of a ritual nature from the fact that for a very long time everything of that kind was restricted to using what was traditional...all forms of ritual that are extant today are actually very ancient, merely changed slightly in the one or other respect" (Stuttgart, June 14, 1921, CW 342).

From this it follows that whoever undertakes to found a ritual, if it is to be a true image of what is happening in the spiritual world, must stand in close relationship to that world of the spirit. We must also possess artistic ability, for ritual forms, as the images of spiritual events, are in no way to be compared with photographs, but are independent configurations produced by physical means. A supplementary explanation for this seems to have been provided by the this statement: "When we lift ourselves to the next stage of existence, pictures appear to us that we cannot now apply as we would our thoughts by asking: How do these pictures correspond to reality? Rather, things appear in pictures consisting of colors and shapes, and we have to interpret through our imagination the beings that are thus presented symbolically" (Berlin, Oct., 26, 1908, CW 107). That is illustrated concretely by the funeral rite and has the following remark appended to it: "It could be expressed in a more complicated way, but in its simpler form what has to be won through inner struggle can be thus won" (Dornach, June 27, 1924, CW 236). The term *erobert* (conquered) expresses once more how difficult it must be to initiate a ritual.

He explained the reason for simplicity—a striking characteristic of all his rituals—by saying that a complicated ritual would not satisfy the people of today and that he therefore had to make it extremely simple (Stuttgart, June 14, 1921, CW 342). But it is just the simplicity that bears witness to artistically creative ability. Now art and ritual are closely connected in respect of their origin, as they both come from the same spiritual region: "During humankind's evolution ritual is evolved as the living picture of the spiritual world that reaches into the domain of artistic production. For art is also a product of the astral world—and ritual turns to beauty" (Paris, June 6, 1906, CW 94). An interesting occurrence in this connection was recorded by Emil Bock: "When, early in 1923, I received from him the Burial Service for children, he was himself radiant with thankfulness for this special form of creativity, which was at the same time the highest art of receiving. Twice he came to me on that day—it was during a conference—with the words: 'Is not the text beautiful!'"[28]

Another Characteristic Arises from the Esoteric Principle of Continuity

> *May what is to come*
> *rest upon what has gone before;*
> *May what has gone before*
> *carry what is to come*
> *to strong existence in the present.*[29]

Wherever possible he linked what he had recently investigated to the old tradition for the sake of the continuity of progress; likewise in the creation of rituals. The necessity of taking past currents into account was once formulated by him in the following manner: "In

---

28 From Emil Bock, *Wir erlabten Rudolf Steiner. Erinnerungen seiner Schüler* (We experienced Rudolf Steiner. Recollections by his pupils), Krück von Portuzyn, Stuttgart 1956.

29 From "Zwölf Stimmungen" (Twelve moods), in *Wahspruchworte*, CW 40 (German ed.).

order to preserve the continuity of human development it is still necessary today to link, as it were, to ritual and symbolism" (Dornach, Dec. 20, 1918, CW 186). And as these rituals were preserved by tradition "something was preserved that can and will be wakened into life when human beings have discovered how to bring into all their deeds the power that streams from the Mystery of Golgotha" (Dornach, Sept. 29, 1922, CW 216). The following words point to the current of the future, which is only beginning to manifest today: "It is only possible to arrive at symbols in our day by immersing ourselves lovingly in the universal secrets of existence; and it is actually only through Anthroposophy that a ritual or symbol can proceed" (Stuttgart, June 14, 1921, CW 342). In this same sense we are told, in a lecture about different rituals, that rituals today have to include what modern spiritual-scientific training can reveal of the laws of universal spirituality and that in creating such a ritual "all we can expect is that we shall have to start right at the beginning again" (Dornach, Sept. 11, 1923, CW 350).

The connection between elements coming from the past and those coming from the future as they are presented in the ritual now in use in the movement for religious renewal (The Christian Community) "takes humanity's historical evolution fully into account and thus represents in many of its single details as well as in its overall aspects a carrying forward of the historical aspect. But its every aspect also bears the imprint of fresh revelations, which the spiritual world can only now begin to make to our higher consciousness" (Dornach, March 3, 1923, CW 257).[30] In a similar manner he expressed himself regarding the reformulation of the Catholic Mass for the Reverend Schuster who had asked him to "put the ritual text of the Roman Catholic Church into a form corresponding to what

---

30 With this reference to historical development the four parts of the Mass are obviously alluded to—The Gospel Reading, Offertory, Transubstantiation, Communion—which represent "the path that the pupil of the ancient pagan mysteries had to take in undergoing initiation" (Dornach, Jan. 11, 1919, CW 188; Munich, Nov. 4, 1906, CW 94).

originally lay within it, not the strange translation that is widely extant today," and then "something new" could arise, even though it is only a matter of translation. He also said in this connection about the funeral service: "Naturally, one must connect with the usual funeral rites, but because the usual ritual is translated properly, and not just according to the dictionary, a different result is achieved" (Stuttgart, June 14, 1921, CW 342).

The following statement also points to a characteristic feature of rituals: "One can only properly embody a single ritual from the spiritual world at any one time."[31] The question as to how the various ritual forms correspond with this single possible "ritual" could be answered by saying that the rituals given for the various circles—the Cognitive Ritual of the Esoteric School, services for the free religion lessons of the Waldorf school, the Communion service for The Christian Community—must be essentially the same in their deeper aspect. This appears to be confirmed by a statement by Emil Bock, according to which the third of the school services (*Opferfeier*) was an attempt to introduce an equivalent of the Act of Consecration of Man of The Christian Community, insofar as this could be carried out by lay persons, that is to say, by those who were not consecrated priests. Maria Röschl-Lehrs added to this in the previously quoted passage: "What constantly recurred in the evolution of Christianity as the urge and longing for lay priesthood—but, to be sure, was constantly persecuted and finally also extirpated—has been re-sown by Rudolf Steiner [in the *Opferfeier*]." It is obvious from the foregoing that in Rudolf Steiner's eyes the esoteric Cognitive Ritual, the free religious ritual of the Waldorf school and the Act of Consecration of Man of The Christian Community stood in no kind of contradiction to one another. On the one hand, it was because, in religious matters, as in all other things, the freedom of the individual was

---

31 Carl Unger, "Zur Frage des Verhältnisses der Christengemeinschaft zur Anthroposophischen Gesellschaft" (Relationship between The Christian Community and the Anthroposophical Society), in *Schriften II* (Writings II), Stuttgart, 1964.

of paramount importance and only true Christianity was allowed "complete religious freedom" (Zurich, Oct. 9, 1918, CW 182). On the other hand, because it is only through the spread of ritual into all branches of life that the way to the high ideal of the consecration of the whole of life may be attained. The necessary prerequisite for that is that certain inner thoughts and feelings "shall interpenetrate and spiritualize our inner being, thoughts and feelings as fully consecrated as in the best sense of inner Christian development the Holy Communion has spiritualized the human soul and filled it with the Christ." When this becomes possible—and according to Rudolf Steiner it will become possible—we shall have progressed a stage further in evolution and thereby the "real proof will again be provided" that Christianity is greater than its external form (Karlsruhe, Oct. 13, 1911, CW 131).

11

THE MEANING AND SPIRITUAL ORIGIN
OF THE COGNITIVE RITUAL

It is impossible to make real progress in penetrating the higher worlds without going through the stage of *Imagination* knowledge.¹ The motif of the temple—for both Goethe and Rudolf Steiner—is to be a vessel for the suprasensory ritual, which Goethe allows the three kings to fulfill and Steiner lets speak at the three altars.² A decisive reason for any work with ritual symbols lies in the primary knowledge that events that take place in the higher world immediately bordering on the physical (the astral, or imaginative, world) are symbolic expressions of astral facts, just as all that can be observed in the physical world are expressions of physical facts. In this sense, working with the symbolic ritual is to be regarded as a practical means toward getting to know the astral world. Rudolf Steiner expressly emphasized the fact that in no other way than by means of symbolic ideas can the way into the higher worlds be found—literally:

> The opinion often prevails in the various esoteric streams of today that there can be an ascent to higher worlds by other means than by applying imaginative and symbolical ideas. And there is a kind of fear, yes, even an aversion, to ascending

---

1   *The Stages of Higher Knowledge* (CW 12), p. 18.
2   E. A. Karl Stockmeyer, a member of the cognitive–ritual circle, in his essay "Concerning the Unity of Temple and Ritual in Connection with the Goetheanum Building-Idea," in *Rosicrucianism Renewed: The Unity of Art, Science, and Religion* (CW 284), p. 219.

into the astral worlds with the help of symbolic signs or other esoteric educative principles by people of the present day. One might ask: Are such attitudes of fear justified? One can answer yes and no. In a certain sense, they are justified and in another they are not at all appropriate; no one can truly rise to the spiritual worlds without passing through the astral world. (Cologne, Dec. 29, 1907, CW 101)

In the letter of August 15, 1906, is a statement on the spiritual origin of the Cognitive Ritual: "This ritual can be no more than a reflection of a fact on the higher plane."[3] This is connected with an important addendum to lectures from 1924 that describe this fact pertaining to the spiritual world: "At the end of the eighteenth and beginning of the nineteenth century a great suprasensory event consisting of suprasensory ritual acts—unfolding mighty pictures of the spiritual life—hovers close to the physical world of the senses." This suprasensory ritual and action flowed into Goethe's spirit. Transformed and changed in miniature, we have this picture set down by Goethe in his fairytale *The Green Snake and the Beautiful Lily* (Dornach, Sept. 16, 1924, CW 238). One of the most central themes of the fairytale is the temple with the three kings, the representatives of wisdom, beauty, and power (or strength). Steiner also describes it as a path of initiation—the Gancient King's power of perception coming from the Imagination faculty, that of the Silver King from objectivized feelings, and that of the Bronze King from the will (Berlin, Oct. 24, 1908, CW 57). The three altars with their acolytes, both in the Cognitive Ritual and the temple scenes of the mystery dramas, are in full accordance with that. And when in the letter of August 15, 1906, it is further stated that the ritual appropriate to European conditions, recognized by esotericists during the last 2,300 years[4] has been prepared by the "Rosicrucian masters," the connection

---

3   A letter from Steiner to A. W. Sellin, Aug. 15, 1906 (in the addendum of chap. 3 of this volume).

4   According to a statement by Günther Schubert, Rudolf Steiner once told him that all this refers to Melchizedek.

with the suprasensory ritual becomes evident through the following words: "The Rosicrucians (said): 'shape the world in such a way that it contains wisdom, beauty, and strength, then will wisdom, beauty, and strength be mirrored in us. If you have used your time to this end then you will depart from this life taking with you the mirror image of wisdom, beauty, and strength. Wisdom is the image of manas; beauty, piety, goodness, the image of buddhi; strength is the image of atman.... It is not through idle contemplation that human beings progress on Earth, but by incorporating wisdom, beauty, and strength into the Earth'" (Berlin, Oct. 24, 1905, CW 93a).

Goethe's "mystery fairytale" appeared at the end of the eighteenth century (1795). One century later, 1899, when the so-called Kali Yuga, the spiritually dark period, came to an end and once more a spiritually bright period was about to begin, Rudolf Steiner made the far-reaching decision, in the sense of the decisive words "The time is at hand!" in Goethe's fairy story, to give public expression to the esotericism that lived within him. And in accordance with the esoteric principle of preserving continuity, he linked to the fairytale *The Green Snake and the Beautiful Lily,* the pictures of which had lived with him in his meditation for twenty years. On the 150th anniversary of Goethe's birth, on August 28, 1899, Steiner published the essay "Goethe's Secret Revelation," and a year later, autumn 1900, he carried the interpretation of Goethe's Apocalypse, begun therein, a stage further with a lecture to Berlin theosophists and so became "completely esoteric."[5] Twenty years later, on the eve of the first gathering in the first Goetheanum, the "First High

---

5   *Autobiography,* CW 28. Marie Steiner made the following entry in a notebook (Archive no. 21): "When Rudolf Steiner first made his public appearance with the intention of removing the veil of esotericism, he took Goethe's fairytale as his starting point and spoke about the altars of Wisdom, Beauty and Strength. He placed them in the temple of his mystery dramas and spoke to us once more and in greater depth about their significance. And again, he placed them into our Esoteric School and let us approach again and again the various aspects of thinking, feeling and willing, which are an expression of these altars."

School Course," as he called this lecture, recalled the development of the anthroposophic movement, its "primal cell."[6]

Through that it certainly may not merely be construed that the anthroposophic movement had its outward start with this lecture, but that, implicitly too, a start had been made in fulfilling the central demand of Goethe's fairytale: to bring the mysteries—that is the Temple—from obscurity into the full light of day, to the attention of the public. For it is in this deeper sense that anthroposophic Spiritual Science has been developed to act as a herald to humankind of the newly dawned Epoch of Light. And therefore, in the last year of his lecturing activity, Rudolf Steiner, in connection with his description of the suprasensory ritual, spoke these weighty words: "What is Anthroposophy in reality? Yes, dear friends, if you comprehend all the wonderful, majestic imaginations that were present as a suprasensory ritual in the first half of the nineteenth century [and at the end of the eighteenth century] and translate them into human concepts, that is Anthroposophy" (Dornach, July 8, 1924, CW 237).

Consequently, there is a direct line from the perception of the ritual in the suprasensory world—which is certainly connected with the ancient ritual prepared by the Rosicrucian masters—leading by way of Goethe's fairytale to the translation of these images of the spiritual life into the scientific concepts of Anthroposophy and to the creation of the Cognitive Ritual.

In this sense, according to Marie Steiner, the cognitive cultus and its three altars represented the sign and seal of Rudolf Steiner's activity, brought from the depths of the Temple—where it had been since the time of the mysteries first existence—and handed over to humankind.[7]

---

6 Dornach, Sept. 25, 1920. *Blätter für Anthroposophie* (News for Anthroposophy), 1955, 7th edition, no. 3.

7 Marie Steiner's commemorative address on the first anniversary of Rudolf Steiner's death (CW 265).

Why the Cognitive Ritual Was Practiced in Brotherly Union

> *It is not just one person, plus a second and a third, but something quite different when people unite.*[8]

To answer the question of why ritual symbolism was practiced in brotherly union, certain spiritual facts must be considered. One of these has to do with the character of such unions, which Rudolf Steiner described the day before he became a member of Memphis-Misraim Freemasonry:

> Union makes it possible for a higher being to express itself through the members. That is a general principle in the whole of life. Five people who come together having thoughts and feelings in harmony with one another, are more than $1+1+1+1+1$, they are not just the sum of five, just as little as our body is the sum of its five senses. The living with one another and in one another signifies something very similar to the coexistence of the cells in the human body. A new higher being exists among the five, yes, even among two or three. "Where two or three are gathered together in my name, there am I in the midst of them."
>
> It is not the one and the other and the third, but something quite new that comes about through the union. But it only comes about when the one lives within the other, when the one does not produce one's forces merely from the self, but also from the others. That, however, is only present when a person lives unselfishly within the other person. Thus unions where human beings work together are the hidden places into which the higher spiritual beings descend to work through the individual members in the same way that the soul works through the members of the body.
>
> This will not be easily believed in our materialistic civilization, but in the spiritual–scientific worldview it is not

---

[8] Lecture, Berlin, Nov. 23, 1905, CW 54.

merely a figurative form of speech, but something eminently real. Hence the spiritual scientist does not speak in abstractions when he talks about the folk spirit or the folk soul, or the family spirit, or the spirit of another community. This spirit that is at work in a community is not outwardly visible, but it is there all the same, and it exists through the brotherly love of the people who are active in the community. Just as the body possesses a soul, likewise a guild or brotherhood also has a soul, and I repeat: It is not said in a figurative sense but should to be taken literally.

Those who do work together in brotherhoods are magicians because they draw higher beings into their circle. One does not need to call upon the machinations of spiritualism if one is working together in a community in brotherly love. Higher beings are manifested therein. If we devote ourselves to a brotherhood, this dedication, this merging into the whole confers power on our organism, giving us the strength of steel. When we then speak or act as a member of such an organization it is the spirit of the organization that acts or speaks through us, not the individual soul. It is the secret of the progress of future humanity to work through communities.

As one epoch hands over to the next and each epoch has its own task to perform, so does the medieval epoch stand with regard to our own and our epoch to the one that will follow it. The medieval brotherhoods acted directly in practical life through the founding of the useful arts. They only showed signs of leading a materialistic existence when the fruits of their labors had been reaped and when the basis of their consciousness—their brotherhood namely—had more or less disappeared, because the true feeling of unity within the community had given place to the state principle or to abstract spiritual life.

It is the duty of future generations to found brotherhoods once again, brotherhoods from the spirit, from the highest ideals of the soul. The life of humankind has brought the most diverse associations to maturity until now; it has caused a terrible fight for existence, which has now reached its high point. The spiritual–scientific view of the world strives to bring about the highest good for humankind through the principle of brotherhood. Thus, you may see that the worldwide spiritual–scientific movement wishes to replace the struggle for existence by the principle of brotherhood. We must learn to lead a communal life. We should not imagine this or that person is able to achieve some goal or other on his or her own.

Perhaps you might wish to know, each one of you, how a struggle for existence and brotherly love are compatible with one another. That is very simple. We shall have to learn how to replace fighting with positive work, to exchange war for an ideal. But today that is all too little understood. People do not know which war is referred to, because all one talks about is fighting when one speaks about life. There is a social war, a war for peace, a war for the emancipation of women, a territorial war, and so on. Whichever way we turn we see struggles.

The spiritual–scientific view of the world strives to put positive work in the place of this struggle. Whoever is familiar with this outlook on life knows that fighting will not produce the right result in any sphere of life. Try to discover what, according to your experience and knowledge, is the best to be promoted in life without attacking your opponent. It might be only an ideal, of course, as the spiritual–scientific principle has to be introduced into the life of the present day. People who unite with others to work for the good build the foundation for future healthy development.

The Theosophical Society wants to set an example in this direction. It is not therefore a society based on propaganda like other societies, but is a brotherhood. One's own work in it is the outcome of that of every one of its members. That should be rightly understood. Those who are most effective are those who do not push their own opinions onto others, but take account of what they read in the eyes of their companions; those who search the thoughts and feelings of others and put themselves at the others' service. Those who never defend their own opinions in life are best able to work in such a circle of people. If we try to understand that our best forces spring from our union with others and that such a union must not be thought of as only an abstract idea, but as something to be applied first and foremost in a theosophical way in our every action and every moment of our lives, then we shall make progress. But we must not be impatient about our progress.[9]

Another spiritual fact that is the basis of working together in a symbolic way is that when thought forces are employed in a ritualistic fashion over a period of time, they become so enhanced that they change into outward reality. It is in this way that progress is made. Everything proceeds from within, not from without: "What at one time are thoughts and feelings become outer forms at a later time. The individualities who guide the evolution of humankind have to implant into our minds the thought forms that thousands of years later will turn into outer reality. There you can see the functioning of thought forms, inspired by symbolical representations, ranging from a depiction of Noah's Ark and Solomon's Temple to the apocalyptic figures of Human Being, Lion, Bull and Eagle...pictures that, if we ponder them...will lead us to a participation in the world immediately bordering our own." This is expressed in a lecture given in Cologne on December 28, 1907 (CW 101), in which it is explained, by way of chief example, that the concepts of Noah's Ark and Solomon's Temple affect the new form of the human frame.

Through spiritual–scientific knowledge, the following statement on Freemasonry also acquires clarity: "If you ask me what the essence of Freemasonry is, I would have to answer in abstract terms: It is a body whose members think the things that will benefit the world several centuries before they manifest," some of which have nevertheless already come to pass (Berlin, Jan. 2, 1906, CW 93).

If the general spiritual progress of humankind is helped by such brotherly symbolic–ritual cooperation, so, too, is individual progress. This is verified by Rudolf Steiner's statement that true consciousness of immortality is connected with the exercise

---

9   Steiner, "Brotherhood and the Struggle for Existence," in *Die Welträtsel und die Anthroposophie* (CW 54), Berlin, Nov. 23, 1905.

of fraternity. The standard rule concerning the consciousness of immortality may be expressed this way: Only what one does not strive for merely on one's own to gain full knowledge of the immortality of the spirit will contribute to gaining such knowledge (Berlin, Dec. 23, 1904, CW 93).

It is well known that the realization of ideals requires great patience. Steiner explained this and comforted his hearers in the following lesson.

Instruction Lesson, Berlin, October 28, 1911

Perhaps there are some among you who feel oppressed by the fact that you cannot convert what you have learned here into practical work, but are continually only absorbing spiritual teachings. Now you have to ask: Am I not a gourmet of spiritual delicacies? To that the Wise Masters of the East answer: By absorbing spiritual teachings you do something that has eternal value. If there were no souls into which they could pour their teachings, the spiritual development of humanity could not progress through the activity of "yesterday's spirits," whether human beings who have lived in former times or gods who preceded us in earthly evolution. It is like the seed of a plant; insofar as it remains a blossom or fruiting body, it has no value; unless it is placed into the earth it will be unable to sprout. Those who absorb into their souls artworks such as *The Sistine Madonna*, the *Faust* drama, and so on are far more important for Earth's evolution than are the artists themselves.

If Raphael had painted only the *Sistine Madonna* and no one else had ever seen that work, it would have had importance only for him and not for eternity. Only when people allow works of art or other spiritual products to work upon them will something result that will outlast the Earth evolution and be taken up into the Jupiter condition. The one who creates is not the most important person. Of far more importance is the observer, the reader, and so forth. When artists or writers receive inspiration for their work from the spiritual world, until the moment of conception it is of eternal importance to them. However, from the moment they get to work with pen or paintbrush they are working only for what is temporal; it is of importance only for them. Everything produced for the world comes under the sway of the temporal. Only what is stimulated within the human breast remains. The greater weight is therefore not where the intellect would expect it to be. The fact that the Evangelists wrote their Gospels was important to them, but it would have meant nothing for eternity if there had not been innumerable hearts upon which the Gospels have worked. It is of far greater value to read a classical work of antiquity and let it affect you than to write an inferior book yourself.

Those who think that they must produce something for the world should wait until destiny calls them to carry out one or another piece of work. And those who, for instance, have had a spiritual vision and ask themselves if they ought to divulge it to the world, they can apply the following rule in forming an opinion: If to divulge the vision were to be a source of pleasure to them then they certainly ought not to divulge it. Only what causes pain in the telling is of any value. Humorists who derive pleasure from their strokes of wit do not provide anything that is of significance for humanity; only those who have endured with pain the foibles of humankind and have transmuted them into humor, provide something of lasting value for history. Nothing but "devotion to the spiritual world" can produce fruitful results for work on Earth.

People may have accumulated treasure and feel the need to use it in the service of humanity, but without esoteric insight it will be impossible to know if the one or other philanthropic institution will presently lead either to the welfare or the downfall of humankind. People can engage in ever so many Samaritan works and make ever so many men and women happy, but it can be—and without the aforementioned devotion toward the spiritual world, it most probably will be—that, for example, great misfortune will befall the children of those men and women: that is, the next generation.

Here, in our lodge, because the members are present with their thoughts, more is done for the wellbeing of the world than in all philanthropic works. Physical values will be destroyed if one uses them for one's own ends; spiritual values will on the other hand be generated if they are taken up and used. Thus, the one who creates is not at all the most important person. If one were to refer to the akashic record concerning the time of Raphael, Michelangelo, and so on, and give one's attention only to these figures, one would not gain a true picture. Likewise, if while investigating Atlantean times by means of the akashic record, and if one were to pay attention only to what existed in the souls of the great leaders of the mysteries (which is difficult to do, by the way), one would get a correct vision only by paying attention to what awakes in the hearts and souls of those who were taught.

Whoever is able to write a fairly tolerable book, would accordingly also be able to grasp the contents of a good classical work from the past and would do far more good with it than by writing his or her own mediocre book.

Thus, it is not for unauthorized pleasure when members are busily occupied with grasping what is offered to them here. Without the acceptance of the members nothing can be achieved for the future spiritual progress of humankind. Humanity would have to succumb to materialism; subsequent generations would then be ill in body and soul. Children who would be born do not find in their spiritual surroundings the thoughts they need for proper development unless there are circles of people to take up spiritual knowledge, even when it has not been made public. Materialism does so much harm that it is impossible to do much in this way to prevent it being exaggerated. Even if ten or a hundred times more study were undertaken than actually happens, it would still be insufficient to counterbalance the evil of materialism.

12

ESOTERIC RESEARCH INTO THE HIRAM–JOHN INDIVIDUALITY

The central instruction in the Cognitive–Ritual Section is "The Temple Legend" and its main figure, the master builder Hiram Abiff. Information about the reincarnation of Hiram Abiff as Lazarus–John and Christian Rosenkreutz in "Explanations of the Temple Legend" (CW 265) requires additional remarks, because it contains only a portion of what we can call Rudolf Steiner's research into the reincarnations of the Hiram (respectively, John) individuality, since this refers not only to the individuality of Lazarus–John, the Evangelist and writer of the Apocalypse, but also to John the Baptist and the mysterious union of the two.

Such research into reincarnation, which encompasses both the John figures equally, occupies an outstanding position in Steiner's work because it appears as Alpha and Omega at the beginning and the end of his spiritual–scientific lecturing activity and, above and beyond that, like a red thread running through the whole of his work (Marie Steiner).

The first results of his research in connection with the threefold defense of Christianity as a mystical fact and as the central event of human evolution are found at the beginning of his spiritual–scientific lecturing activity (1901/02) in his lecture cycle *From Buddha to Christ*; in the avant-garde literary circle *"Die Kommenden"* (the coming ones) in Berlin; in his series of lectures to the circle of Berlin theosophists on the Egyptian and Greek mysteries and Christianity; and in his book *Christianity as Mystical Fact* (CW 8). These three accounts culminate in the interpretation of St. John's Gospel, beginning with the raising of Lazarus as an initiation carried out by Jesus Christ and with an assertion that the awakened Lazarus wrote St. John's Gospel. According to Rudolf Steiner's lecture in Dornach, June 11, 1923 (CW 258), his lecture course *From Buddha to Christ* ends with this motif. In copies of this lecture series given to theosophists, it is dated March 15, 1902. The book *Christianity as Mystical Fact* does not state explicitly that Lazarus is the author of St. John's Gospel, though it is clear from the whole context.[1]

Immediately after commencing his defense of Christianity, Steiner began to introduce his teaching on reincarnation and karma into European spiritual life, because all spiritual–scientific investigation depends on that.[2] This applies especially to his teachings on history, since reincarnating human souls, who carry the results of their life in one epoch into their lives in other epochs, create history. Because this applies to the spiritual leaders of humankind, as well, their active impulses during different periods form an essential chapter in the broad subject of history and reincarnation, much of which is devoted to the two John figures.

Rudolf Steiner first spoke about the earlier lives of these two leading figures of Christianity in 1904, beginning with John the Baptist. In public lecture in Berlin on Christianity and reincarnation, January 4, 1904 (CW 52), he states that reincarnation was always taught in the mysteries and about Christ, who, as the Gospels relate, pointed out to his intimate pupils that John the Baptist was the reincarnated prophet Elijah. Further statements followed at the turn of the year 1908/09. Marie Steiner described the background from which he arrived at this statement in a memorial essay following Rudolf Steiner's death:

---

1 Rudolf Steiner pointed to this in his final address, given Sept. 28, 1924. In the lecture on July 25, 1904, Steiner said that, according to the akashic record, the awakened Lazarus was the writer of St. John's Gospel and the the disciple whom the Lord loved and who stood beneath the Cross.

2 See *Reincarnation and Karma* (CW 135).

It happened when Rudolf Steiner encouraged me to continue ever further with my recitation. I had tried then to wrestle my way through to Novalis. I informed him that I would not find it easy, and that I had not yet found the key to Novalis. He advised me to immerse myself into the mood of the Holy Nuns. The nuns did not help me—quite the opposite. I did not know what to do with them. Then all of a sudden it became clear: Raphael's figures surrounded me. The Child shone in the arms of his mother with his world-penetrating eyes. "I see you in a thousand forms," Mary, lovingly expressed. All around, sounding world ocean, and color harmonies. I said to Rudolf Steiner, "The nuns did not do the trick, but another person helped me: Raphael. Novalis is transparent to me now." Radiance spread over Rudolf Steiner's gentle features. A few days later he revealed to us for the first time the mystery of Novalis–Raphael–John–Elijah.[3]

A "few days later" cannot be dated exactly.[4] The first certain date has been handed down in a description from memory of a Novalis celebration that took place in Munich on January 6, 1909, of which it is said, "I saw and heard Marie von Sivers recite verses by Novalis for the first time under the Christmas tree in the Munich Branch room, surrounded by colored reproductions of Raphael's paintings. It was the turn of the year 1908/09. The whole room was decked out in rose-red satin, and a rose cross (then still with twelve red roses) hung in the center above the speaker's podium, from which we had

---

3   From: "On the Eve of Michaelmas," in *Events in the Anthroposophical Society: News for the Members*, year 2, 1925.

4   "The Songs of Mary" by Novalis were recited by Marie Steiner for the first time at the Christmas celebration in the Berlin Branch on Dec. 22, 1908. Thus this "few days later" could have been the lecture on Dec. 28, 1908 (no written record), in which this theme was introduced, which was described as a highlight of Spiritual Science, but on which occasion Rudolf Steiner had not allowed notes to be made. The fact that it is unlikely that just in Berlin, the main center of activity at that time, it would not have been spoken about, strengthens the argument in its favor. For in the Berlin lectures this series of incarnations was mentioned much later and as if already known.

just heard Rudolf Steiner speak about the being who incarnated as Elijah, John the Baptist, Raphael, and Novalis."[5]

It must have been the occasion of a very solemn event. Likewise, six months later, during the lecture course *The Gospel of St. John and Its Relation to the Other Gospels*, a Novalis matinée was again celebrated (Cassel, July 4, 1909, no notes), from which only later notes by a participant remain: "After a musical introduction, Rudolf Steiner announced that Marie von Sivers would recite poems by Novalis. Marie von Sivers spoke with deep empathy in her own developed way of speaking. Later, Steiner began his lecture, in which he told us about the incarnations of Elijah–John the Baptist–Raphael–Novalis as the sequence of lives of one individuality.... Steiner spoke afterward about the mood of that recitation with unusual warmth, intensity, and even solemnity. The lecture had a completely inward and sacred character.... Thus, at the end of the lecture—the sole content of which was this sequence of repeated earthly lives—a deep emotion came over his audience, and many eyes glistened with tears, more restrained by the men but uncontrolled by the women."[6]

The process of reincarnation is not so simple, however, as one might imagine:

> Everyone, including theosophists, usually accept the mystery of reincarnation in a way that is far too simplistic. We should not imagine that a soul incarnated in its three bodies today was simply incorporated in a previous incarnation and then in an earlier one, and that this always proceeded according to the same plan. The hidden matters connected with this are far more complicated.... It is often impossible to bring a historic figure into line with such a scheme. This work must be taken up in a far more complicated way if we are to understand it (Leipzig, Sept. 12, 1908, CW 108).

---

5   Max Gümbel-Seiling in *Gedenkblatt für Marie Steiner-von Sivers* (Memorial for Marie Steiner-von Sivers), Stuttgart, 1949.

6   From notes by memory from Rudolf Toepell in the Archive of Rudolf Steiner's Estate (Nachlaßverwaltung).

That was an announcement, so to speak, of what was going to be started from the end of 1908 onward as a more advanced chapter of the teaching about reincarnation. Illustrations were given from concrete examples of historical personalities to show that, conditional on the law of spiritual economy for the preservation of what was of spiritual value for the future, not only the human "I" but also other members of the human being can reincarnate, even in other individualities. The descriptions of such "penetration" incarnations in the case of great spiritual teachers, the highest of whom are the so-called bodhisattvas, comprise one of the main subjects of the years 1909 to 1914.[7]

Among the figures thus portrayed we find John the Baptist time and again. The lecture cycle *The Gospel of St. Mark* (Sept. 1912) not only allots broad space to John the Baptist but also alludes to a life previous to the Elijah incarnation. Since that time five spiritually historic incarnations of his are known: Pinehas (during the time of Moses), Elijah, John the Baptist, Raphael, and Novalis. It is all the more surprising, therefore, that a year later, in *The Fifth Gospel* lectures (1913/14, CW 148), he makes this remark about John the Baptist: "I am not saying this now as part of *The Fifth Gospel* [results of akashic research into personalities of the Gospels], since research has not yet reached as far as John the Baptist in connection with *The Fifth Gospel*. I say it from knowledge that can be acquired in a different way" (Berlin, Jan. 13, 1914, CW 148). On the grounds of all the investigation that had been made before then about the Baptist, this remark can refer only to research into "penetration" incarnations, as they had already been investigated and recorded in the case of other Gospel personalities. A reason why this research into John the Baptist did not occur until years later was given by Steiner during the war years (1914 to 1918) when he was asked in connection with *The Fifth Gospel* if the theme could be taken further. He said

---

[7] See: *The Principle of Spiritual Economy*, CW 109; *According to Luke*, CW 114; *Esoteric Christianity and the Mission of Christian Rosenkreutz*, CW 130; *The Gospel of St. Mark*, CW 139; *The Fifth Gospel*, CW 148.

that, as a result of the ongoing war, the spiritual atmosphere was far too turbulent for such research. When the war ended, he was asked this again; he answered that other tasks were then more urgent.[8] Later, however, Rudolf Steiner's "Last Address" on September 28, 1924, showed that the possibility must have presented itself.

During the years from 1904 onward, there were also five spiritually historical important incarnations given for the other John figure, Lazarus–John: Hiram Abiff, Lazarus–John, Christian Rosenkreutz in the thirteenth and fourteenth centuries, and the Count of St. Germain in the eighteenth century.[9] It was explained in the Berlin lecture of November 4, 1904 (CW 93) that the Count of St. Germain was a reincarnation of Christian Rosenkreutz; the connection with Hiram Abiff is clear from the context of the whole lecture, though it was not stated directly. The reincarnation of Hiram as Lazarus–John was first given in a cognitive–ritual working connection at Easter 1908; in the two lectures on September 27 and 28, 1911 (CW 130); in Neuchâtel the two incarnations of Christian Rosenkreutz in the thirteenth and fourteenth centuries were described. The only thing that cannot be exactly dated is the first mention of the connection between Lazarus–John and Christian Rosenkreutz from the point of view of reincarnation, as this was recorded verbally without reference to an exact date.[10]

At Easter 1908, even before any mention of a cognitive–ritual work connection of Lazarus as the reincarnated Hiram Abiff, the Lazarus–John research had been documented in a very special way. This consisted of displaying the Lazarus–John initiation experience of the Apocalypse through the esoteric seals and pillars at

---

8   Friedrich Rittelmeyer in *Rudolf Steiner Enters My Life*.

9   This name was also given to other people, however, "so that not all that is told about the Count of St. Germain can be attributed to the real Christian Rosenkreutz" (Neuchâtel, Sept. 27, 1911).

10 Stated personally by Marie Steiner to Günther Schubert and by the latter to the editor, Hella Wiesberger. Later in 1923, Rudolf Steiner spoke about it again to a small group (c.f. M. Kirschner-Bockholt, *What Is Happening in the Anthroposophical Society*, 1963, nos. 48 and 49).

the Munich Conference at Pentecost 1907. It also formed a fundamental element of the new building plans. In addition, it was made known through pictures and words that the authoritative course of instruction for Western humanity was that of the Christian Rosicrucian way founded by Christian Rosenkreutz.[11] In the lecture during the Congress and in subsequent lectures in 1907, Rudolf Steiner refers repeatedly to this course of instruction and to its founder Christian Rosenkreutz, the great spiritual leader of the West. In one place it is said: "...he has always lived among us and is still with us today as our leader in spiritual life" (Munich, June 1, 1907, Esoteric lesson, CW 264).

The spiritual connection revealed during the Munich Congress between the individuality of Lazarus–John and the new building plans was seen again some years later, also in connection with the new building plans, in Rudolf Steiner's intention to introduce a new way of working together that, in the way it was presented, is directly attributable to the individuality we have known "since earliest times in the West as Christian Rosenkreutz" (Berlin, Dec. 15, 1911, in CW 264). This founding attempt was solemnly announced shortly beforehand on a cognitive–ritual occasion in Stuttgart on November 27, 1911.[12] As nothing else besides this fact has been preserved, it can only be supposed that at that time—it was shortly after the two lectures about the life and work of Christian Rosenkreutz in the thirteenth and fourteenth centuries (Sept., 1911, CW 130)—the incarnation connections of Lazarus–John and Christian Rosenkreutz had been announced for the first time.[13]

---

11   *Rosicrucianism Renewed* (CW 284).

12   Reported by Imme von Eckhardtstein.

13   Certain confirmation of this assumption can be seen in the triptych *Grail* by the artist Anna May, which was painted, according to a statement by Marie Steiner, after the lectures in Neuchâtel. In the middle section it shows the Golgotha scene with Joseph of Arimathea who collects the blood of Christ; on the left side panel are the figures from the Temple Legend; King Solomon, the Queen of Sheba and Hiram Abiff; on the right panel is the initiation of Christian Rosenkreutz in the 13th century, first described

The extent to which the individuality of John the Baptist can also be seen in connection with the building scheme is shown by the following procedures. When the founding ceremony for the building (originally intended to be built in Munich) was planned to take place on May 16, 1912, Rudolf Steiner spoke repeatedly during his time there about the known four incarnations: Elijah, John the Baptist, Raphael, and Novalis; and finally, in Munich, and indeed, on the very day that the founding ceremony would have taken place. As a result of difficulties caused by the authorities, it did not happen there after all. In place of it, however, what underlies the idea of the building (the plan to create a modern, "public" mystery temple) was dramatically and artistically created that summer with the first scenes of the mystery drama, *The Guardian of the Threshold*. This scene takes place in the antechamber of the rooms of a mystic league and many of its members have been invited to be informed of the fact that, through a recently published scientific work, the necessary conditions have now been created for many people not previously admitted to the Sanctuary—because not initiated into its secrets—to now attend. The grand master of the mystic league accounts for this fact in a speech about the continuity of humankind's spiritual leadership, which, following a stage instruction by Rudolf Steiner, takes place in front of the portraits of Elijah, John the Baptist, Raphael, and Novalis hung at the back of the stage. His speech begins with these words:

> In that same spirit's name, which is revealed
> To souls within our sacred shrine, we come
> To those who until now might never hear
> The word that does here secretly sound forth...

In autumn 1920, eight years later, when the building on the Dornach hill near Basel had meanwhile been erected and was in use,

---

by Steiner in Neuchâtel. He also gave Anna May certain instructions about it. See Margarete Hauschka in *Das Goetheanum*, 1975, no. 24, with a monochrome reproduction of the painting; see also Adrian Anderson, *Rudolf Steiner's Esoteric Christianity in the Grail painting by Anna May: Contemplating the sacred in Rosicrucian Christianity* (2017)

Rudolf Steiner reconstructed this same speech into the first person singular, which is a very uncommon form for him to use, and gave it to Marie Steiner to recite from the organ gallery into the two cupola rooms during the first event to take place there:

> In that same spirit's name, which is revealed
> To souls within our place of striving, do I come
> To those who now are eager to accept
> The word that resounds here within their souls.

Through the text, which was included in the artistic program from *The Chemical Wedding of Christian Rosenkreutz, anno 1459*, a different John individuality, Lazarus–John, was also included in this first event taking place in the building.

Then, when Rudolf Steiner ceased his spiritual-scientific lecturing activity in September 1924 (it was exactly four years after the first performance had taken place in the new building in Sept. 1920), the significance of his studies of John came once more vividly to expression. For when, on Sunday, September 28, 1924, the eve of St. Michael's Day, he recovered sufficiently from his serious illness to address the members who were present, what was his concern? The two John individualities! In a deeply moving way he spoke about the four incarnations: Elijah, John, Raphael, and Novalis, in order then to lead on to the results of his new John research—the mysterious connection between the two at the time of the raising of Lazarus. However, his strength did not allow him to explain the results of his new investigation. It was only touched on through the fact that he did not refer, as he had always previously done, to John the Baptist, but to Lazarus–John as the reincarnated Elijah. As this could not be further elaborated it made it difficult for his audience to understand him. Some friends who were able to ask him about it recorded what he said as follows:

> At the awakening of Lazarus, the spiritual being, John the Baptist, who since his death had been the overshadowing Spirit of

the disciples, penetrated from above into Lazarus as far as the consciousness soul; the being of Lazarus himself, from below, intermingled with the spiritual being of John the Baptist from above. After the awakening of Lazarus, this being is Lazarus–John, the disciple whom the Lord loved.

And as further explanation it is recorded:

> Lazarus could develop fully from the earth forces at this time only insofar as the intellectual or mind soul; the Mystery of Golgotha took place during the fourth post-Atlantean period and at that time the intellectual or mind soul was being developed. Therefore, another cosmic being had to lend him the forces from the consciousness soul upward: manas, buddhi, and atman. Through that a human being confronted Christ who extended from the depths of Earth into the highest Heaven and who bore the physical body in perfection throughout all its members into the spiritual bodies of manas, buddhi, and atman, as they will one day be developed by all humankind in a far-distant future.[14]

Concerning the still-unanswered question as to how the union of the two individualities can be understood in the light of succeeding incarnations, Marie Steiner gives the following explanation:

> We are ever and again led to it [the Novalis–Raphael–John–Elijah secret] from the most varied angles. The last, most difficult riddle, because it is intercepted by the line of another's individuality, was given to us on Michaelmas Eve—and then was broken off. Rudolf Steiner did not say all he wanted to say. He gave us the first part of the mystery of Lazarus—at that time he not only said to me, but later wrote it on the cover of the first copy: Do not give it to anyone until I have given the second half. One nevertheless got it from him, as with so

---

14 See Steiner's last address, Sept. 28, 1924, in *Karmic Relations,* vol. 4; also, in German, the study by Adolf Arenson: "Elias–John–Lazarus," contained in *Ergebnisse aus dem Studium der Geisteswissenschaft Rudolf Steiners* (Results of the study of Rudolf Steiner's Spiritual Science), Freiburg im Breisgau, 1980, as also the article by M. Kirschner-Bockholt in *What Is Happening in the Anthroposophical Society,* 1963, nos. 48 and 49.

many other things. Now he will never give the second half. It will be left to our powers of judgment to distinguish between the incarnation and incorporation secrets, the line of interception of individualities. He ended with what had run like a red thread through all his revelations of wisdom, with the mystery of Novalis, Raphael and John.[15]

With that Rudolf Steiner's research into the Hiram–John connection and the mystery of the merging of the two Johns, indicated in his last address, becomes a spiritual legacy that calls upon us to strive continually for an explanation. It is moreover a question, the solving of which is of particular importance for the future. This has been preserved as one of the last utterances of Rudolf Steiner.

Now, indeed, a fully valid answer to the question asked by Marie Steiner about being able to distinguish between the secrets of incarnation and those of incorporation will have to be left to future spiritual investigation. Nevertheless, from the results of research as they are presented here, some light can be shed on the question as to the meaning attached to the merging of the two John individualities. If one brings together the statements made by Rudolf Steiner on various occasions, it becomes apparent that a decisive factor of this explanation will lie in the importance of the Mystery of Golgotha as the "conquest over death by the life of the spirit" (Berlin, Oct. 23, 1908, CW 107). What is to be understood by that follows from the basic explanation of the relationship between individuality and personality.

> One easily confuses the concepts individuality and personality nowadays. The individuality is eternal and persists from one life to the next. Personality is what a person brings to a single life on Earth for its improvement. If we wish to study the individuality we must look at the human soul. If we wish to study the personality we have to look at how the innermost part of our being expresses itself. The innermost part of our being is incarnated into a race and into a profession. All of that determines the inner configuration and makes it personal. In

---

15   See footnote number 3.

the case of those who are at a lower stage of development, one will notice little of the work upon their inner being. The mode of expression, the kind of gestures and so on conform to those of their race. Those who produce their mode of expression and gestures from their inner being, however, are more advanced. The more the inner being of a person is able to work on the exterior the more developed he or she becomes. One could say that the individuality thereby comes to expression within the personality. Those who have their own gestures, their own physiognomy and even have an original character in their way of doing things and in their environment, possess a decided personality. Is that all lost for posterity at death? No, it is not. Christianity knows quite exactly that this is not the case.

What is understood by the resurrection of the flesh or the personality is nothing else than the preservation of what is personal throughout all following incarnations. What we have won as a personality remains in our possession, because it is incorporated into our individuality and is carried forward by it into the following incarnations. If we have made something of our body that is of original character, so will this body and the force that has worked upon it be resurrected. Just so much as we have worked upon ourselves, and what we have made of ourselves, is preserved. (Berlin, March 15, 1906)

The real consciousness of immortality is connected therefore with the personalization of the individuality, the higher spiritual members of the human being. And the fact that this process also signifies the Christianizing of the human being is indicated in the following short commentary to a passage from the so-called Egyptian Gospel:

> There is an ancient writing in which the highest ideal for the development of the "I," Jesus Christ, is characterized by saying, "When the two become one, when the exterior becomes as the interior, then the human being has attained Christ-likeness within himself. This is the meaning of a certain passage in the Egyptian Gospel. (Munich, Dec. 4, 1909, CW 117)

The meaning of what is within and what is without, of individuality and personality, is made even clearer by the interpretation that Rudolf Steiner gives in his lecture in Berlin on May 6, 1909 (CW 57), to the provençal saga of Flor and Blanchflor. This saga stands in close connection with the Hiram–John research, because it relates that the soul renowned as Flor reincarnates in the thirteenth and fourteenth centuries as the founder of Rosicrucianism, the mystery school that has as its task the cultivation of the new Christ Mystery appropriate to the present day. This saga tells the story of a human pair, born on the same day, at the same hour, in the same house, brought up together and united in love from the very beginning. Separated through the ignorance of others, Flor goes in search of Blanchflor. After difficult and life-threatening dangers they are ultimately reunited until their death, which takes place on the same day.

Rudolf Steiner interprets these scenes in the following way: Flor signifies the flower with the red petals, or the rose, Blanchflor is the flower with the white petals, or the lily. Flor, or the rose, is

> the symbol for the human soul that has taken into itself the personality or "I"-impulse. This allows the spirit to work from its individuality that has brought the "I"-impulse down into the red blood. But in the lily one perceives the symbol of the soul, which can remain spiritual only insofar as the "I" remains outside it and only approaches as far as the border. Thus, rose and lily are two opposites. Rose has self-awareness completely within it, lily has it outside itself. But the merging of the soul that is within and the soul that works from without and enlivens the world as the world spirit, was present. The story of Flor and Blanchflor expresses the discovery of the world soul, the world-"I," by the human soul, the human "I." ... What can unite with the Mystery of Golgotha was envisaged in the union of the lily soul and the rose soul. (Berlin, May 6, 1909, CW 57)

When it is said that the uniting of the soul that is within and the soul that enlivens the world from without as the world-spirit "was present," it is surely the uniting of the Christ principle as the highest spiritual principle with the personality, the earthly body of Jesus of Nazareth, that is referred to. For only through the fact that these two have fully united as far as the physical could earthly death be truly conquered.

How far the contrast of the rose soul and lily soul can be applied to the two John individualities is shown by the fact that Hiram-Lazarus is always characterized as the representative of the forces of personality, whereas the Elijah-soul is often described as such a highly spiritual being that he can only be loosely connected with his earthly vessels, as was also the case with John the Baptist.[16] If the uniting of the rose soul and lily soul can lead to union with the Mystery of Golgotha, so may we conclude—in view of the merging of the two John souls at the raising of Lazarus by Jesus Christ—that the disciple whom the Lord loved has become the being to whom the Christ secret of the overcoming of death had become attached and remains so, as expressed in the words that refer to Christian Rosenkreutz: "With this individuality and its activity since the thirteenth century [by having experienced another initiation] we connect all that includes for us the continuation of the impulse given by the appearance of Jesus Christ on Earth and through the accomplishment of the Mystery of Golgotha" (Berlin, Dec. 22, 1912, CW 141).

A further aspect follows from this if we combine the words from the Egyptian Gospel: "When the two become one and the exterior becomes the interior" with the second half of the saying: "and the male becomes like the female, so that there is neither masculine nor feminine." This latter word points to the fact that there will be no more death when sexuality ceases, for death and sexuality are mutually dependent on one another. Hiram Abiff already was promised in the Temple Legend that a son would be born to him, who, even though he would not see him himself, would give rise to

---

[16] See the lecture in Berlin, Dec. 14, 1911, CW 61; also Steiner, *The Gospel of St. Mark* (CW 139).

a new race of human beings, which, according to Rudolf Steiner, would not know death, because propagation would come about by means of speech and the word connected with the heart and not by means of death-bringing sexuality (Berlin, Oct. 23, 1905, CW 93). Thus, according to the lecture in Cologne on December 2, 1905 (CW 97), the perfecting of the human race will come about through the raising of the forces of propagation from the womb to the heart, and the "soul power of John" will be the force that will raise "streams of spiritual love" to ray forth from the loving heart. This is hinted at in the Gospel when it describes the scene at the Last Supper in which the disciple whom the Lord loved, who knew the secret of evolution, raised himself from the lap of Christ to His breast.

Against this background all the documents that recount the initiation experiences of the Hiram–Lazarus–John individuality in the various incarnations,[17] as well as the cosmic deed of Christian Rosenkreutz at the beginning of the seventeenth century—by which it was to have been made possible to overcome the polarity of Cain and Abel, both in the single human being as well as in humanity as a whole[18]—point to the central Christian secret of the conquest of death.

Rudolf Steiner himself also saw the goal of his activity along these lines. That shines out in what he said at the founding of the Cognitive–Ritual Working Group when he said that the significance of the theosophical [anthroposophic] movement, lay in the fact that neither purely male nor purely female, but wisdom that is beyond sex [or gender], should be prepared there on a spiritual level, which would later take place on the physical plane: "The Reunification of the Sexes" (Berlin, Oct. 23, 1905, CW 93). In addition to that, not only the fully equal cooperation between men and women, which has everywhere been put into practice by him even in ritual matters, but also the words he spoke during the same lecture: "I have

---

17   See *The Temple Legend,* CW 93.
18   See *Esoteric Christianity and the Mission of Christian Rosenkreutz,* CW 130.

reserved for myself the task of uniting the members of Abel's race with those of Cain," receives a very special meaning in the context of practical application.

And through this it becomes understandable again why the Hiram–John research stands like Alpha and Omega at the beginning and end of his spiritual–scientific lecturing activity and runs through the intervening years like a red thread through the whole of his life's work.

13

WAS RUDOLF STEINER A FREEMASON?

Marie Steiner

We are shown in the work of Rudolf Steiner that in ancient times mysteries existed for initiation, through which human souls were raised up to a participation in the life of the spirit. From them were derived the impulses from which sprang the great civilizations of the past that are known to us. In them was practiced the secret knowledge, the science of the spirit, which was at the height of its development in those days and found its outward expression in the polytheistic religions. The counselors of kings and those great leaders of humankind who were chosen to be the innovators of new cultural achievements came from these mysteries. The wisdom that they acquired was the unifying bond amid the comings and goings and repercussions of nations. The fruits of every civilization were watched over and preserved for the progress of humankind and handed on from generation to generation. They formed a second current alongside what flowed directly from spiritual sources but faded in the consciousness of the majority of people to the same degree as the knowledge of the physical objects became more acute and comprehensive. The soul lost all memory of its origin. The time arrived when not only the single nations but the whole of humankind would have succumbed to decadence if the Christ event had not taken place.

To point out the significance of the Christ event in the revivifying of humanity with all that it implied was the task to which Rudolf

Steiner dedicated his life. For that, he had to draw together all the wisdom that had been collected by humankind until that moment and to irradiate with his light every branch of this learning, both exoteric and arcane. To the arcane knowledge belong the ancient lost mysteries: the dust that had settled over them had to be cleared away, in a figurative sense, like the archaeologists who have to clear away the dust from ancient temple sites. But the most important thing to be saved was the living substance that still coursed through the mysteries, resting on old tradition but already falling ever more into rigidity and decay through their human exponents. Without revivification through the infusion of Christianity, without an understanding of this greatest of all mysteries, the ancient wisdom could only lead to aberration in the course of time.

Rudolf Steiner had a comprehensive insight into these connections, because of his philosophically based and organically developed Spiritual Science. That is the reason why he regarded it as his task at that time, when approached by such circles as practiced the ancient esoteric knowledge—either from tradition or because of fresh stimulation—to make his knowledge available to them, not rejecting what they asked of him but accepting it cautiously. He never sought contact with such circles, but wherever they approached him for elucidation or instruction, he did not refuse to provide them with it. That was a service to humanity on his part.

The efforts made by those who represented the Theosophical Society, who would have liked to see him in their midst, were initially rejected emphatically by him, for the Theosophical Society worked along one-sided Eastern lines and in many cases moved in a medium of dilettantism, or psychic phenominalism. But a basis for an understanding of true Christian esotericism was especially lacking. Only when German theosophists wished to found an independent section under his leadership and consequently on the basis of Western Christian esotericism, did he feel it his duty to comply with their request.

Was Rudolf Steiner a Freemason?

After a number of years, when Annie Besant, the later president of the Theosophical Society, tried to prevent this work for living Christianity, the separation from the Theosophical Society took place and the Anthroposophical Society was established. Rudolf Steiner details these events in his *Autobiography*.

The other suggestion came from the direction fostered by Medieval Christian esotericism on the basis of ancient mystery knowledge. It laid value on its historical continuity stretching back to the times when esoteric knowledge was engendered in Egyptian temples. In their manifold ramifications, which developed over the course of centuries, the circles coming from the various mystical currents took what seemed spiritually appropriate and beneficial to them, especially the impulses of the Crusades, the "Bauhütten" unions (working masons' clubs), etc. They survived under various names, such as Freemasonry Union, Order of the Illuminati, and so on.

As time went on, however, they began to lose their erstwhile knowledge and drift further and further from their original goals. They then succumbed to rationalism and often to atheism, and their unions started to serve political, commercial or charitable ends. The disappointment of those who joined them to gain a knowledge of the spirit became ever greater. Ever more frequently those who were disappointed came to Rudolf Steiner to tell him that they only now understood, through his publicly given lectures on Spiritual Science what lay behind the symbols, which none of their members understood. Many deplored the fact that they were serving untruth because they repeated time-honored formulas that manifest a belief in a divine spirit, but at the same time they were completely skeptical about the content of what they professed. And one could encounter a great longing to experience something of the solemnity with which the ancient rites had been connected at one time. Freemasonry was revealed as a current that was obsolete and becoming submerged, whose outer organism was vulnerable to the powers of opposition, yes, had even fallen prey to them already.

However, what had been preserved of the truth in these thousands of years old endeavors would and must continue to serve the rehabilitation of humanity in a changed form. That was the task that confronted Rudolf Steiner when it was suggested to him by those circles that he should found an independent organization on the strength of historically legal documentation. This suggestion was made to him by a spiritually aspiring person who had formed the opinion that Rudolf Steiner knew more about spiritual matters than all the others put together. The suggestion was then officially confirmed by someone who was more concerned with practical advantage and possessed a very indifferent attitude toward spiritual aspects. It was not Rudolf Steiner's task to pry into this person's past, nor was it his intention to maintain a relationship with him.

Many of the officials, not only of esoteric societies but also the dignitaries of the Church and other institutions, often prove unworthy of their high office. The fact that the various Freemasonry orders (as it now appears from their writings) do not acknowledge one another is something they have in common with other human institutions, and it would take much time and pains, as well as legal ingenuity, to sort it out. Rudolf Steiner, however, had to take into account something that is of decisive importance to everyone who represents spiritual truths—the historical connection to an ancient, time-honored (though *time-altered* in form) spiritual current—in order to rescue it from decadence, insofar as he could. By accepting it he could preserve what truth it contained and waken it to new life in order for it to serve the progress of humankind in accordance with the forces of consciousness that now prevail. In terms appropriate to the consciousness soul, the ancient symbols could be made to live again through the medium of art to inspire the whole of humanity.

Rudolf Steiner made one condition. He would implement the historically legal union, within the degrees appointed him to carry out the work independently—with that, however, their relationship should end. No further claim should be made on him either in respect of their cooperative activities or in human, social, or organizational matters. Nothing but an outward, non-obligatory formality should be practiced, no work at all done in conjunction with one another! The newly founded, completely independent circle, which had been recruited from those theosophists who desired to approach this kind of Western esotericism in this way, were introduced to the ancient symbols, first in a graphically explicit manner and then increasingly according to their inner nature until they had been worked through by consciousness. In this way their connection with vague and mystical feeling was severed and artistic and scientific life was made available to them. *When war broke out in August 1914, Rudolf Steiner declared that the study group formed in this way under the name* Mystica aeterna *had been annulled, and as a sign thereof he tore up the relevant document.*[1] The group never met again in this connection.

With that is clearly stated the reason for the seeming contradiction that some people say Rudolf Steiner was a high-degree brother, whereas others state that he never belonged to the brotherhood at all. Rudolf Steiner in fact never belonged to the Order of Freemasons. He was completely estranged from their company and was even

---

[1] It must strike anyone who tries to arrive at the truth concerning Freemasonry literature that Rudolf Steiner is never mentioned therein, except in cases of outright rejection, and except for three isolated examples (out of a possible 200 publications) his writings do not appear in the great *Bibliography of Freemasonry Literature* by Wolfstieg (4 vols., 1911–1926), which encompasses the contents of all Freemasonry lodge libraries with 54,320 entries. Experts should also be aware of the fact that such titles as Misraim, Memphis, OTO (Oriental Templar Order), referring to the documents in question, were for Rudolf Steiner just empty husks robbed of their content and long since reduced to mere names. (This footnote is not from Marie Steiner, but from the editor of the *Newsletter,* C. S. Picht, who had never seen the aforementioned document. It did not exist in Marie Steiner's manuscript preserved in the archive, nor was it her way to search through 54,000 entries of a bibliography to find exactly three titles. Picht, however, was a very capable person, who performed a great service in developing the bibliography for Rudolf Steiner's work.)

strongly attacked by them, for since the beginning of his theosophical–anthroposophic activity he had revealed through his teachings what they regarded as the secrets that gave them their authority and respect. He laid bare esoteric knowledge because humanity was in need of it, and it is a requirement of the age we live in. He at the same time kindled an understanding for it. In order to bring new life into the ancient symbols in a proper fashion through a formally constituted work group attached to a historical current, he pledged himself by an outward contract and stood aside from any dealings with Freemason brothers. Thus the term *high-degree brother*, which his enemies liked to bandy about, since it was no longer possible for them to label him a "Jew," is actually misleading. Because Rudolf Steiner had never had any connection with any sort of Freemasonry order, but the name "Freemason" was to have made it look as though he had, a certain mood was thereby to have been created so that people would not try to come to terms with the Spiritual Science founded and developed by Rudolf Steiner. If they had done so, the contrast to Freemasonry would have become immediately clear to them. From his knowledge of the fact that the present-day inclination of the human soul is such that one cannot inwardly accept the esoteric and that what is hidden must be brought to light, Rudolf Steiner made his Spiritual Science fully public.

Through that he made possible a true understanding of Christianity and showed the way and the method by which modern human beings can fulfill their life's tasks through a realization of spiritual facts. It will be of decisive importance for the destiny of the future how Rudolf Steiner's Spiritual Science, which is not restricted to secret circles nor practiced from the point of view of power politics but is available to all people, will be accepted in the consciousness of the present day.[2]

---

2   Originally published in *Anthroposophie. Zeitschrift für freies Geistesleben* (Anthroposophy. Magazine for independent spiritual life), year 16, vol. 3, Apr.–June, 1934, Stuttgart (C. S. Picht, ed.).

14

CLARIFYING RUDOLF STEINER'S CONNECTION WITH THEODOR REUSS

Rudolf Steiner's chapter in his *Autobiography*, as well as Marie Steiner's article, "Was Rudolf Steiner a Freemason?" (both of which deals with the second part of the Esoteric School[1]) have avowedly an apologetic character. This, together with certain difficulties of understanding, led to the fact that authors such as Möller and Howe,[2] even anthroposophic authors, have not actually taken what was said there seriously. To politically colored thinking today, it seems difficult to understand that one can oppose a false claim merely because it is not true; it believes that one must look for an attempted cover-up or hidden motive in such an objectively presented defense.

The libel and slander just mentioned, to which Rudolf Steiner refers in chapter 68 of his *Autobiography*, have as their real core the fact that he entered a contract with Theodor Reuss (1855–1923) that allowed him to set up the second part, or section (of the Esoteric School), in connection to the stream of the high-degree Freemasonry

---

1   Both are included in this volume.
2   Helmut Möller and Ellie Howe, *Merlin Pelegrinus: On the Background of the West* (1986). The authors of these extensive monographs on the life and activities of Theodor Reuss belong to the Freemasonry research lodge, Quatuor Coronati.

represented by John Yarker (1833–1913).³ The slanderers and libelers assumed from this that he had a close working relationship to Reuss, which led to who knows what. In fact, however, Reuss's significance for Rudolf Steiner's activity was purely accidental. Significance of this kind was had by every railroad official who sold him a train ticket to wherever he held a lecture.

Originally, the slander and libel were invented by Max Kully, the priest in Arlesheim (the village next to Dornach), who persecuted Rudolf Steiner through ardent hatred. From his malicious writings, his claims went on into the "literature" of the opponents, right on into Frick's *Licht und Finsternis* (Light and darkness), and beyond.

At the same time, it is easy to understand why no word of the slander and libel is true. Thus, for example, Möller and Howe come to the conclusion in their book (published in 1986) that Rudolf Steiner's relationship with Reuss was merely of a "superficial nature," although they pulled chapter 68 of *Autobiography* to pieces. One will have to grant them in this connection that they did not know about the documents that would have been so important for their examinations but were not published until 1987 (in CW 265), and that this chapter 68 (as well as others) must remain difficult to understand for thinking that cannot conceive of spiritual realities. Möller and Howe do not substantiate their conclusion further, because in this area it is normally somewhat awkward and complicated to prove the nonexistence of something. One must therefore assume that this conclusion resulted from data that was generally available up to 1986. This was negative; Rudolf Steiner's name appeared only twice in editions of the *Oriflamme*,⁴ the house periodical by Reuss that contained "official announcements" of the "Order of the Ancient Freemasonry of Scottish, Memphis and

---

3   This lecture is included in CW 265 and as a facsimile in Peter-R. König's *Der grosse Theodor Reus Reader* (The large Theodor Reuss reader), 1997.

4   To a great extent, printed again by Peter-R. König. the *Oriflamme* can be found only in *Der Kleinen Theodor Reuss Reader* (The small Theodor Reuss reader) by the same author, Munich 1993, but not as a facsimile.

Clarifying Rudolf Steiner's Connection with Theodor Reuss

Misraim Rite." These two times were the announcement at Easter 1906 of the permission granted for the establishment of the Mystica aeterna chapter.[5] At the same time, in the advertising section of the *Oriflamme*, there was an ad for the magazine *Lucifer*, published by Dr. Rudolf Steiner. It is not known whether the advertisement was a paid ad or a friendly gesture on the part of Reuss or just an attempt to make a big show. However, Rudolf Steiner's name did not appear in the "schema" of the *Oriflamme* of December 1909, in which Reuss listed all of the important officials of the order. Moreover, Steiner did not appear in the photo gallery of the prominent people of the order in the *Oriflamme* of 1912. It is significant that Steiner's name never surfaced in any of the announcements given in the *Oriflamme* by Reuss and the great officials of the order. From this absence alone it follows that no common bond existed with Reuss, much less any collaboration.

One of the problems that Möller and Howe, and others, have with this issue is the question of why Rudolf Steiner became involved with Reuss in the first place.[6] The answer is quite simple. The *problem*, however, arises naturally only in the aftermath. When Rudolf Steiner negotiated with Reuss, Reuss's reputation was not the best, but not nearly as bad as it was many years later after he connected with Aleister Crowley. Reuss's somewhat poor reputation in 1905 had *absolutely nothing* to do with Rudolf Steiner,[7] for whom the *person* of Reuss played absolutely no role. Reuss was simply the man authorized by Yarker to handle things in Germany; one could not go around him in a fair way of working.

Despite that, it would be interesting to learn how this meeting of the two came about. Rudolf Steiner gave the main details about it in chapter 68 of his *Autobiography*, and there is no rational reason to doubt the truth of this presentation, even if given in

---

5   Included in CW 265.
6   Möller and Howe.
7   Letter to Sellin in CW 265 and in the addendum to chapter 9 in this volume.

an apologetic connection. However, only a little is known about the exact, though unimportant, details. One will have to connect this bit of knowledge with what can otherwise be known: John Yarker in England was the Grand Master of the Memphis–Misraim Rite and of some other Orders. Reuss, together with Dr. Franz Hartmann and Heinrich Klein, had received his charter for Germany from him. Hartmann and Reuss were long-time members of the Theosophical Society. Yarker, a friend of H. P. Blavatsky and Garibaldi, was a significant person for the theosophical and Freemasonry connections; he even participated in the founding of the Theosophical Society in 1875.[8]

After *Isis Unveiled* was published, he admitted H. P. Blavatsky into his High Degree Freemasonry and awarded her the highest degree in the Rite of Adoption.[9] She negotiated with him for the introduction of a ritual in the Theosophical Society, which, however, never came about.[10] Annie Besant sought to be admitted into the Memphis–Misraim Rite, but she was turned down because Mrs. Alice Leighton Cleather objected.[11]

In 1891, she was in the Council of the "Esoteric School of Theosophy" under H. P. Blavatsky, but in 1895 she went with Judge to became an active member in the "Theosophical Society in England," which was under his direction.[12] She must have been apparently quite influential in the Memphis–Misraim Rite and naturally, because of the Judge case,[13] had nothing good to say about Annie Besant. (After this rejection, Annie Besant joined the "Droit Humain" in Paris.) Another member of the Council of the Esoteric School of

---

8   CW 265 and here in chap. 9, concerning the interrelationship of Blavatsky, Garibaldi and Yarker; also Sylvia Cranston, *H.P.B.*

9   Sylvia Cranston.

10 Josephine Ransom, *A Short History of the Theosophical Society.*

11 From the postcard from Reuss to Rudolf Steiner on Feb. 14, 1906.

12 N.N., *The Theosophical Movement 1875–1925*, New York 1925.

13 About this, see chapter 7 of this volume.

Theosophy in 1891 was W. Wynn Westcott.[14] He, too, belonged to Yarker's Order complex. He was, among other things, Director of the "Societas Rosicruciana in Anglia" (Rosicrucian Society of England) and was the intermediary for the coming together of Reuss and Yarker.[15] All of this demonstrates how close the relationship was between Blavatsky's Theosophical Society and Yarker's orders. There is an inner consequence from the fact that Rudolf Steiner connected his symbolic–cultic work to the Yarker stream, just as when he connected the first Section of the Esoteric School to Blavatsky's Esoteric School after he decided to place his teaching activity into the framework of the Theosophical Society. With the continuation of the impulse in these three characteristics of spiritual life, he fulfilled one of the laws for esoteric teaching: continuity.

In her previously mentioned essay, Marie Steiner reports on how Rudolf Steiner came to encounter the Memphis–Misraim Rite:

> That was the task that confronted Rudolf Steiner when it was suggested to him by those circles that he should found an independent organization on the strength of historically legal documentation. This suggestion was made to him by a spiritually aspiring person who had formed the opinion that Rudolf Steiner knew more about spiritual matters than all the others put together. The suggestion was then officially confirmed by someone who was more concerned with practical advantage and possessed a very in different attitude toward spiritual aspects. It was not Rudolf Steiner's task to pry into this person's past, nor was it his intention to maintain a relationship with him. Many of the officials, not only of esoteric societies, but also the dignitaries of the Church and other institutions, often prove unworthy of their high office.

When it was said, "officially confirmed by someone," Reuss is meant. However, neither the date nor the name of the person who

---

14 N.N., *The Theosophical Movement*.
15 Möller and Howe.

made the original suggestion were given. Also, there is nothing more to be found in the Rudolf Steiner Archive, except that Marie Steiner had reported that he was Czechoslovakian. Apparently, this person was a member both of the Memphis–Misraim Rite and the Theosophical Society and must have been part of the Rudolf Steiner's audience in Germany, since Steiner's lectures in Prague began in 1907. Perhaps this person was even in the German Esoteric School.

Steiner describes this initial encounter:

> A few years after the beginning of the activity in the Theosophical Society, Marie von Sivers and I were offered, from a particular side, the leadership of a society that was of the kind that had preserved the old symbolism and cultic events in which the "old wisdom" was incorporated.... I therefore took the Certificate of the Society mentioned that lay in the stream represented by Yarker.

He abbreviated his presentation here by passing over the details and uniting the initiatives of the Czechoslovakians with Reuss. With the "leadership" is most likely meant one that was yet to be created, and not one that already existed. One could also read it differently, because Reuss, who was about to leave Germany, intended to give the "jurisdiction over all of the existing organizations of the Rite and the Order in the German realm" to Rudolf Steiner. This is how it is according to the contract that Reuss and Rudolf Steiner entered into on January 3, 1906, and which regulated the relationship between Rudolf Steiner's chapters of Mystica aeterna and Reuss's order. Reuss kept this contract hidden from his order, and it was made public only in 1987 in the framework of Rudolf Steiner's Collected Works with the documents concerned with the cognitive–ritual section. The important stipulations of the contract are:

1. Rudolf Steiner was entitled independently to admit members into his Chapter according to his choice and had sole jurisdiction over these.

2. For each candidate for membership an entrance fee of 40 Marks was to be paid to Reuss. Reuss was not obliged to report on the use of these funds.
3. Once Rudolf Steiner paid the fee for 100 members, he should receive full jurisdiction over the whole order, as quoted.

The text of the quite long-winded, complicated contract certainly comes from Reuss and is his paraphrasing of what was negotiated orally. Although there is no record of it, we know what Rudolf Steiner wanted: to create a formal historical connection to the Yarker stream with the right to set up independently a symbolic–cultic activity of his own creation. Independence meant here, among other things, not to be bound organizationally as part of the Reuss Order. That corresponded to the third stipulation that, in Reuss's eyes, would solve two problems at the same time. However, Reuss had presumably not understood what Rudolf Steiner wanted. As he absolutely did not bother any further about the Order and even denied the rest of the members of the Order admittance to his events,[16] Reuss found an excuse to separate the three united Rites: the Scottish Rite, the Memphis Rite and the Misraim Rite[17] and confer upon Rudolf Steiner the office of Grand General Master only of the Misraim Rite. That this separation is connected with Rudolf Steiner is quite clear; it fit exactly in the time plan. In fall 1906 it was foreseen that the stipulated number of 100 members in the Mystica aeterna would be reached in the spring. The edict of September 10 about the separation fixes the date of the separation at June 24, 1907.

On October 1, 1906, Reuss wrote to Marie von Sivers: "I hope you will have the 'hundred members' by St. John's Tide, on June 24, 1907, so that the office is then officially conferred upon you."

This separation of the Misraim Rite in 1907 did not hinder Reuss from continuing to refer to himself as the Grand Master also

---

16 Letter to Sellin, CW 265 and in chapter 9 of this volume.
17 Edict of Sept. 10, 1906, in the *Oriflamme*, July–Dec. 1906. CW 265.

of the Misraim Rite. The following shows just how dubious his titles were. In 1902 Westcott authorized him to install a German branch of the "Rosicrucian Society of England." This branch was, however, already declared to be closed in 1907 by the High Council in London.[18] Thus also here, Reuss did not keep to the facts and continued to use the title "Supreme Magnus of the Brotherhood of the Rosy Cross."[19]

After Easter 1906, Reuss published the grant of permission for the Mystica aeterna in his *Oriflamme*. This act must have been felt to be in violation of the agreements, as it represented an attempt to draw Rudolf Steiner into the Reuss organization. It was possibly one of the reasons that Rudolf Steiner broke off all contact with Reuss in the summer of 1906. The reason Marie von Sivers continue any contact at all was because of the necessary correspondence concerning admittance fees. In his letter to Marie Steiner; Sellin called this publishing of the permission an "indiscretion." In June 1907, Reuss sent the document containing the conferring of the Misraim Rite upon Rudolf Steiner. This is the last official document in connection with Reuss.[20] It was not published in the *Oriflamme*.

In addition to the official documents, there are the letters (or postcards) from Reuss in the Rudolf Steiner Archive. It appears that they have all been almost completely preserved, with one exception yet to be discussed. There are three letters to Steiner from spring 1906; one letter of February 11, 1910; and twenty-one letters to Marie von Sivers from 1906 to 1918. All of the letters were brief—none more than a page—and almost all were handwritten. The letters to Reuss are not there, because at that time both Rudolf Steiner and Marie von Sivers almost always wrote their letters by hand and

---

18 Möller and Howe.

19 CW 265; and Peter-R. König.

20 Printed in CW 265 and as a facsimile with Peter-R. König.

made no copies. Apparently, the Reuss estate in which one would look for the originals was lost. There are, however, four drafts of letters from Marie von Sivers to Reuss that have been preserved. From 1906 until the outbreak of World War I in 1914, Reuss had lived in London and visited Germany only occasionally.

The content of the letters from Reuss were quite banal, having to do almost only with requests for money, receipts, New Year's greetings. One must consider this correspondence as a whole—one can find hardly anything meaningful in the individual letters. Therefore, the following relevant passages are brought out.

Above all, these letters are informative because of what is missing in them, especially: Reuss never once mentions a conversation that had taken place or a single letter he received from Rudolf Steiner. Reuss was quite accurate in his correspondence. He confirmed the receipt of the letters from Marie von Sivers explicitly each time, even with their dates. It is reasonably certain that Reuss received no letter from Rudolf Steiner after the spring of 1906, and apparently not before that either.

And the other way around, Rudolf Steiner seems to have tossed into the wastebasket the few letters—unanswered—addressed to him from Reuss after the summer of 1906, with the exception of the letter in 1910. Two such letters were mentioned in correspondence with Marie von Sivers—one was even sent as certified mail. Reuss complained that he had not received a reply to them, and these letters are not in the archive. This is the previously mentioned exception. One should note this break, this important point, in the summer of 1906.

In letters to Marie von Sivers, Reuss asked repeatedly for a personal conversation with Rudolf Steiner: on October 1, 1906—on February 9; March 3, 1907; February 24, 1908; and July 17, 1909. In the beginning, he used an urgent tone and eventually expressed resignation. "Wouldn't a meeting be useful" (Feb. 24, 1908). "On September 3, I go to Germany for four weeks and would very much like to speak with Dr. Steiner *anywhere!* Please request of Dr. Steiner that he kindly let me know when and where we could meet" (July 17, 1909). As stated, there is nothing in the letters to indicate that his request was granted.

A letter of February 2, 1907, is especially significant. "I find his [Steiner's] previous conduct to be extremely prudent, as it was the only weapon for protecting his work from the flashing serpent's tongue. Because of that there will be no communication by letter; but I must speak with him because we need to reach an understanding about a certain point. Be so kind as to let me know where and when I can meet Dr. Steiner on April 11, 12, or 13."

Beyond this letter, the relationship between Reuss and Rudolf Steiner was mentioned only once more. This was in a letter of February 11, 1910, and was perhaps the reason it landed in the wastebasket—and probably through Marie von Sivers.[21] In this letter, written in English, Reuss reports that Dr. Franz Hartmann, who had not been active in Freemasonry matters for four years, got in touch with him and had intended to make things difficult for Rudolf Steiner. Reuss went on to say, "I beg to add for your information and guidance that no one (except Heilbronner and Klein), not even Dr. Lauer, is in my confidence as to our actual relations, or as to our written agreement of January 1906." Thus, only Klein and Heilbronner knew the content of the contract of January 3, 1906, and that was the independence of the Mystica aeterna from Reuss and the 40-Mark admittance fee—a quite significant private source of income for Reuss that he certainly did not want to see endangered.

Strictly speaking, there is yet another letter about this relationship to Reuss—*not about how it was, of course, but rather how Reuss imagined it in the beginning.* It is the second of the three letters in the spring of 1906, and for the purpose of illustration it is presented here in its entirety.

---

21 The whole letter is printed in Peter-R. König.

Grand Orient of the Ancient and Accepted Scottish Rite, 33°
Sovereign Sanctuary of the Order of the Old Freemason
Rites of Memphis and Misraim

London, March, 1906

Honorable Brother Dr. Steiner,
Dear Sir and Brother,

I hereby request that you send all of your correspondence and fee remittances to: Theodor Reuss, c/o Henry Klein, Redcote, Burwood Park Road, Walton-on-Thames, where you should also kindly send the list of the candidates who have been admitted up to now. Mr. Emil Adriányi (who was admitted at the time free of charge, due to a lack of funds, into the Order and into the Degree of Sovereign Sanctuary) spreads false reports that the Grand-Orient and the Sovereign Sanctuary of Berlin no longer exist! I am sending letters immediately to counter this and ask that you do the same. I will let the Supreme Councils know that you represent me.

With brotherly greetings,
Theodor Reuss

Since nothing is known about this communication to the Supreme Councils, it may be that Reuss was prevented at the right moment from sending it. However, this letter shows how Reuss considered the situation to be.

On February 14, 1906, Reuss wrote to Rudolf Steiner: "Please kindly tell me which candidates I should enter into the Order's register." And on April 12, 1906, he wrote, "I sent the certificates by certified mail to you for your first four members. I could not send the certificates for the other sixteen, because you have not yet sent their names to me." He last time he asked about those names was in a letter to Marie von Sivers on May 19, 1906: "I hereby confirm to you gratefully the receipt of 400 Marks for ten candidates and allow myself to ask politely for the communication of their names."

This is the last letter in which the certificates and names were mentioned, and all of these letters were from before the decisive point of the summer of 1906. The names of the members were not sent to Reuss, in keeping with the agreed-upon autonomy of the Mystica aeterna. It is no longer possible to reconstruct how the first four names came to be known. However, one must draw the conclusion that these four certificates were not handed out by Rudolf Steiner, but were destroyed instead.

The admittance fees were no longer sent with each admission, but Marie von Sivers sent a payment on account once a year. The work of the Mystica aeterna was stopped with the outbreak of World War I in the summer of 1914, after more than six hundred members had been admitted. In spite of the fact that there are letters from as late as 1918 that had to do exclusively—with one exception—with the final invoicing, he continued to find something more that he believed he could demand. The exception is the letter he wrote to Marie Steiner on July 12, 1917, in which he had the insolence to give her an invitation to go, as a faithful representative, to the Congress of the OTO in Ascona.

As we can see, this correspondence consists of only banalities; from a higher perspective, even the slightest philosophical, literary, artistic reflection was absolutely, completely missing. This is not surprising, of course, since Reuss naturally sensed the superiority of Rudolf Steiner and Marie von Sivers. His tone was thoroughly polite and respectful; the tone had no similarity to that of the letters between Reuss and his friends that were printed in the *Oriflamme*. It is wholly through the inquiry that common intentions could have formed a basis for any work in common. It was even stated explicitly that no written (personal) contact or relationship took place. An oral relationship of any significance was impossible, since Reuss was in England the whole time. Even for insignificant, rarely possible agreements to "meet Dr. Steiner anywhere for an hour," there is no evidence.

Clarifying Rudolf Steiner's Connection with Theodor Reuss

Among the documents that have been preserved, the only fact that can be found is that Rudolf Steiner ended his relationship with Reuss during the summer of 1906. Unfortunately, the reason and how it occurred were not given. It was clear from the beginning that their connection did not require a working relationship, at least from Rudolf Steiner's side. It was also clear that Reuss was undependable.[22] This would not have precluded a simple written contact, as it did in fact begin at first. Something must have happened in the spring or summer that caused Rudolf Steiner to tell Reuss or directed that Reuss be informed that he did not wish further contact with him and that he should contact Marie von Sivers concerning fees. Certainly this was formulated in Rudolf Steiner's characteristic polite and friendly way; drafts of Marie von Sivers' letters were of this nature. Consequently, Reuss did not actually perceive the earnestness behind the words and thus repeatedly tried to make contact. We have only assumptions about the reason or reasons for Rudolf Steiner's withdrawal. One reason that might have been Reuss's worsening reputation at the beginning of 1906. Along with this is what Rudolf Steiner wrote to A. W. Sellin in August 1906:

> What I have established, therefore, has nothing to do with what formally pretended to hold "Memphis and Misraim degrees." And what goes on around the Order of Reuss and his associates is absolutely no concern to me. There have even been naïve people coming to visit me in order to bargain with me about what they know of Reuss, or even to "warn" me about him. But actually that does not affect me in the least.[23]

An important reason might have been that Reuss did not honor the agreement and tried to claim Rudolf Steiner for himself and his Order, as shown in the unreasonable requests that he serve as Reuss's representative in Berlin and in the indiscreet publication of the grant of permission for the Mystica aeterna at Easter 1906.

---

22 Letter to Marie von Sivers in CW 265 and in chapter 9 of this volume.
23 Letter to Sellin, CW 265 and in chapter 9 of this volume.

The slander and libel mentioned at the beginning peaked with the claim that Rudolf Steiner had played a role as Grand Master of Reuss's Ordo Templi Orientis, the OTO. That this claim is false is nearly proven by what has already been said up to this point; this OTO must only yet be characterized somewhat.

There is no trace of a normal establishment of the OTO. It seemed to come into existence with the September 1912 Jubilee edition of the *Oriflamme*. The myth of the origin of this order is as follows:

> The Rosicrucian, esoteric teachings of the Hermetic Brotherhood of Light were reserved for the few initiated of the occult inner circle. The cognitive stages of this inner circle ran parallel with the highest degrees of the Memphis–Misraim Rite, and those "'initiates" form the secret core of the Oriental Templar Order [OTO].

That is pure pseudo-esoteric pretentiousness with jargon borrowed from Reuss's superficial acquaintance with Theosophy—neither with the teaching nor with the occult circle was there sufficiency. This Jubilee Edition includes paradoxically a photo gallery of those secret, "initiated ones": Reuss, Heinrich Klein, Dr. Carl Lauer, Andreas Ullmer, Paul Kirmiss, Aleister Crowley—and posthumously, Dr. Carl Kellner, and even the well-known Dr. Franz Hartmann who had just died and with whom Reuss had already been feuding since at least 1906.[24] If Reuss had gained the opportunity to receive Rudolf Steiner into the assembly in order to draw other people—which he had done in an unauthorized fashion with Hartmann—he certainly would have done it.

As of 1912, Möller and Howe say:

> Unfortunately, it also remains unclear exactly when the Occult Inner Circle became the OTO. Nonetheless, in the account of the Jubilee Edition, there is a claim by Adriányi that, although

---

24 See both letters about Hartmann in Peter-R. König.

at the beginning no one "initiated" had held a high rank in the Memphis and Misraim hierarchy, "until the appearance [of the Jubilee Edition]...nothing was known about the existence of an OTO" (*Weimar Freimauer Zeitung* [Weimar Freemason newspaper], no. 11, 1979). Also [Paul] Eberhardt, who, as Grand Master of the Scottish Rite associated with Reuss from 1906 to 1909, put the date of the OTO as 1912 in his 1914 Winkel lodge book. This was ascertained directly or indirectly by the corresponding contemporaries. By contrast, immediately after the appearance of Eberhardt's book, Reuss turned to *Die freimauerische Presse Deutschlands* [The Freemason Press of Germany] with an explanation: He himself had sent Eberhardt a copy of the "Constitution of the Order [thus, in 1912] from this he must see that the Constitution of the...Order of the Oriental Templars [OTO] is dated January 1906." Adriányi believed this...to be predated.[25]

Meanwhile, there appears on page 14 of the Jubilee edition the likely actual reason that the OTO had formed. A foundation document of June 1, 1912, was made known for the National Grand Lodge in Great Britain and Ireland—with Aleister Crowley as "National Grand Master" of the highest degree.

This *proves quite clearly* that the OTO *was something absolutely different* from the Scottish Rite A &A, Memphis, Misraim. There already existed a grand lodge for these in England, indeed with John Yarker as grand master, from whom Reuss himself had received his authorization. Therefore, it would be impossible, according to the customs of Freemasonry, to declare a vacancy in England and to set up a new Grand Lodge for these rites.

In the Jubilee edition there was a history of "our order" that was probably completely and intentionally confused with the intention of unjustly claiming the members of the three rites for the OTO. Even the observant reader will find it difficult to decide at any one time just who is meant as "our order"—the OTO, the three rites,

---

25 There is no proof that this Constitution really originates before 1912.

or even an order from prehistoric times. This confusion was very successful and continues on in the anthroposophic literature. It is to be attributed to this confusion that retrospectively the three rites in Germany were referred to with this slogan-like abbreviation.

The only thing that existed in 1905, when Rudolf Steiner dealt with Reuss, was the Memphis–Misraim Rite. There is not a single document concerning the OTO with this name (not even in Reuss's fantasy titles)[26] that can be detected as having appeared before 1912. And with this OTO an illegitimate offshoot proceeded from the stream of the old secret societies, representing a last stage of the decadence. The doctrines of the "ancient wisdom" there are completely in ruins; remaining are only empty titles, empty words and substance, and these are replaced by sexuality.

The Memphis–Misraim Rite was a form in which the old, preserved substance slumbered, and Rudolf Steiner awakened it to new life and brought it to a real blossoming and real fruit. Not only did the Misraim Service affect the development of the soul life of many participants very deeply—as is shown by the few witnesses in the archive[27]—but it was directly connected with the whole of the anthroposophic movement's significant impulses of art and the new form of the social life.[28] In contrast, the OTO involved a purely private founding by Theodor Reuss and was, like its founder, completely unreal, having no being or substance and almost no members.[29] It is

---

26 Certainly there are allusions to a Templar Order in Reuss's announcements before 1912. If one looks at the relevant places in the *Oriflamme* more closely—also Reuss's usual letterhead as of winter 1906—one sees that it is only decoration coming from Reuss's fantasy in the description for the three Rites. For this, Reuss has naturally reached back into the past for the name of the OTO.

27 See chapter 16; participants did not speak of the Misraim Service then.

28 See chapter 9.

29 In the *Oriflamme* of 1912, Reuss mentions 500 members in "our order." Those are, however, the total members of the three rites, and at that, Reuss

confused thinking to believe that Rudolf Steiner, who did not maintain relations with the Memphis–Misraim Order, could have been concerned over Reuss's "illegitimate child."[30]

Now, there are two places in the printed documents in CW 265 (*Freemasonry and Ritual Work*) that apparently could point to a membership of Rudolf Steiner in the OTO. Neither of these, however, are authentic and both come from a later time. The first place is the footnote in Marie Steiner's essay from 1934, "Was Rudolf Steiner a Freemason?" We can now state with certainty that this footnote *is not* from Marie Steiner but from the publisher of the magazine. Marie Steiner's manuscript that lies in the Archive does not have this footnote. In addition, the footnote contained statistical details that Marie Steiner would never have thought of investigating. (For more about this, see the footnote on page 215 in this volume. Möller and Howe are also included in the footnote.)

The second place is in the text of the "oath" that Rudolf Steiner supposedly signed when he entered the Memphis–Misraim Rite. Reports in the Archive relate the following: According to Möller and Howe, in 1921 the "Executive Council of 3" of the OTO consisted of three people: A. Ullmer, Alice Sprengel, and Mrs. Adeline von Wrangel, whom Reuss named in 1917 as Grand Master of the OTO Lodge on Monte Verità near Ascona, Switzerland. Helena Kober from Arlesheim visited Mrs. von Wrangel in 1925 and had her burn the original of the "oath" in her presence, which was a very

---

also generously counted more than 400 members who did not belong to them but to the Mystica aeterna.

30   The nonsense was maintained that the OTO was an "aggregate-Order," which had taken into itself the Memphis–Misraim Rite. Through this Rudolf Steiner was supposed to have inadvertently become a member. This comes from the atmosphere of the often-confused thinking of the time that did not read with exactitude and confused the "wisdom" with the organization. The Constitution of the OTO prescribed that one could become a member only by written application. Rudolf Steiner had never signed such a document.

unfortunate act. Now there is a copy—or perhaps a forgery—of this document that Alice Sprengel produced. This woman, because of her machinations, was expelled in 1915 from the Anthroposophical Society. She left Dornach and went to Ascona and settled there near Reuss on Monte Verità, where she served as his secretary. A copy of this copy reached Emil Bock in Stuttgart by way of Frau Baader, an acquaintance of Alice Sprengel. Then through Erich Gabert, it came into the Archives in 1966. As the not-so-conscientious Alice Sprengel made the copy, she replaced the formulation, which was probably so similar to the contract of January 3, 1906, with that of her familiar *"Alten und Primit. Ritus von M. u. M. OTO"* [Ancient and Primitive Rite of Memphis and Misraim OTO] of the order on whose council she herself served. The abbreviations themselves show that it cannot be the original text. In documents, names are always written in full. Consequently, this text is also not proof of Rudolf Steiner's possible membership of in the OTO.

To summarize, our examinations yield the following facts:

- In January 1906, Rudolf Steiner executed, through his contract with Theodor Reuss as authorized representative of John Yarker, the formal–historical connection to his Misraim Rite.
- In the summer of 1906, Rudolf Steiner broke off personal contact with Reuss.
- From the summer of 1907, Rudolf Steiner was the sole legal leader of the Misraim Rite in Germany.
- Rudolf Steiner built up his symbolic–cultic foundation with complete independence, without being subject to any directives from outside—especially from Yarker or Reuss. This founding was completely his own work and had only his own esoteric pupils as members.
- The work in the sphere of the Misraim Rite was stopped in 1914 with the outbreak of World War I, and Rudolf Steiner never started it up again in this organizational form.

- A collaboration with Reuss never took place, especially not in the sphere of the OTO, which Reuss made public only in 1912—six years after Rudolf Steiner broke off his relationship with Reuss.
- This OTO was a purely private establishment by Reuss. The only thing it has in common with the historical Scottish A & A, Memphis and Misraim Rites is that its founder originally had a charter for these three rites in Germany from John Yarker.

These given facts show clearly that Rudolf Steiner had absolutely nothing to do with Reuss's OTO, neither in form nor content. The claim that he had done anything with Reuss is simply not true. Their intention is best described by Schiller's words:

> The world loves to blacken the radiance
> And drag the sublime into the dust.[31]

---

31 *The Maid of Orleans*, verse 3.

Rudolf Steiner, 1918

15

The Esoteric School
and a New Beginning after the War

World War I had become a fiery symbol to Rudolf Steiner that new forms would have to be devised for a fruitful continuation of the general, as well as the esoteric social life. He must have been under much more pressure with regard to reestablishing his esoteric activity than he was before the war, on the one hand because of the necessarily contradictory endeavors to preserve continuity in adherence to previously held principles, and on the other hand to conform to the needs of the new age—that is, to introduce democratic principles and openness into the esoteric work. This is made clear by the two following statements. The first was said immediately after the war ended: "...to maintain the continuity of human evolution at the present time, it is necessary to connect with ritual and symbolism" (Dornach, Dec. 20, 1918, CW 186); the other comment was given in response to a question about Freemasonry from a worker at the Goetheanum:

> Today all such matters are really no longer appropriate. What should we mainly reject in this connection? We have to reject its isolationism through which a spiritual aristocracy would soon develop, which should not happen. The democratic principle, which must increasing gain influence, is at odds with the Freemasonry alliance, just as it is with the priesthood. (Dornach, June 4, 1924, CW 353)

At the time this last remark was made Rudolf Steiner had already undertaken the remodeling of the Society and the Esoteric School, by which he wanted publicly to merge into a higher synthesis the antithesis between the old hierarchical way of working and of the modern demand for democracy. The steps that he made in this direction between the end of the war and his death were somewhat as follows.

Steiner was asked on several occasions in late autumn 1918, soon after the war ended, to restart the esoteric instruction, but he refused initially. One reason was because of the frequently occurring and inappropriate attitudes; the other was the fact that appropriate new forms had not been worked out yet. However, a year later, in late 1919, he was asked again at the school in Stuttgart whether a religious service could be arranged on Sundays for the pupils of the free-religion lessons, he answered that it would in that case have to be in the form of a ritual, adding: If this ritual could be provided, it would thus be the first reconnection with the esotericism interrupted by the war[1]—apparently, insofar as it related again to a non-ecclesiastical ritual.

Soon after the ritual and the "Sunday service" were inaugurated and took place for the first time (Feb. 1, 1920),[2] this remark was recorded at a teachers' conference in Stuttgart on November 16, 1921: "A ritual is the most esoteric event one could imagine." Following a five-and-a-half-year pause, Rudolf Steiner once again took up the esoteric work within the Anthroposophical Society. First, this took place in Dornach with two esoteric lessons on February 9 and 17, 1920. It was not continued, although that had been the intention, because various members had acted improperly again. That is why, in the teachers' conference on November 16, 1921, when he was again asked about the esoteric lessons, he answered that it would be very difficult to arrange them and that he'd had to drop them

---

1   Told by one of the two first religion teachers; reported by Herbert Hahn.
2   See *Faculty Meetings with Rudolf Steiner*, introduction (CW 300a/b).

The Esoteric School and a New Beginning after the War

because everything to do with esotericism had been "shamefully abused." Esotericism was a "painful" chapter for the anthroposophic movement. He wanted to think about it, however; first, the appropriate mode had to be found.[3] Soon after (December 4, 1921), he held an esoteric lesson in Norway, where lectures could be held again for the first time since the outbreak of war during the summer of 1914. During that stay in Norway, a gathering of the cognitive–ritual section members also took place; although two or three new members were accepted—the circle was solemnly pronounced closed,[4] just as this had happened immediately after the outbreak of war in 1914. Through that, however, the "old" was not dead (as he explained in Oslo) but would rise again in a metamorphosed form. Two esoteric lessons also took place in London during 1922, one during his stay in April and the other during his stay in November.

Three esoteric lessons also took place through the initiative of several members who were especially interested in the contents of the earlier cognitive–ritual work. Rudolf Steiner designated this circle the "Wachsmuth–Lerchenfeld Group" for the main speakers. This group of approximately fifteen people met in Rudolf Steiner's Dornach home, the "Hansi House," twice before and once following the Christmas Conference: Dornach, May 27, October 23, 1923, and January 3, 1924 (notes from these lessons are in CW 265). The known names of the participants (however, not a complete list) were: Maria Röschl, Marie Steiner, Harriet von Vacano, Elisabeth Vreede, Ita Wegman, Margarita Woloschin, Jürgen von Grone, Kurt Piper, Otto von Lerchenfeld, Albert Steffen, Guenther Wachsmuth, and Wolfgang Wachsmuth and his wife.

Between the first and second lessons, yet another was planned, to which Friedrich Rittelmeyer was invited. Rudolf Steiner canceled this lesson, however, because he considered the publication of the Rittelmeyer–Lemp discussion in the magazine *Anthroposophy* to be

---

3 *Faculty Meetings with Rudolf Steiner*, vol. 2 (CW 300b/c).
4 See CW 265.

a grave error (see CW 259). Just as with these three lessons, so, too, the lesson on September 30, 1923, in Vienna followed the content of the earlier cognitive–ritual section of the Esoteric School. The participants of these lessons following the war were either members of the earlier Esoteric School or those to whom Steiner had already provided personal meditations.

Yet a different circle was formed in the autumn of 1922 in Stuttgart during the Pedagogical Youth Course[5] by and for mostly young people: the so-called Esoteric Youth Circle. After it was founded, two esoteric lessons were also held for the participants: in Stuttgart on July 13, 1923, and in Dornach, December 30, 1923 (CW 266/3).

The esoteric, and particularly the cognitive–ritual way of working, which had necessarily undergone a metamorphosis as a result of the changed conditions of the times, as was indicated in Christiania in December 1921 on the occasion of the ceremonial closing of the circle, is addressed by Rudolf Steiner in the lecture given on December 20, 1918, in Dornach immediately after the war ended. Already at that time it was stated that the passage of time necessitated that a renewal of many things must take place. For from now on, and becoming increasingly obvious as time progresses, new revelations break through the veil of events into the soul and spiritual horizon of humanity. As these new revelations are the expression of a new creative principle resting on the spirits of personality, the stamp of the personality impulse will become increasingly decisive for the future. In connection therewith the fundamental difference between the old and the new revelation has been explained and the symbolism and ritual, through which one formerly communicated has been characterized. This old symbolism has had no essential part to play in anthroposophically oriented Spiritual Science. If symbols are mentioned, it is only in the sense of "borrowed symbolism" to exemplify one or another thing or to prove the correspondence of "what has been newly discovered, which is of use to new humanity,

---

5   See *Becoming Michael's Companions* (CW 217).

and that which is antiquated and belongs to the past" (Dornach, Dec. 20, 1918. "In the Changed Conditions of the Times").

The wording of this lecture—which emphatically describes anthroposophic Spiritual Science as belonging to the *new* revelation—is apparently partly because of requests from various friends that he should again take up the esoteric and, especially, the cognitive-ritual work. The following words seem to verify this:

> Some of you know that in our circles, too, we have in no way hesitated to set forth the life of symbolism and ritual that has remained since ancient times. But we have always done so in a very different spirit. Generally the greatest value is attached, in an antiquated spirit, to the symbolism and ritual itself. To maintain the continuity of human evolution, it is still necessary to establish a connection, as it were, with symbolism and ritual. But in our circles, symbolism and ritual have never been presented in any other way than as something that should lead us to the spiritual reality itself and to its immediate incorporation into the living value of our time. Hence it is just in anthroposophic Spiritual Science that we find the explanation of many, nay, in fact of all the principles of ritual and symbolism from the past. We show how humankind received by other paths a Wisdom that in our time is antiquated and out of date. This Wisdom brought us, in a certain sense, into an unfree condition. Today we must set out on new paths of Wisdom.... It is immensely important, my dear friends, to bear this in mind. To be able to be, in the deepest sense of the word, a human being who identifies with what the new revelations of the Heavens are wanting from the Earth development—this is the thing that matters. (Dornach, Dec. 20, 1918, CW 186)

This is the reason it will be no good to conceive of everyday life in the future as a miserable, profane existence, and then retire to the Church or a Masonic temple and leave these two worlds entirely separate from each other.

Since then Rudolf Steiner must have pondered how the esoteric work should receive an up-to-date form, so that the outmoded principle of secrecy could be replaced by something else. Marie Steiner reports how at that time he often pondered over the form that the new should take, so that it would encompass something binding and solid to overcome mediocrity and yet be compatible with the freedom of all. "He was not of the opinion that one could practice esotericism as in former times, in deep isolation and with strictly binding vows. These things were not compatible with the feeling of freedom of the individual. The soul had to appear before its own higher 'I' and recognize the obligation of respectful silence that is due toward this 'I' and to the spiritual world."[6]

These considerations arise from the changed conditions of the times—the tragic loss of the Goetheanum building through the fire on New Year's Eve 1922 and the necessary but difficult reorganization of the Society; they bring the decision at the refounding of the Society at Christmas 1923 to a head, not only to reconstitute it on a completely public basis, but also to give the Esoteric School a form compatible with the new consciousness of the time.

This also led to the release of printed manuscripts of his lecture cycles, which had been available only to members of the Society until then. The "old ways of thinking about things" were no longer appropriate. "One simply does not understand the conditions of our present social life if one believes that such things must be kept secret forever. We can no longer do that today. In this connection, our age has indeed also become spiritually Democratic." This was said in Dornach on March 4, 1923 (CW 257).

Accordingly, as the "Free High School for Spiritual Science" it was to be built up in three classes and with several scientific and artistic sections. It would be incorporated in the Statutes of the Society as the "central point" of its activity, to which every member had the right to apply for admission after having been a member of the Society for a certain length of time.

---

6   Marie Steiner's memorial words printed with the first edition of the lectures about the karmic connections of the anthroposophic movement, Dornach, 1926; reprinted in *Beiträge...* (Contributions...), no. 23, Christmas 1968.

In numerous articles, Rudolf Steiner explained that he wanted this new Esoteric School to be understood as the "Free High School for Spiritual Science." He said that this High School would differ from the usual high schools and would therefore not try to compete with them in any way whatsoever, nor would it become a substitute for them. Nevertheless, one should be able to receive in the Esoteric School what the ordinary high school could not provide—esoteric deepening for which the soul has strives in its search for knowledge. For those who were searching for a path into the spiritual world in a general human way, there was a general section. For those who were looking for an esoteric deepening in a particular scientific, artistic, or other direction, other sections would try to show the way. Thus all seeking human beings can find what they are looking for at the "High School at the Goetheanum" according to their special needs. The High School was not to be a purely scientific institution but rather a purely human one that also fully covers the esoteric needs of both the scientists and the artists. Rudolf Steiner said that he himself would see to it that people were fully informed about what was going on.[7]

Thus, just as in the beginning of the movement it was connected for reasons of continuity with what already existed historically, it was likewise connected with what came earlier at the Christmas Conference of 1923. In the opening lecture on December 24, 1923 (CW 260), of the Christmas Conference for the reestablishment of the Anthroposophical Society he made a statement while reading statute number 5, which begins, "The Anthroposophical Society sees the Free School for Spiritual Science in Dornach as the center of this work. This [School] will consist of three classes...." He said, "Please do not be shocked at these three classes, my dear friends! The three classes were already there originally in the Anthroposophical Society, only in a different form until 1914."

---

7 See Rudolf Steiner, *Constitution of the School of Spiritual Science;* also, *The Foundation Stone: The Life, Nature & Cultivation of Anthroposophy.*

On the following day, December 25, 1923, the Foundation Stone of the General Anthroposophical Society was laid. The connection with the earlier was fulfilled symbolically by three strokes of a gavel:

> Rudolf Steiner did not open the Christmas Conference with words but with symbolic strokes, and with this he brought the law of continuity into effect. For everyone who belongs to the institution, which Rudolf Steiner describes in chapter 68 of his *Autobiography*, these three strokes said: "The *New* that I want to give you I connect here with what existed earlier, in keeping with the law of esotericism." Also, here there is no possibility for a petty interpretation for those who know these opening strokes. It hardly needs to be stressed that this connecting with the earlier contains the possibility to bring something completely new—yes, even a new leap forward—as with the plant, the blossom connects to the leaf structure and yet is something completely new.[8]

Carl Unger, a leader who experienced all the phases of the Society's development, pointed to something concretely new of this kind. He detected a "momentous difference" in relation to Rudolf Steiner's earlier manner of lecturing. Earlier, Steiner had spoken to the members of the Society—that is, to a specific audience at a specific place and time. And at the same time what arose from the members as soul need, as spiritual yearning, was given full consideration, as he describes it in his *Autobiography* (chapter 67). Now, however (according to Carl Unger), he spoke from all soul situations and to the whole of humanity.[9]

The Esoteric School was also no longer geared to the individual, as it had been before the war. Everyone received the same meditations and these were explained for everyone at the same time. Also, the Masters were no longer spoken of. It was still stressed that the

---

8   From Adolf Arenson, member of the three classes of the Esoteric School of 1904–1914, in a letter to Albert Steffen on Dec. 24, 1926. See the letter at the end of chapter 16.

9   Carl Unger, *The Language of the Consciousness Soul*, introduction.

School was founded through the will of spiritual powers, for only in this way could an esoteric school rightly exist. This means further that, through everything connected with the impulse of the Christmas Conference, the possibility was given that the School was founded through the Michael-being. Michael is the spiritual power who (as shown about him for many years) has led human affairs since the last third of the nineteenth century (CW 270).

Despite this difference from the earlier period, one can see continuity. During the lecture cycles on karmic relationships in 1924 it was described how Anthroposophy in its reality is what many who are incarnated today experienced in the spiritual world before their birth under the direct leadership of Michael as a suprasensory training and as a ritual flowing in powerful cosmic imaginations translated into human concepts. From this, something like small mirror images descended into Goethe's mystery fairytale, *The Green Snake and the Beautiful Lily*. From all of this it becomes clear that the lecture about this fairytale for the Berlin theosophists in 1900, the original cell of the anthroposophic movement, was the first interpretation of the initiation wisdom of the new Michaelic Age.[10]

Because Rudolf Steiner was immensely overburdened and became severely ill in the autumn of 1924, only the first of the intended three classes and a few of the intended scientific and artistic sections could be established. How the second and third class would have been arranged, and whether the ritual element would have been a part of it, has only been hinted at. Fred Poeppig reports, "Alexander Strakosch told me that Dr. Steiner told him that the stage of the new Goetheanum was to have an opening in the stage floor for unconventional appearances and disappearances for ritual purposes, as is usual by the admission into the Third Degree."[11] Marie Steiner mentions in a letter much later that he had said to her that "in

---

10   Dornach, July 8, 1924 (CW 237); and Arnheim, July 18 & 19, 1924 (CW 240).
11   Typescript, Verlag Die Pforte, Basel 1966.

Class 2, much of what he had given us in the M.E. [Mystica aeterna] would flow into it imaginatively, and that in Class 3 this would have been transformed into moral strength."[12] In her notes for an address to be given at a memorial ceremony for the anniversary of Rudolf Steiner's death on March 30, 1926, it is stated:[13]

> He left us before he was able to complete the work he started—before he was able to give us what he described as the second and third classes. In the second he wanted to give us the ritual, which would have corresponded to the revelations that had flowed from the imaginations of the suprasensory School of Michael at the [end of the eighteenth and beginning of the nineteenth centuries].

Destiny did not allow him to complete this grandly conceived work for the future. Nevertheless, in keeping with a passage in his mystery drama, "as an example for humanity [it] would have been placed—just once—upon Earth. In spirit, it will continue to work, even if it does not survive in earthly life. It will contribute a small part of the power to the Earth and one day will bring about the marriage of spiritual goals with earthly actions."[14]

---

12 Letter from Nov. 8, 1947, to Helga Geelmuyden, Norway.
13 Notebook, Archive no. 133.
14 See *The Souls' Awakening*, scene 1, in *Four Mystery Dramas*, CW 14.

16

Adolf Arenson: A Circular to the Members and a Letter to Albert Steffen

Circular from Adolf Arenson[1] to the Members, 1926

My Dear Friends!

Through the whole situation of our movement, a consideration connected with the inner history of our Society has come about that I believe would be of value to our members. These matters may not be suitable to put into print for everyone, because they could be used in an oppositional sense. Yet, precisely the positive ideas that result from them should be able to flow into our work, because they arise from the active experience of all the events of our movement and our Society since the beginning of the work of our honorable leader, Rudolf Steiner.

In this sense I ask you to be willing to receive the following thoughts.

With anthroposophic greetings,
Connstatt, in October 1926
Adolf Arenson

---

1   Adolf Arenson (1855–1936) was among Steiner's earliest and most important students in the Esoteric School.

Eighteen months have passed since our teacher and leader Rudolf Steiner departed from us. Increasingly, the knowledge has come to light about how, through his death, the situation has changed from the ground up for us with one stroke, and we are obliged to maintain his work in purity and carry it forward. What one continued to hear often at the beginning—that everything will remain as it was, because he is still among us—has gradually died away. Facts are merciless; it is just not the same as before; the rich stream of revelations no longer flows from the spiritual worlds; the wise counsel; and gone is the soothing hand that repeatedly brought balance to negative situations among the members. The work with the School that began with the First Class Lessons was intended to continue with the establishment of the Second Class, but it ended abruptly.

This knowledge is unvarnished and harsh, but it is healthy, as it can lead us to take firm responsibility for our task, the core of which must be to bring the living seed contained in his every word and deed to full flower in us. Only in this way can we truly acknowledge and be grateful for what has been given to us; only through this can we pass the treasure of wisdom with which he has entrusted us into the world so it becomes the shared possession of humanity.

As a precious legacy, he left us the "Leading Thoughts,"[2] which had been published weekly in the *News for Members*. They must not lie fallow; the life flowing in them must not become hard and fixed. They must be grasped with honest effort; the seed must be brought to blossom and to fruit in us. Rudolf Steiner expressed clearly how he thought about this work in his address to the members in the *News for Members* of August 10, 1924, number 31 (CW 26): "The following point of view, however, is probably the most important. The point is not that Anthroposophy should simply be listened to or read but received into the living soul. It is essential that what has been received should be worked on in thought and carried into

---

2   See Rudolf Steiner, *Anthroposophical Leading Thoughts: Anthroposophy as a Path of Knowledge* (CW 26); also Carl Unger, *The Language of the Consciousness Soul: A Guide to Rudolf Steiner's "Leading Thoughts."*

the feelings; the "Leading Thoughts" are actually intended to stimulate this in connection with the lecture courses already in print and circulation."

This is also true of the wisdom given in the revelations of the Class lessons. They are communicated to the members of the First Class through the content that is read aloud. Through this, all will (sooner or later) be given the opportunity to familiarize themselves with the content. For the future, however, we must never tire of our work with them. They, too, must be seeds of the spirit that we fill with soul and enliven through our own creative work. The words that the spirit of Benedictus speaks to the Monk in "The Trial of the Soul" apply also for us in the most eminent sense:

> Our brothers hold themselves obliged to hasten
> the downfall of this sin against the spirit.
> In this they are supported
> by words that formerly I spoke on Earth.
> They do not dream;
> these very words can be renewed only
> if they are nurtured for their further growth
> by those who are successors in my work. (p. 235)

Whether the time is ripe for this work, I will not say. The important thing is to point it out already now in order to strengthen the initiative in us so that the living stream does not gradually stagnate. It is necessary for this that we contemplate clearly our situation today, that we eliminate prejudices, that we correct wrong opinions—in a word, that we try to live in the truth and reality, "without which a healthy esotericism cannot thrive."

Until the Christmas Conference the Anthroposophical Society was the framework for the anthroposophic movement. The tremendous thing about the Christmas Conference was that both should from then on form a unity. In order for this to be possible, Rudolf Steiner placed himself at the head of the Society. Now true esotericism flowed directly into the Society through him. Now there was the guarantee that the actions of the Executive Council would always be in accord with the goals of the spiritual world whose earthly representative was Rudolf Steiner.

Today we are alone and have become lonely. It is a matter of acquiring what he gave us through patient, devoted work. How do we find the way to that?

He showed us the way himself. To grasp the "Leading Thoughts" correctly and continue them, he himself pointed toward this spiritual wealth in the lecture cycles from 1906 to 1920.[3] The connection between what was given before the Christmas Conference and the new—this is the solution. If we carefully read the address in number 31, which was already mentioned, we cannot help but know that it is impossible without the earlier spiritual content to exhaust fully all that can be attained from the "Leading Thoughts."

Shouldn't there be something similar in the realm of esotericism? There is, of course, a great lack of knowledge of the facts here. For example, a passage is inserted here that appeared in the Christmas edition of the *Oesterreichische Blätter für Freies Geitesleben* (Austrian newspaper for independent spiritual life) and insofar as I know has not been contradicted yet. It is an examination of setting up the Class lessons and states, "The essential character of the course of teaching that Rudolf Steiner developed for this School is that he included in it only what he could give as personal instruction up to that time. What he separated from the personal and formed into an objective, systematic path of schooling could now be communicated to everyone who becomes a member [of the School]."

Thus, it is said here that, until the Christmas Conference, one could receive esoteric instruction only through personal contact with Rudolf Steiner. This is absolutely contrary to the facts! Since 1904, there have been groups that Steiner trained intentionally for the esoteric, which then presented this "systematic path of schooling."

---

3   This refers to the lecture cycles printed during Rudolf Steiner's lifetime.

Steiner had indicated this on various occasions and stated it clearly in a discussion of the Class lessons: "The three Classes were originally already there, though in a different form in the Anthroposophical Society until 1914."[4] Moreover, one of those "Schools" was indicated clearly in chapter 68 of Steiner's *Autobiography*. The following statements characterize this institution, which played an important role in the development of esotericism within the Anthroposophical Society.

It was an institution in which there were various degrees to which the participants were promoted according to their souls' karmic right to the content of that particular degree. The promotion to a higher degree took place partially in forms that were also similar to what was practiced in occult societies (for instance, the Freemasons)—not, however, in imitation of such orders, but because they resulted from the spiritual research. Rudolf Steiner was the head of the School and the communication of the spiritual realities; at his side stood Marie von Sivers as comrade and colleague.

Here is an indication that, owing to my advanced age, I consider my duty to speak of, since there are only a few people still living who witnessed this scene.

During an action or event in a higher degree, at which only a small number of participants were allowed to be present, Rudolf Steiner proclaimed that collaboration with Marie von Sivers was to be accepted as fully justified. It was not just symbolic as it was for the rest of us. Indeed, *a reality was indicated that goes beyond death and birth.*

It is easy to see that by climbing to higher degrees the esoteric impulses flow with increasing riches, and that in nearly a decade of events—until the outbreak of World War I—many participants experienced these lessons as deeply significant for the development of their soul life.

---

4   In CW 260, on Dec. 24, 1923, in the morning at 11:15 am.

That is what can be said within this framework about an institution that, under Steiner's leadership, offered the members the possibility of ascending to ever-higher stages of esoteric life. Such societies no longer exist; they had to end when the war began. However, what the individual souls attained in content and deepening during the decade of earnest esoteric work belongs to the spiritual substance of our Society.

There has always been what Rudolf Steiner called "tests of humanity's maturity." One such test was the stream that came over Europeans at the end of the eighteenth century. It degenerated into the French Revolution with its grotesque worship of the "Goddess of Reason." Another test is the appearance of Spiritual Science. Future development will bring the sort of attitude humanity should have toward it.

However, within the Anthroposophical Society the maturity of the Society itself was tested. The first attempt to present karma in a real form reaches back to 1904, but only today can karma be discussed openly.

One earnest test was the establishment of the Independent Anthroposophical Society in 1912, followed by an attempt to introduce to humanity the threefolding of the social organism; it tested the maturity of the Society *and* humanity as a whole. Then came the great test of the Christmas Conference, intensified by the death of our leader and teacher.

We are now in the midst of this test, whose results will depend on our attitude about whether we will gain the forces to stand beside Michael in a helpful and supportive way in the greatest and most decisive test, which will begin with the end of the century.

Michael expects this help from us. May we manage not to disappoint him.

A Letter from Adolf Arenson to Albert Steffen[5]

Connstatt, December 24, 1926
Dear Mr. Steffen:

My October circular has led to unpleasant results—neither intentional nor foreseen—that I must nevertheless consider good in the interest of truth. I have no reason to go into the individual opinions that arose. I have said what I considered my duty to say and do not need to take back one word of it. However, I want to supplement for you the point on esotericism in my circular. I did not think it necessary to add my explanations [in the circular], but I want to do so for you, Dear Mr. Steffen, as you might be interested.

In opposition to the view that one often heard—that the Christmas Conference voided everything given before it—I have proved indisputably, in my opinion, that Rudolf Steiner himself referred to the spiritual content of the earlier lecture cycles with the "Leading Thoughts." Steiner's words in the *News* (1924, no. 31), which I quoted in my writing, is not open to interpretation. I let the words follow: "Shouldn't something similar be found in the realm of esotericism?" With a simple report of the facts, I left it to the members' judgment to form their own opinions. To avoid impinging on the freedom of others, I went no further.

For you, however, I wish to add this: In the esoteric communities preceding the World War, two laws were repeatedly stressed to us. One was that of absolute truth, without which all esoteric efforts would be without foundation and meaningless. The other law was that of continuity—that is, connecting with what existed earlier.

Rudolf Steiner opened the Christmas Conference not with words but with symbolic strokes that fulfilled the law of continuity. To all who belonged to the institution described in chapter 68 of his *Autobiography*, these strokes said, "The New that I want to give you, I herewith connect to what existed earlier in accordance with the law

---

5   Albert Steffen was the President of the General Anthroposophical Society at that time.

of esotericism." Here, too, there is no room for interpretation for those who understand the opening strokes.

It hardly needs to be stressed that this connection to what came earlier contains the possibility of bringing something completely new, even a leap forward, as a plant on which the blossom connects with the leaf and is nonetheless something completely new.

My indication of the continuity as regards our work on the "Leading Thoughts" and on the esoteric content of the Class lessons, to which we are obliged in the future, was absolutely in the sense of what Rudolf Steiner gave us.

Even though these communities had to cease with the outbreak of the war, both of these laws—truth and continuity—should continue to live in our souls, and it is our sacred duty to look after Rudolf Steiner's legacy in the sense of these laws.

I held it to be important to communicate this to you and add only that I leave it to your judgment as to how you use the content and wording of this letter.

I include a copy of the final draft of my writing, and as ever, I send this with heartfelt anthroposophic greetings,

Adolf Arenson

17

Concluding Remarks

The Problem of Movement and Society in Rudolf Steiner's Work

A sense for what is tragic is the key to an understanding of human evolution.[1]

Like a red thread, running through these documents is one problem—if not the decisive one—in Rudolf Steiner's spiritual-scientific activity as the polarity between *movement and Society*. Until the Christmas Conference of 1923/24, Steiner had held to the principle of keeping the leadership of the movement and the Esoteric School strictly separate from that of the Society. This was because it was difficult "to combine what is demanded currently by an official position in the outer world—even chairman of the Anthroposophical Society—with the occult duties related to the revelations of the spiritual world" (Torquay, Aug. 12, 1924, CW 260a). Another time he said: "The anthroposophic movement—really a spiritual current guided by spiritual powers and spiritual forces from the suprasensory world, only having their reflection here in the physical world—must not be confused with the Anthroposophical Society, which is simply an administrative society that, as much as possible, takes care of the anthroposophic impulse" (Berne, Apr. 16, 1924, CW 260a).

From the beginning he drew people's attention to this with particular urgency concerning the inner constitution of his Esoteric School:

---

1   Basel, Dec. 21, 1916, CW 173.

These aspects must be kept strictly separate; they must never be mixed together. When one talks about the external Theosophical Society, one must never even mention the esoteric individualities who stood over its inception. The powers that live on the higher planes—that live for the sake of human evolution outside of the physical body—never interfere in these affairs. They never impart anything other than impulses. Whenever we are engaged practically in extending the Theosophical Society, the great individualities we call the Masters are standing by our side; we may turn to them and allow them to speak through us. When it concerns the propagation of occult life, it is the Masters who speak. When it concerns only the organization of the Society then they leave it to those living on the physical plane. This distinguishes the occult current from the framework of the theosophical organization. Allow me to express the difference between the inwardly flowing spiritual stream and what manifests through individual personalities; it can perhaps best be expressed: When it concerns spiritual life, then the Masters speak; when it concerns only organization, since error is possible, the Masters remain silent. (Berlin, Oct. 22, 1905, CW 93)

After the theosophical movement and the Society were united in 1907 (when Annie Besant, the leader of the Esoteric School, became president of the Society), Rudolf Steiner corrected this, as far as it concerned him, by taking his first Esoteric Working Committee from Annie Besant's Esoteric School.

Rudolf Steiner tried in no uncertain terms to clear up the problem of the polarity (movement vs. Society). In 1912, with the impending exclusion of the German Section from the Theosophical Society and the founding of an independent Society, he neither took office nor became a member of it. He worked as a completely independent spiritual teacher, and officially had nothing more to do with the administration of the Society. But soon World War I (1914–1918) began, which greatly impaired the life of the Society. Through the establishment of daughter foundations in the postwar years, a strong opposition grew up against Anthroposophy, culminating in the burning of the first Goetheanum on New Years's Eve (1922). It became evident that the Society was not equal to the fight, and the polarity of the "movement vs. Society" problem became incomparably more difficult. The question as to how this divergent situation could be resolved now became a decisive personal problem for Rudolf Steiner. Marie Steiner reports that, in many difficult moments of failure, faced with the base conduct of opponents, he said, "Who knows if it would not be better to continue the movement without the Society? I am responsible for all the shortcomings of the Society, and the movement suffers as a result."[2]

The reorganization of the Society began in early 1923 through the founding of national societies, and the decision was made to rebuild the Goetheanum and begin an International Anthroposophical Society on Christmas 1923. Rudolf Steiner held eight lectures in Dornach in June 1923 on "The History and Requirements of the Anthroposophic Movement in Relation to the Anthroposophical Society" (CW 258). He intended to arouse people to self-reflection, to make them aware that the consciousness within the Society demanded that one should find one's way from external things connected with society into the genuine spiritual reality, for "an anthroposophic movement can exist only in an Anthroposophical Society that is a reality" (lecture 6). Just then, he was still wrestling with a solution to the problem of movement and Society. As late as November 1923, while in Holland for the founding of the Dutch National Society, he still had grave doubts whether "a continuance with the Society as such was still possible at all." He complained that no one seemed to understand what he was getting at—that it might be necessary to continue the work with very few people in a strict circle."[3] After having

---

2   Memorial words from Marie Steiner's as the foreword to the 1st ed. (1938) of *The Anthroposophic Movement*, CW 258. See also *Beiträge...* (Contributions...), no. 23, Christmas 1968.

3   F. W. Zeylmans van Emmichoven: *Entwickelung und Geisteskampf 1923–1935* (Development and spiritual struggle), 1935.

concluded soon after to cut the Gordian knot by accepting the personal responsibility for the leadership of the Society—in addition to his activities in the field of spiritual investigation and teaching—he appended the announcement of his decision: "It is a fact that things at the moment must be taken extremely seriously—in bitter seriousness—to avert what I have often spoken about, specifically, that I will find it necessary to withdraw from the Anthroposophical Society" (Dornach, Dec. 23, 1923, CW 259).

To preserve both movement and Society, Rudolf Steiner concluded, "after difficult inner conflicts" (Dornach, Dec. 24, 1923, CW 260), to break with the previous occult rule of keeping the leadership of the movement and the Esoteric School separate from the Society. Whenever he spoke about the new constitution in 1924, he declared that this decisive change was its underlying thought and emphasized that, because he himself had become Chair of the Society, the movement and the Society had become identical. For him that had the practical implication that, apart from the teaching and the spiritual investigation "to give active expression on the earthly plane to what the spiritual worlds wished to reveal,"(CW 260a), he had to accept the whole heavy burden of outwardly running a large organization. It was clear to him what this involved after ten years as General Secretary of the German Section of the Theosophical Society.

Beyond this, the decision at the Christmas Conference signified for him "the undertaking of new responsibilities toward an anthroposophic movement directly from the spirit realms" (Breslau, June 9, 1924, CW 260a), and that something completely new would be inaugurated. For the Society, as well as for the Esoteric School, administrative forms had to be created so that Anthroposophy could be portrayed to the world as fulfilling its "world mission" of providing the necessary soul to the material civilization of our planet Earth (Paris, May 25, 1924, CW 260a). He regarded that giving full publicity to the Society and the Esoteric School was one of the main prerequisites for this, along with simultaneous safeguards of conditions essential for the life of the esoteric work. In this way the Society was to become the most modern esoteric society in the world, right down to its constitution (Berne, Apr. 16, 1924, CW 260a). That is why the lecture courses that had previously been only for members (of an intimate circle) were made available. The new Esoteric School was to be similarly arranged in a way that it would not have any of the characteristics of a secret society. Although the School had not had a proper outward organization between 1904 and 1914, it would now be declared in the statutes a "Free High School of Spiritual Science," with three classes and with sections for the different scientific and artistic branches as the center of activity of the Society, whose members were to be given the right to apply for membership, and people would be informed in detail about what occurred (Dornach, Jan. 30, 1924, CW 260a).

We can clearly assess once more the intense quality of Rudolf Steiner's attitude toward the guiding spiritual powers by looking at his momentous decision to resolve the earlier discrepancy between the movement and the Esoteric School and Society by personally intervening to bring about a new synthesis. According to his own statement, he had taken a great risk, not knowing how those spiritual powers that guide the anthroposophic movement from the spiritual worlds would react—yes, he even had to consider the danger that, by taking on the external management, the source of his spiritual enlightenment "that we all rely on entirely when it comes to the matter of spreading Anthroposophy" might dry up (Paris, May 23, 1924, CW 260a). It was certainly proved later that he took the correct action, since his decision was kindly accepted by the guiding spiritual powers, and the stream of revelations became even stronger than before. Nevertheless, because of that, strong forces of opposition simultaneously arose; forces of opposition on a spiritual level "that make use of people on Earth for their own ends" (Paris, May 23, 1924, CW 260a). He experienced this in his own body—during the days when the Society and the Esoteric School were still new—through an attempt to poison him.[4] He could, indeed, repulse this attack on his physical forces at the time, but they were greatly impaired. For nine months he continued to produce an extraordinary amount of teaching activity and created new administrative forms for building up the Society; then he became seriously ill and, on March 30, 1925, was called away from his physical work on Earth. The esoteric–social work belonging to the future, begun by him in ambitious style, had to be left unfinished.

For, as with anyone of exceptional spiritual stature, Rudolf Steiner's life was also full of tragedy; but for him it was tragedy of a different kind. Aristotle defined the essence of tragedy as the *state of tension* arising from the inevitable connection that human beings have with the powers that, warring among themselves, decide human fate. What differentiates the tragedy of Rudolf Steiner's life from this is that, in complete *free will*, he placed himself into the tensions to balance and to bridge the differences, until even his strong powers had become completely exhausted.

The significance of his superhuman effort to resolve the conflicting relationship of the movement and the Society, which led to premature death, can perhaps best be approached by means of a comparison with the polarity of point and circle. The underlying aim of his work can be demonstrably attributed to a cognitive experience, a kind of archetypal intuition, revealed by the polarity of the point and circle.[5] This archetypal intuition—"intuition is centered in a point"[6]—is evidently the same as the first, the most far-reaching of the seven great mysteries of life, for the commentary to this mystery

---

4   See "The Chronicle" in *Die Konstitution der Allgemeinen Anthroposophischen Gesellschaft* (The constitution of the General Anthroposophical Society), CW 260a, untranslated.

5   See "Rudolf Steiners Lebenswerk in seiner Wirklichkeit ist sein Lebensgang" (Rudolf Steiner's life work is in its reality his biography), in Beiträge... (Contributions...), no. 49–50, Easter 1975.

6   The Hague, Apr. 1922 (exact dates unknown), questions and answers in "Die Bedeutung der Anthroposophie in Geistesleben der Gegewart" (The

Concluding Remarks

reads as follows: "Consider how the point becomes the sphere and still remains itself. If you have understood how the infinite sphere is, after all, merely a point, then return, for then the infinite will appear as finite within you."[7] The inner experience of this polarity is described by a technical term appropriate to this great life mystery: "the plunge into the abyss," for to progress from the center to the periphery an abyss (called "turning inside-out" by Steiner on other occasions) must be crossed. Only then can the way to a true understanding of humanity's greatest polarity—the "I"-being and external world—be made accessible.

When Rudolf Steiner discovered during his early student days, 1879 to 1880, through his study of synthetic geometry, that it can actually be calculated and demonstrated that a point lying infinitely distant at the right is the same as a point lying infinitely distant at the left—in other words, the circle is qualitatively the same as the point—the spiritual concept of the mutually interacting double current underlying time—evolution and involution—became mathematically conceivable to him. The idea of the threefold principle underlying world creation in the sense of a balancing of polarities came to him at that time, and was later worked out methodically.

It can be concluded from this that Rudolf Steiner must have acquired his knowledge of the relationship of *"I"* to *world* through his experience of "turning inside-out" the polarity of point and periphery. This is clearly seen in the case of three of his most representative creations: 1) In the realm of scientific knowledge, the two books that form a polarity in this sense: *Intuitive Thinking as a Spiritual Path: A Philosophy of Freedom* and *An Outline of Esoteric Science*. 2) In the artistic–sculptural realm: the double cupola of the first Goetheanum. 3) In the esoteric–social sphere of the

---

importance of Anthroposophy in the spiritual life of the present day), Dornach 1957.

[7] Letter to Günther Wagner, Dec. 24, 1903.

formation of the Society: the double cupola concept of the "spiritual" Goetheanum.

Rudolf Steiner stated that *The Philosophy of Freedom* and *An Outline of Esoteric Science* belong together as the main representatives of "I"-wisdom and world knowledge in the sense of the polarity of point to circumference. When he wrote *The Philosophy of Freedom*, Steiner was asked if he had been aware of the spiritual world-architects (the hierarchies described in *An Outline of Esoteric Science*), he replied that he was aware of them but that the language he spoke at that time gave him no way to formulate it; that only came later. Nevertheless, even though the hierarchies are not formulated as such in *The Philosophy of Freedom*, they are still contained in it. For, if one penetrates the experience of freedom as Steiner described it there, one becomes aware not only of the human being as a spiritual being, but also of the hierarchies, because they are all contained within human beings. And then the decisive sentence follows: "In spirit vision what is within human beings appears as spiritual environment."[8]

Similarly, at the end of a lecture cycle in which he summarized his arguments (*The Spiritual Hierarchies and the Physical World*, CW 110), he drew attention to the point–periphery intuition compared to knowledge of the "I" vs. knowledge of the world:

> We have...raised the spiritual question of the significance of the human being. And we have tried to establish the significance of the human being, the point at the center of the universe, according to the teachings of the mysteries. In so doing, we tried to solve the riddle of the center, the human being, from the periphery—the enigma of the point from the perspective of the circumference! By doing so, we place our knowledge within the sphere of reality.... Our knowledge is real when it

---

8 From a conversation between Rudolf Steiner and W. J. Stein: "Ein Beitrag zu Rudolf Steiners Lebensgeschichte" (A contribution to Rudolf Steiner's life story), in *Korrespondenz der anthroposophischen Arbeitsgemeinschaft* (Correspondence of the anthroposophic working community), 1934, no. 5.

steps in front of our eyes as the structure and process of the entire cosmos.

The fact that the formative laws underlying the human form can also be detected in the dynamics of the polarity between point and periphery, follows from his statement that one can approach human beings only if one can comprehend in a "completely inward" way that a circle is a point and a point a circle; for the truth is fulfilled in human beings that "the 'I'-point in the head becomes the circle that forms naturally in the limb system" (Dornach, July 5, 1924, CW 317).

In the same way that nature fashions the human form from the dynamics of point and periphery, Rudolf Steiner also constructed the plan of the first Goetheanum in the form of two intersecting circles, and with that he characterized it: "And the building becomes the human being."⁹ We can even see from the history of the building concept how this building plan developed in Rudolf Steiner's mind. In 1907, when the concept of the building was first envisioned at the Munich Congress, the assembly hall was still arranged as a single room corresponding to the Rosicrucian initiation temple. It remained this way for the Munich-inspired model building for Malsch. But, even during the preparatory work for Malsch in 1908, Rudolf Steiner had the intuition of extending the single-cupola hall into a double-cupola room. The importance attaching to this extension becomes understandable from the modern esoteric–historical task of bringing suprasensory knowledge to the public cultural life and its thus-far hidden center for the work of initiates (that is, the temple) to involve the public. What arose from this esoteric–historical task—as the problem of the discrepancy of the "movement" with its necessarily aristocratic character, and the "Society" with its public–democratic character—was the solution brought by Rudolf Steiner through the construction of a ground plan of two intersecting circles. He once characterized their differing constructions (large cupola room, as auditorium, from ordinary circle construction; small

---

9   One of the "window-words" in *Truth-Wrought-Words*, CW 40.

Weltenwerden ist Verschwinden des Geistes auf einer Seite in den <u>Abgrund</u> und aufglänzen auf der anderen Seite aus dem <u>Abgrund</u>.

Was du nach außen verlierst, mußt du von innen gewinnen.

<u>Gieb, so wird dir gegeben.</u>

Man hat einen Satz des Menschenlebens erst begriffen, wenn man ihn als Specialisierung eines anthropogenetischen und eines universellen, oder kosmischen Satzes begriffen hat. —

Genau ebensoviel als eine Sonne von sich objectiviert in einem Planetensystem, lebt als Seele der Sonne subjectiv <u>in</u> der Sonne <u>Innere</u>. Dieses Innere ist der <u>wahre</u> Sonnenlogos. Ihn nimmt wahr als Sonnenwesenheit, wer <u>mental</u> schauen kann.

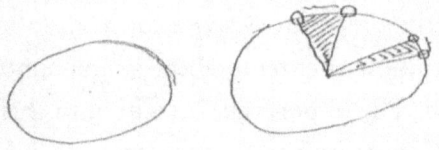

Die Bahnen, die Geschwindigkeiten u.s.w. der Planeten sind die Thaten der Sonnenseele (des <u>Sonnenlogos</u>)

Notebook page, archive 634

cupola room, to be used as a stage and for ritual purposes, from calculating the division of a circle), in connection with the polarity of point and periphery as the "new architectural–artistic idea" (Dornach, June 28, 1914, CW 286). The burning of the building on New Year's Eve 1922–1923, nullified this attempt to reconcile the opposing principles of "I" and the world, or movement and Society, through artistic forms. In spite of this great misfortune, rebuilding was never questioned. Rudolf Steiner maintained the thought of the reshaping of the building for a year, until the idea of the intersection of two circles occurred to him in quite a new way.

At the same time, during the destiny-filled year of 1923, the idea of shaping the long overdue reconstitution of the Society also evolved from the point–circle intuition. In the struggle toward that end, which he continued after the burning of the building until the reestablishment of the Society on Christmas 1923, the resolve was born to overcome the polarity of movement and Society by placing himself in the center. The concept of the floor plan of the building also became the forming principle of the social body. The Christmas Conference of 1923–24 for reestablishing the Society and the Esoteric School became the "ideal foundation stone" of a new social double-cupola construction. The Esoteric School in the form of "the Free High School for Spiritual Science" under the sole direction of Rudolf Steiner was intended to serve as the "small cupola," as it were, and was to be connected with the "large cupola" of the democratic–public Society. With this hazardous undertaking, Rudolf Steiner apparently wanted to bridge the abyss that had existed until then between the aristocratic life of the occult movement and the democratic life of the public society. The awareness of this abyss must have lived within him especially strongly in 1923, while he was still wrestling to evolve the new social form. For, according to existing phrases passed on from an esoteric lesson of that year, he spoke of this abysmal situation as a "heroic tragedy" in the history of modern humanity.

The decision at Christmas 1923 cost Rudolf Steiner his life. Marie Steiner has often referred to the "infinite tragedy" connected with the Christmas Conference.[10] From the tremendous importance he attached to the polarity of movement and Society, it almost goes without saying that Rudolf Steiner could not appoint a successor for the continuation of the impulse inaugurated at that time: "that henceforth the anthroposophic movement will be formed so that it gives no further attention to anything but what the spiritual world requires of it" (Dornach, Apr. 12, 1924, CW 260a). No one else could act as its mediator, because, as he said in this connection, "of course the Anthroposophical Society would be something quite different, depending on whether it was under my leadership or someone else was in charge" (CW 260a).

Although this can be experienced as deep tragedy, it is, nevertheless, a tragedy that summons us to active knowledge and further fruitful work. For what is decisive from Rudolf Steiner's perspective might best be expressed in a meditation he once wrote: "Earthly embodiment is spirit vanishing into the abyss, on the one side, and shining forth from the abyss, on the other.[11]

---

10 Marie Steiner in *The Christmas Conference for the Foundation of the General Anthroposophical Society, 1923/1924*, CW 260.

11 No. 634 in the Archive notes.

Index of Names

Abel 210
Adriányi, Emil 227, 231
Alcyone (Krishnamurti) 139
Annie 93
Arenson, Adolf 7, 204, 244, 247
Aristotle 260
Avalon, Arthur 44, 46, 49

Barth, Otto Wilhelm 121
Belyi, Andrei 91
Besant, Annie ix, 31, 38, 78–80,
    82, 84, 95, 96, 98, 100, 101,
    104–113, 124, 126, 132, 139,
    213, 220, 256
Blavatsky, Helena Petrovna (HPB)
    viii, ix, 3, 19, 21, 46, 60–65,
    68, 70, 73, 76–79, 93, 95–97,
    101–105, 109, 110, 124, 126,
    220, 221
Bock, Emil 141, 178, 180, 182, 234
Böhme, Jakob 66
Bredow, Eugenie von 60
Bresch, Richard viii
Bright, Esther 82
Brockdorff, Count and
    Countess von viii
Broek, Roelof van den 45
Buddha, Gautama 53

Cain 210
Cleather, Alice Leighton 220
Cooper-Oakley, Isabel 84
Coulomb, Emma and Alexis 101–104
Cranston, Sylvia 220
Crowley, Aleister 230

Darwin, Charles 15

Eberhardt, Paul 231
Eckhardtstein, Imme von 201
Elias 204
Elijah 196–199, 202, 203

Fichte, Johann Gottlieb 16
Frick, Karl R. H. 218

Gabert, Erich 234
Garibaldi, Giuseppe 126, 220
Geelmuyden, Helga 246
Geyer, Johannes 136, 176
Goethe, Johann Wolfgang von vii,
    8, 16, 17, 20, 21, 22, 32, 87,
    133–187, 245
Grimm, Herman 116
Grone, Jürgen von 239
Gümbel-Seiling, Max 198

Haeckel, Ernst 8, 15
Hahn, Herbert 238
Harrison, C. G. 65
Hartmann, Franz 102, 124, 220, 226,
    230
Heise, Karl 130, 135
Hilarion 58
Hiram Abiff 195, 200, 201, 208
Hodgson, Richard 102, 103
Howe, Ellie 217
Hübbe-Schleiden, Wilhelm 10, 19

Jahn, Rudolf 132
Jesus 56, 58, 91, 139, 196, 206, 207,
    208
Joachim, Herman 116
Joachim, Joseph 116
John the Baptist 195, 196, 198, 199,
    201–204, 208, 209
John the Evangelist 53, 136, 144, 197,
    200
Joseph of Arimathea 201
Judge, William Quan 79, 101, 104,
    105, 220

Kalckreuth, Countess Pauline von 81
Keightley, Bertram 82, 106, 110–112
Kirmiss, Paul 230
Kleeberg, Ludwig 91
Klein, Heinrich 124, 220, 230
Kober, Helena 234
Kolbe, Adolf 82
König, Peter-R. 217, 218, 224, 226,
    230

Krishnamurti, Jeddu 139
Kully, Max 218
Kut Hoomi 56, 58, 60, 75, 91

Lauer, Carl 230
Lauer, Hans Erhard 167, 226
Lazarus 195, 196, 200–204, 208, 209
Leadbeater, Charles Webster 82, 107, 110, 139
Leinhas, Emil 11
Lerchenfeld, Count Otto von 239

Mahatmas, the 60, 107, 109
Maikowski, René 174
May, Anna 201, 202
Mayreder, Rosa 5, 12, 13
Mazzini, Giuseppe 126
Mead, George R. S. 84, 106, 111, 113
Mead, Laura 84
Melchizedek 185
Menes, King 120
Meyer, T. H. 90
Michelangelo 194
Minsloff, Anna 111
Misraim, King 121
Möller, Helmut 217–219, 230, 233
Morya 56, 58, 91
Moses 199
Moudra, Paula 134

Nietzsche, Friedrich vii, 8
Nikhilananda, Swami 44
Noah 120, 129, 191
Novalis 197, 198, 199, 202–205

Olcott, Henry Steel 3, 95, 101–105, 107, 109–111
Ormus 121

Paracelsus 66
Parzival 123
Paul, St. 71
Picht, Carlo Septimus 215, 216
Pinehas 199
Piper, Kurt 239
Poeppig, Fred 245

Ransom, Josephine 126, 220
Raphael 194, 197–199, 202, 203–205
Reuss, Theodor 124–127, 131, 134, 143, 145–148, 217
Rittelmeyer, Friedrich 55, 58, 60, 165, 200, 239, 240
Röschl-Lehrs, Maria 177, 178, 182, 239
Rosenkreutz, Christian 56, 58, 91, 195, 200–203, 208
Ruthenberg, Wilhelm 175, 176

Schirmer-Bey, Jenny 90
Scholem, Gershom G. 45
Scholl, Mathilde 81, 82, 84
Schubert, Günther 11, 185, 200
Schuré, Édouard 66, 86, 93, 95, 106, 108
Schuster, Hugo 175, 181
Sellin, Albrecht Wilhelm 119, 121, 124, 125, 131, 136, 143, 144, 146, 147, 185, 219, 223, 224, 229
Serapis 58
Sinnett, Alfred Percy 75, 87, 96, 97, 107
Sivers, Marie von 81
Solomon 201
Soro, Vincenzo 126
Sprengel, Alice 233
Steffen, Albert 7, 239, 244, 247, 253
Steiner, Marie (throughout)
Steiner, Rudolf (throughout)
St. Germain, Count of 58, 200
Stinde, Sophie 81
Stockmeyer, E. A. Karl 184
Strakosch, Alexander 246

Tingley, Catherine 105, 106
Toepell, Rudolf 198
Ullmer, Andreas 230, 233
Unger, Carl 118, 182, 244

Vacano, Harriet von 239
Vreede, Elisabeth 90, 239

Wachsmuth, Guenther 239
Wachsmuth, Wolfgang 239
Wagner, Amalie 81, 87
Wagner, Anna 52, 82, 83, 92, 109
Wagner, Günther 61–63, 67, 68, 73, 74, 81–84, 261
Walther, Clara 127

Index of Names

Walther, Kurt 136
Wandrey, Camilla 170
Wegman, Ita 239
Westcott, William Wynn 220, 224
Wiesberger, Hella 11
Woloschin, Margarita 239
Woodroffe, Sir John 44, 46
Wrangel, Adeline von 233

Yarker, John ix, 114, 116, 124–127, 217, 219–223, 231, 234, 235

Zarathustra 53, 64, 90
Zeylmans van Emmichoven, F. W. 257

Bibliography and Recommended Reading

Anderson, Adrian. *Rudolf Steiner's Esoteric Christianity in the Grail Painting by Anna May: Contemplating the Sacred in Rosicrucian Christianity.* Porthill, ID: Threshold Publishing, 2017.

Blavatsky, H. P. *The Secret Doctrine: The Synthesis of Science, Religion, and Philosophy* (2 vols.). Pasadena: Theosophical University, 2014.

Cranston, Sylvia. *H.P.B. The Extraordinary Life and Influence of Helena Blavatsky, Founder of the Modern Theosophical Movement.* New York: TarcherPerigee, 1993.

Goethe, Johann Wolfgang von. *The Fairytale of the Green Snake and the Beautiful Lily.* Hudson, NY: Anthroposophic Press, 1991.

Kleeberg, Ludwig. *Wege und Worte: Erinnerungen an Rudolf Steiner.* Stuttgart: Mellinger, 1990.

Lindenberg, Christoph. *Rudolf Steiner: A Biography.* Great Barrington, MA: SteinerBooks, 2017.

Meyer, T. H. *The Bodhisattva Question: Krishnamurti, Rudolf Steiner, Valentin Tomberg, and the Mystery of the Twentieth-Century Master.* Forest Row, UK: Temple Lodge, 2010.

———. *Rudolf Steiner's Core Mission: The Birth and Development of Spiritual-Scientific Karma Research.* Forest Row, UK: Temple Lodge, 2010.

Nikhilananda, Swami. *Hinduism: Its Meaning for the Liberation of the Spirit.* New York: Ramakrishna-Vivekanada Center, 1992.

Prokofieff, Sergei O. *Anthroposophy and the Philosophy of Freedom: Anthroposophy and Its Method of Cognition.* Forest Row, UK: Temple Lodge, 2009.

———. *The Esoteric Nature of the Anthroposophical Society.* Stourbridge, UK: Wynstones Press, 2015.

———. *Rudolf Steiner and the Founding of the New Mysteries* (2nd ed.). Forest Row, UK: Temple Lodge, 2017.

———. *Rudolf Steiner and the Masters of Esoteric Christianity.* Stourbridge, UK: Wynstones Press, 2019.

Ransom, Josephine. *A Short History of the Theosophical Society.* Wheaton, IL: Theosophical Publishing House, 1966.

Rittelmeyer, Friedrich. *Rudolf Steiner Enters My Life.* Edinburgh: Floris Books, 2013.

Scholem, Gershom G. *Jewish Gnosticism, Merkabah Mysticism, and the Talmudic Tradition.* New York: Jewish Theological Seminary of America, 1960.

———. *On the Kabbalah and Its Symbolism,* New York: Schocken, 1996.

Selg, Peter. *The Anthroposophical Society: The Understanding and Continued Activity of the Christmas Conference.* Great Barrington, MA: SteinerBooks, 2018.

———. *The Michael School: And the School of Spiritual Science.* Great Barrington, MA: SteinerBooks, 2016.

———. *Rudolf Steiner, Life and Work: 1861–1925* (7 vols.). Great Barrington, MA: SteinerBooks, 2015–2019.

———. *Rudolf Steiner and the School for Spiritual Science: The Foundation of the "First Class."* Great Barrington, MA: SteinerBooks, 2012.

———. *Rudolf Steiner as a Spiritual Teacher: From Recollections of Those Who Knew Him.* Great Barrington, MA: SteinerBooks, 2009.

———. *Rudolf Steiner's Foundation Stone Meditation: And the Destruction of the Twentieth Century.* Forest Row, UK: Temple Lodge, 2012.

———. *Rudolf Steiner's Intentions for the Anthroposophical Society: The Executive Council, the School for Spiritual Science, and the Sections.* Great Barrington, MA: SteinerBooks, 2011.

Steiner, Rudolf. *The Anthroposophic Movement: Its History and Life-conditions in Relation to the Anthroposophical Society* (CW 258). London: H. Collison, 1938.

———. *Anthroposophical Leading Thoughts: Anthroposophy as a Path of Knowledge: The Michael Mystery* (CW 26). London: Rudolf Steiner Press, 1973.

———. *Anthroposophy and the Inner Life: An Esoteric Introduction* (CW 234). Forest Row, UK: Rudolf Steiner Press, 2015.

———. *The Apocalypse of St. John: Lectures on the Book of Revelation* (CW 104). Spring Valley, NY: Anthroposophic Press, 1985. Great Barrington, MA: SteinerBooks, 2000.

———. *Architecture, Sculpture, and Painting of the First Goetheanum* (CW 288). Great Barrington, MA: SteinerBooks, 2017.

———. *Autobiography: Chapters in the Course of My Life, 1861–1907* (CW 28). Great Barrington, MA: SteinerBooks, 2000.

Bibliography and Recommended Reading

———. *Becoming the Archangel Michael's Companions: Rudolf Steiner's Challenge to the Younger Generation* (CW 217). Great Barrington, MA: SteinerBooks, 2006.

———. *Briefe Band II: 1890–1925* (CW 39). Dornach: Rudolf Steiner Verlag, 1953.

———. *Calendar 1912–1913: Facsimile Edition of the Original Book Containing the Calendar Created by Rudolf Steiner for the Year 1912–1913* (CW 40). Great Barrington, MA: SteinerBooks, 2004.

———. *Calendar of the Soul* (CW 40). Hudson, NY: Anthroposophic Press, 1988.

———. *The Christ Impulse: And the Development of Ego-Consciousness* (CW 116). Great Barrington, MA: SteinerBooks, 2015.

———. *Christianity as Mystical Fact: And the Mysteries of Antiquity* (CW 8). Great Barrington, MA: SteinerBooks, 2006.

———. *The Christmas Conference: For the Foundation of the General Anthroposophical Society, 1923/1924* (CW 260). Hudson, NY: Anthroposophic Press, 1990.

———. *The Connection between the Living and the Dead* (CW 168). Great Barrington, MA: SteinerBooks, 2017.

———. *Constitution of the School of Spiritual Science: An Introductory Guide.* Forest Row, UK: Rudolf Steiner Press, 2013.

———. *Cosmic Memory: The Story of Atlantis, Lemuria, and the Division of the Sexes* (CW 11). Hudson, NY: Anthroposophic Press, 1987.

———. *Cosmology, Religion, and Philosophy: Ten Lectures* (CW 25). London: Rudolf Steiner Press, 1984.

———. *Esoteric Christianity and the Mission of Christian Rosenkreutz* (CW 130). London: Rudolf Steiner Press, 2001.

———. *Esoteric Lessons 1904–1909: From the Esoteric School,* vol. 1 (CW 266/1). Great Barrington, MA: SteinerBooks, 2007.

———. *Esoteric Lessons 1910–1912: From the Esoteric School,* vol. 2 (CW 266/2). Great Barrington, MA: SteinerBooks, 2012.

———. *Esoteric Lessons 1913–1923: From the Esoteric School,* vol. 3 (CW 266/3). Great Barrington, MA: SteinerBooks, 2008.

———. *Faculty Meetings with Rudolf Steiner,* 2 vols. (CW 300a/b). Hudson, NY: Anthroposophic Press, 1998.

———. *The Fifth Gospel: From the Akashic Record* (CW 148). London: Rudolf Steiner Press, 1985.

———. *The First Class Lessons and Mantras: The Michael School Meditative Path in Nineteen Steps* (CW 270), T. H. Meyer, ed. Great Barrington, MA: SteinerBooks, 2017.

———. *The First Class of the Michael School: Recapitulation Lessons and Mantras* (CW 270), T. H. Meyer, ed. Great Barrington, MA: SteinerBooks, 2018.

———. *The Foundation Stone: The Life, Nature, and Cultivation of Anthroposophy.* Forest Row, UK: Rudolf Steiner Press, 1997.

———. *Founding a Science of the Spirit* (CW 95). Forest Row, UK: Rudolf Steiner Press, 1999.

———. *Four Mystery Dramas* (rev. ed; CW 14). Great Barrington, MA: SteinerBooks, 2015.

———. *"Freemasonry" and Ritual Work: The Misraim Service* (CW 265). Great Barrington, MA: SteinerBooks, 2007.

———. *From the History and Contents of the First Section of the Esoteric School: Letters, Documents, and Lectures: 1904–1914* (CW 264). Great Barrington, MA: SteinerBooks, 2010.

———. *Der Goetheanismus, ein Umwandlungsimpuls und Auferstehungsgedanke: Menschenwissenschaft und Sozialwissenschaft. Zwölf Vorträge, Dornach 1919.* Dornach: Rudolf Steiner Verlag, 1982.

———. *Der Goetheanumgedanke inmitten der Kulturkrisis der Gegenwart: Ausgewählte Aufsätze 1921–1925* (CW 36). Dornach: Rudolf Steiner Verlag, 1982.

———. *Goethe's* Faust *in the Light of Anthroposophy: Spiritual–Scientific Commentaries on Goethe's* Faust, vol. 2 (CW 273). Great Barrington, MA: SteinerBooks, 2016.

———. *Goethe's Theory of Knowledge: An Outline of the Epistemology of His Worldview* (CW 2). Great Barrington, MA: SteinerBooks, 2008.

———. *Goethes Geistesart in ihrer Offenbarung durch seinen «Faust» und durch das Märchen «Von der Schlange und der Lilie»* (CW 22). Dornach: Rudolf Steiner Verlag, 1989.

———. *The Gospel of St. John* (CW 103). Spring Valley, NY: Anthroposophic Press, 1984.

———. *The Gospel of St. John and Its Relation to the Other Gospels* (CW 112). Spring Valley, NY: Anthroposophic Press, 1982.

———. *The Gospel of St. Mark* (CW 139). Spring Valley, NY: Anthroposophic Press, 1990.

Bibliography and Recommended Reading

———. *Guidance in Esoteric Training: From the Esoteric School* (CW 245). Forest Row, UK: Rudolf Steiner Press, 1998.

———. *How Can Mankind Find the Christ Again? The Threefold Shadow-Existence of Our Time and the New Light of Christ* (CW 187). Great Barrington, MA: SteinerBooks, 1984.

———. *How to Know Higher Worlds: A Modern Path of Initiation* (CW 10). Hudson, NY: Anthroposophic Press, 1994.

———. *Inner Reading and Inner Hearing: And How to Achieve Existence in the World of Ideas* (CW 156). Great Barrington, MA: SteinerBooks, 2008.

———. *Intuitive Thinking as a Spiritual Path: A Philosophy of Freedom* (CW 4). Hudson, NY: Anthroposophic Press, 1997.

———. *The Karma of Untruthfulness: Secret Societies, the Media, and Preparations for the Great War*, 2 vols. (CW 173/174). Forest Row, UK: Rudolf Steiner Press, 2005.

———. *Karmic Relationships: Esoteric Studies*, 8 vols. Forest Row, UK: Rudolf Steiner Press, 2002–2017.

———. *Knowledge of the Higher Worlds: How Is It Achieved?* (CW 10). Forest Row, UK: Rudolf Steiner Press, 2009.

———. *Lucifer–Gnosis; Grundlegende Aufsätze zur Anthroposophie und Berichte aus den Zeitschriften «Luzifer» und «Lucifer–Gnosis» 1903–1908* (CW 34). Dornach: Rudolf Steiner Verlag, 1987.

———. *Mantric Sayings: Meditations 1903–1925* (CW 268). Great Barrington, MA: SteinerBooks, 2018.

———. *The New Essential Steiner: An Introduction to Rudolf Steiner for the 21st Century* (R. A. McDermott, ed.). Great Barrington, MA: Lindisfarne Books, 2009.

———. *The Occult Movement in the Nineteenth Century* (CW 254). London: Rudolf Steiner Press, 1973.

———. *Occult Science: An Outline* (CW 13). Forest Row, UK: Rudolf Steiner Press, 2013.

———. *Our Dead: Memorial, Funeral, and Cremation Addresses* (CW 261). Great Barrington, MA: SteinerBooks, 2011.

———. *An Outline of Esoteric Science* (CW 13). Hudson, NY: Anthroposophic Press, 1997.

———. *Philosophie und Anthroposophie: Gesammelte Aufsätze 1904–1923* (CW 35). Dornach: Rudolf Steiner Verlag, 1984

———. *The Philosophy of Freedom: The Basis for a Modern World Conception* (CW 4). Forest Row, UK: Rudolf Steiner Press, 2011.

———. *The Philosophy of Spiritual Activity* (CW 4). Hudson, NY: Anthroposophic Press, 1986.

———. *The Principle of Spiritual Economy: In Connection with Questions of Reincarnation: An Aspect of the Spiritual Guidance of Man* (CW 109). Great Barrington, MA: SteinerBooks, 1986.

———. *Reincarnation and Karma: Two Fundamental Truths of Human Existence* (CW 135). Great Barrington, MA: SteinerBooks, 2001.

———. *Rosicrucianism Renewed: The Unity of Art, Science, and Religion: The Theosophical Congress of Whitsun 1907* (CW 284). Great Barrington, MA: SteinerBooks, 2006.

———. *Secrets of the Threshold* (CW 147). Great Barrington, MA: SteinerBooks, 1987.

———. *Self-education: Autobiographical Reflections, 1861–1893* (CW 25). Spring Valley, NY: Mercury Press, 1985.

———. *The Social Future: Culture, Equality, and the Economy* (CW 332a). Great Barrington, MA: SteinerBooks, 2013.

———. *Soul Exercises: Word and Symbol Meditations, 1903–1924* (CW 267). Great Barrington, MA: SteinerBooks, 2015.

———. *The Spiritual Guidance of the Individual and Humanity: Some Results of Spiritual-Scientific Research into Human History and Development* (CW 15). Hudson, NY: Anthroposophic Press, 1992.

———. *The Spiritual Hierarchies and the Physical World: Zodiac, Planets, and Cosmos* (CW 110). Great Barrington, MA: SteinerBooks, 2008.

———. *Spiritualism, Madame Blavatsky, and Theosophy: An Eyewitness View of Occult History*. Great Barrington, MA: SteinerBooks, 2002.

———. *The Stages of Higher Knowledge: Imagination, Inspiration, Intuition* (CW 12). Great Barrington, MA: SteinerBooks, 2009.

———. *The Temple Legend: Freemasonry and Related Occult Movements: From the Contents of the Esoteric School* (CW 93). Forest Row, UK: Rudolf Steiner Press, 2000.

———. *Theosophy: An Introduction to the Spiritual Processes in Human Life and in the Cosmos* (CW 9). Hudson, NY: Anthroposophic Press, 1994.

———. *Truth and Knowledge: Introduction to the Philosophy of Spiritual Activity* (CW 3). Great Barrington, MA: SteinerBooks, 1981.

Bibliography and Recommended Reading

———. *Truth-Wrought-Words: With Other Verses and Prose Passages* (CW 40). Great Barrington, MA: SteinerBooks, 2010.

———. *Verses and Meditations*. Forest Row, UK: Rudolf Steiner Press, 2004.

———. *A Way of Self-Knowledge: And the Threshold of the Spiritual World* (CW 16/17). Great Barrington, MA: SteinerBooks, 1999.

———. *Die Welträtsel und die Anthroposophie: Zweiundzwanzig Vorträge, Berlin 1905/1906* (CW 54). Dornach: Rudolf Steiner Verlag, 1983.

Steiner, Rudolf, and Marie Steiner-von Sivers. *Correspondence and Documents 1901–1925: Rudolf Steiner–Marie Steiner-von Sivers* (CW 262). Hudson, NY: Anthroposophic Press, 1988.

———. *Creative Speech: The Formative Process of the Spoken Word: A Selection of Lectures, Exercises and Articles* (CW 280). Forest Row, UK: Rudolf Steiner Press, 2013.

Tomberg, Valentin. *Christ and Sophia: Anthroposophic Meditations on the Old Testament, New Testament, and Apocalypse*. Great Barrington, MA: SteinerBooks, 2015.

Unger, Carl. *The Language of the Consciousness Soul: A Guide to Rudolf Steiner's "Leading Thoughts."* Great Barrington, MA: SteinerBooks, 2012.

———. *Steiner's Theosophy and Principles of Spiritual Science*. Great Barrington, MA: SteinerBooks, 2015.

van den Broek, Roelof (ed): *Gnosis and Hermeticism from Antiquity to Modern Times*. New York: University of New York, 1997.

Woodroffe, Sir John. *The Garland of Letters: Studies in the Mantra-Sastra*. Madras: Ganesh, 2004.

——— (Arthur Avalon). *The Serpent Power: The Secrets of Tantric and Shaktic Yoga*. New York: Dover, 1974.

Bibliographic Sources for this Volume

Chapters 1, 3, 5, 6, 7, and 17:
CW 264, *From the History and Contents of the First Section of the Esoteric School: Letters, Documents, and Lectures: 1904–1914* (SteinerBooks, 2010; translated by John Wood). The text of chapter 7 was rewritten by Hella Wiesberger (translated by Marsha Post).

Chapters 2 and 8:
CW 267, *Soul Exercises: Word and Symbol Meditations, 1903–1924* (SteinerBooks, 2015; translated by Matthew Barton).

Chapter 4:
CW 28, *Autobiography: Chapters in the Course of My Life, 1861–1907,* Part Three, "Must I Remain Unable to Speak? Berlin, 1897–1907," chapter 65 (SteinerBooks, 2000; translated by Rita Stebbing, revised).

Chapters 9, 10, 11, 12, 13, 15:
CW 265, *"Freemasonry" and Ritual Work: The Misraim Service* (SteinerBooks, 2007; translated by John Wood). The text of chapter 15 was rewritten by the Hella Wiesberger (translated by Marsha Post).

Chapter 14:
Adapted from an article by Hella Wiesberger and Julius Zoll, «Über Rudolf Steiners Verhältnis oder Nicht-Verhältnis zum OTO» [Rudolf Steiner's relationship or non-relationship to the OTO], in *Das Goetheanum. Wochenschrift für Anthroposophie,* 75, no. 40, Jan. 1997 (translated by Marsha Post).

Chapter 16:
First published as a book for the Rudolf Steiner Archive in Dornach, Switzerland (translated by Marsha Post).

About the Author

Hella Wiesberger, an early and longtime editor of The Collected Works of Rudolf Steiner (Gesamtausgabe, or GA) and a leading figure of the Rudolf Steiner Archive, passed away in Hombrechtikon, Switzerland, in December 2014 at the age of ninety-five. She retained her full mental capacity and continued a full of work schedule until the very end. Ever since 1948, when Marie Steiner died, she devoted all her efforts to administrating the Rudolf Steiner estate.

Born in Bavaria in October 1920, she began her work at the archive as a shorthand typist. "She can do more than work with typewriters," Dr. Robert Friedenthal had said about her in 1948. Thus, she advanced quickly into the circle of editors appointed by Marie Steiner, whereby she benefited from her mastery of the old stenographic systems, since the publication of Rudolf Steiner's lectures is based largely on the notes of attending stenographers.

Hella Wiesberger was committed to Marie Steiner's intention to publish the entire work that Steiner left behind. She became well known beyond anthroposophic circles owing to her bibliography published in 1961 with the title "Rudolf Steiner: The literary and artistic work." This classic reference served as a plan for all subsequent volumes of the collected works and made the archive work public for the first time. Her bibliography remains an indispensable tool for research into Rudolf Steiner's lifework. Among the numerous volumes of the complete edition that she supervised and illumined with her expert commentary, the volumes on esotericism (CW 264–269) deserve to be highlighted and are therefore available for the first time to the public. Also worthy of mention is the new edition of the correspondence between Rudolf Steiner and Marie Steiner-von Sivers, published in 2000, which includes newly discovered letters.

Hella Wiesberger's bibliography is indebted to the writings of Marie Steiner. In her series of studies on Rudolf Steiner, she edited volume 1, *Marie Steiner-von Sivers: A Life for Anthroposophy* (1988), and volume 7, *Rudolf Steiner's Esoteric Teaching Activity* (1997), an important resource for studying Rudolf Steiner's works. She also edited Marie Steiner's collected writings. For the series "Contributions to the Rudolf Steiner Complete Edition," she provided essentials such as basic documentation from 1917 and 1919.

After Hella Wiesberger retired in 1998 from active work in the Archive, she continued to volunteer and contribute her expertise. She devoted herself, above all, to a project that was especially close to Marie Steiner's heart—exploring the last three years of Rudolf Steiner's life, which had been overshadowed in some ways by militant opposition. Even today, some of the events seem murky, contradictory, and even tragic. That research project, funded by two Swiss foundations, was announced by the Archive in December 2014, with Günter Aschoff and Alexander Lüscher as coworkers, both of whom contributed valuable preparatory efforts for the project. Hella Wiesberger assisted the younger researchers until the very end.

Hella Wiesberger's extensive knowledge of meditation was the result of many years' work, characterized by her non-dogmatic nature and a great deal of good humor. She always sought balance and avoided internal squabbles and personal attacks. Anyone who was lucky enough to work with Hella Wiesberger will remember her with gratitude.

A Note from SteinerBooks

SteinerBooks is a 501(c)(3) not-for-profit organization incorporated in New York State since 1928. Its mission is to promote the progress and welfare of humanity and to increase general awareness of Rudolf Steiner (1861–1925), the Austrian-born polymath writer, lecturer, spiritual scientist, philosopher, cosmologist, educator, psychologist, alchemist, ecologist, Christian mystic, and evolutionary theorist. He developed Anthroposophy ("human wisdom") as a path to unite the spiritual in the human being with the spiritual in the universe. To this end, SteinerBooks publishes and distributes books and utilizes other means such as electronic media, conferences, and other activities to make his works available and to explore themes arising from and related to Anthroposophy and the spiritual–scientific movement Rudolf Steiner founded.

- We commission translations of books by Rudolf Steiner not previously published in English, as well as new translations for updated editions.

- Our goal is to make works on Anthroposophy more widely available by publishing and distributing both introductory and advanced works on spiritual research.

- New books are published for both print and digital editions to reach the widest possible readership.

- Recent technology also makes it practical for us to reissue out-of-print works for the next generation in both print and electronic editions.

SteinerBooks/Anthroposophic Press depends on readers for financial support, which is greatly needed, appreciated, and tax-deductible. Consider a donation by check or other means to SteinerBooks, PO Box 58, Hudson, NY 12534. You can also contribute via PayPal at www.steinerbooks.org. For more information about supporting our work or to make a contribution, please send email to friends@steinerbooks.org.

www.ingramcontent.com/pod-product-compliance
Lightning Source LLC
Chambersburg PA
CBHW030103170426
43198CB00009B/479